Lecture Notes in Computer Science   13149

Founding Editors

Gerhard Goos
  Karlsruhe Institute of Technology, Karlsruhe, Germany
Juris Hartmanis
  Cornell University, Ithaca, NY, USA

Editorial Board Members

Elisa Bertino
  Purdue University, West Lafayette, IN, USA
Wen Gao
  Peking University, Beijing, China
Bernhard Steffen ⓘ
  TU Dortmund University, Dortmund, Germany
Gerhard Woeginger ⓘ
  RWTH Aachen, Aachen, Germany
Moti Yung ⓘ
  Columbia University, New York, NY, USA

More information about this subseries at https://link.springer.com/bookseries/7407

Barbara Chapman · José Moreira (Eds.)

Languages and Compilers for Parallel Computing

33rd International Workshop, LCPC 2020
Virtual Event, October 14–16, 2020
Revised Selected Papers

 Springer

Editors
Barbara Chapman ⓘ
Stony Brook University
Stony Brook, NY, USA

José Moreira ⓘ
IBM TJ Watson Research Center
Yorktown Heights, NY, USA

ISSN 0302-9743   ISSN 1611-3349 (electronic)
Lecture Notes in Computer Science
ISBN 978-3-030-95952-4   ISBN 978-3-030-95953-1   (eBook)
https://doi.org/10.1007/978-3-030-95953-1

LNCS Sublibrary: SL1 – Theoretical Computer Science and General Issues

This Springer imprint is published by the registered company Springer Nature Switzerland AG
The registered company address is: Gewerbestrasse 11, 6330 Cham, Switzerland

Preface

The 33rd Workshop on Languages and Compilers for Parallel Computing (LCPC 2020) was hosted by Stony Brook University, NY, USA during October 14–16, 2020. As with so many events in the times of the COVID-19 pandemic, it was a fully virtual event, with live presentations using video conferenceing services. We were happy to have been able to organize this event, despite all the challenges involved in its organization. We were also delighted to have witnessed good participation and interactions from our speakers and attendees.

Since its inception in 1988, the Workshop on Languages and Compilers for Parallel Computing (LCPC) has been a leading venue for cutting-edge research on all aspects of parallel programming systems, from parallel programming models, languages, compilers, runtimes, and tools to results related to new parallel applications or systems. The scope of the workshop is particularly broad: it encompasses foundational results as well as practical experience reports and bold new ideas for future systems. LCPC is a venue that brings together researchers from academia, national labs, and industry. It encourages personal interactions and in-depth technical discussions.

We had a diverse and comprehensive technical program for LCPC 2020, including two invited keynotes, 15 contributed technical papers, two invited short talks, one invited regular talk, and one panel. These were complemented by a special presentation, by Robert Harrison, of the computational facilities at the Stony Brook University Institute for Advanced Computational Science, two live networking sessions, a session on career opportunities, and, after the closing of the workshop, a virtual happy hour.

The 15 contributed technical papers were selected for presentation by the Program Committee from a pool of 19 submissions. Each submissions received three written reviews by members of the Program Committee. The submissions were discussed during a virtual meeting, and the selelcted papers are included in these proceedings.

The two invited keynotes, by J Nelson Amaral and Jeffrey S Vetter, provided an exciting view of the future challenges and opportunities that face the parallel programming systems community. The invited talks covered new developments in computer architecture from Arm and IBM that impact modern compilers, as well as the topic of expressiveness and performance of parallel programming models.

Our unusual and very successful panel deviated from the usual format of having a theme for discussions. Instead, our panel organizer, Rudolf Eigenmann, invited four distinguished members of our community, Mary Hall, Michelle Strout, David Padua, and Vivek Sarkar, to an Ask me anything session. This gave the audience, from aspiring Ph.D. candidates to experienced researchers, the opportunity to cover a broad set of topics, from career development to challenges for the future.

A conference or workshop must be much more than just a venue to present technical work. It must also be an opportunity for the community members to interact and network. With that in mind, we organized two live networking sessions, one to discuss the next technical challenges in the field of parallel languages and compilers, and the other on how to find collaboration opportunities for graduate students and young researchers. We were happy that the networking sessions were well attended and with a vibrant participation. The career opportunities session, moderated by Martin Kong, Riyadh Baghdadi, and Doru Popovici, gave attendees the chance to discuss and ask career related questions to young researchers.

We are in great debt to many people that helped make LCPC 2020 a reality. First, to all the authors and speakers that contributed to our technical program. To the members of the Program Committee and additional reviewers for their hard work in reviewing and selecting the contributed papers to the workshop. To the members of the Steering Committee for their guidance and assistance throughout the entire process. To our Panel Chair, Rudolf Eigenmann, who also happens to chair the Steering Committee. To our Networking Sessions Chair, Martin Kong. We want to give a special thanks to the incredible team of volunteers from Stony Brook University that took care of so many elements of logistics, including our Local Chair, Tony Curtis, and our Publicity/Web Chair, Alok Mishra. Last but not least, we want express our gratitude to the editorial staff at Springer, who patiently worked with us to produce these proceedings.

It was a pleasure to organize this fantastic event. We are looking forward to a future opportunity to host it again in the beautiful setting of Stony Brook University, New York.

October 2020

Barbara Chapman
José Moreira

Organization

Workshop Chairs

Barbara Chapman   Stony Brook University, USA
José Moreira   IBM Research, USA

Steering Committee

Rudolf Eigenmann   University of Delaware, USA
Alex Nicolau   University of California, Irvine, USA
David Padua   University of Ilinois at Urbana-Champaign, USA
Lawrence Rauchwerger   Texas A&M University and University of Illinois at Urbana-Champaign, USA
Vivek Sarkar   Georgia Institute of Technology, USA

Program Committee

Abid Malik   Brookhaven National Laboratory, USA
Alexandre Eichenberger   IBM Research, USA
Ana Varbanescu   University of Amsterdam, The Netherlands
Benjamin Brock   University of California, Berkeley, USA
Dimitrios Nikolopoulos   Virginia Polytechnic Institute and State University, USA
Hari Sundar   University of Utah, USA
Maria Garzaran   Intel, USA
Martin Kong   University of Oklahoma, USA
Mary Hall   University of Utah, USA
Peng Wu   Futurewei, USA
Sam Midkiff   Purdue University, USA
Santosh Pande   Georgia Institute of Technology, USA
Vivek Sarkar   Georgia Institute of Technology, USA
Yonghong Yan   University of North Carolina, USA
Zehra Sura   Bloomberg, USA

Panel Chair

Rudolf Eigenmann   University of Delaware, USA

Local Chair

Tony Curtis   Stony Brook University, USA

Networking Sessions Chair

Martin Kong   University of Oklahoma, USA

Publicity/Web Chair

Alok Mishra   Stony Brook University, USA

Additional Reviewer

Richard Veras   University of Oklahoma, USA

Contents

Performance Analysis

Code Generation

Code and Data Transformations

An Affine Scheduling Framework for Integrating Data Layout and Loop Transformations

Jun Shirako[✉] and Vivek Sarkar

School of Computer Science, Georgia Institute of Technology, Atlanta, USA
{shirako,vsarkar}@gatech.edu

Abstract. Code transformations in optimizing compilers can often be classified as *loop transformations* that change the execution order of statement instances and *data layout transformations* that change the memory layouts of variables. There is a mutually dependent relationship between the two, i.e., the best statement execution order can depend on the underlying data layout and vice versa. Existing approaches have typically addressed this inter-dependency by picking a specific phase order, and can thereby miss opportunities to co-optimize loop transformations and data layout transformations. In this paper, we propose a cost-based integration of loop and data layout transformations, aiming to cover a broader optimization space than phase-ordered strategies and thereby to find better solutions. Our approach builds on the polyhedral model, and shows how both loop and data layout transformations can be represented as affine scheduling in a unified manner. To efficiently explore the broader optimization space, we build analytical memory and computational cost models that are parameterized with a range of machine features including hardware parallelism, cache and TLB locality, and vectorization. Experimental results obtained on 12-core Intel Xeon and 24-core IBM POWER8 platforms demonstrate that, for a set of 22 Polybench benchmarks, our proposed cost-based integration approach can respectively deliver 1.3× and 1.6× geometric mean improvements over a state-of-the-art polyhedral optimizer, PLuTo, and a 1.2× geometric mean improvement on both platforms over a phase-ordered approach in which loop transformations are followed by the best data layout transformations.

1 Introduction

In recent years, the major focus of optimizing compilers has moved from scalar optimizations to transforming the input program so as to extract the ideal granularity of parallelism and data locality that best fits the target architecture. *Loop transformations* represent a major class of program transformations that have been used to address these objectives. The primary goal of loop transformations is to reorder dynamic statement/instruction execution sequences to optimize parallelism and locality, while satisfying dependence constraint for legality.

© Springer Nature Switzerland AG 2022
B. Chapman and J. Moreira (Eds.): LCPC 2020, LNCS 13149, pp. 3–19, 2022.
https://doi.org/10.1007/978-3-030-95953-1_1

More recently, *data layout transformations* have also been receiving attention because of their potential for delivering significant performance improvements due to enhanced cache and SIMD efficiencies [3,6,15,23]. The primary goal of data layout transformations is to rearrange program variables and data structures to optimize spatial data locality, while keeping dependences unchanged. The majority of past work on loop transformations assumes a fixed data layout. Likewise, the majority of past work on data layout transformations assumes a fixed loop ordering. The focus of our paper is on the problem of *cost-based integration* of both classes of transformations, which has received relatively little attention in past work.

There is a large body of past work on loop transformations since the 1980's, e.g., [2,12,16,32,33]. Syntactic/AST-based loop transformation frameworks automatically select a sequence of individual loop transformations, driven by analytical cost models, to achieve a desired optimization goal [18,22,31]. More recently, the polyhedral compilation model has provided significant advances in the unification of affine loop transformations combined with powerful code generation techniques [1,4,5,10,13,24]. The benefits of this unified formulation can be seen (for example) in the PLuTo algorithm [4,5], which has been successfully extended and specialized to integrate SIMD constraints [17].

Data layout transformations represent another class of program transformations that is increasingly being used in compiler optimizations. A number of data layout transformation techniques have been proposed, including permutation of multidimensional array [15,30], conversion between array-of-structs (AoS) and struct-of-arrays (SoA) [6,23], data skewing, and data tiling [21]. However, they are often performed as a pre- or post- pass to loop transformations in past work that tries to incorporate both sets of transformations [11,14,15,21]. On a related note, [23] and [6] addressed the best AoS/SoA selection problem for a given input program, for both CPUs and GPUs, but without considering any loop transformations. Further details are discussed in Sect. 7.

In this paper, we address the problem of integrating loop and data layout transformations, with the goal of exploring the full optimization space so as to select globally optimal combinations of loop and data layout transformations that may be overlooked by phase-ordered approaches. To efficiently explore the optimization space and find the best combination of data layout transformations Φ and loop transformations Θ, our framework employs a cost-based iterative compilation approach. Given a set of candidate pairs of (Φ, Θ), it statically estimates the overall memory and computational cost; and the candidate with minimum cost is selected as the final output. This is in contrast with a phase ordering approach which either first selects the best Φ and then selects the best Θ, or first selects the best Θ and then selects the best Φ. We extend the DL model [9] for memory cost estimation, and build a simple computational cost model based on microbenchmarking and machine parameters. Given a program region applicable to the polyhedral model (i.e., a SCoP region), our compilation framework transforms loop and data layout structures, and the data redistributions between original and new layouts, while preserving the original data layouts outside the SCoP region. In summary, the major contributions of this paper are:

```
#pragma omp for ...
  for (i=0; i<ni; i++) {
    for (j=0; j<nj; j++) {
S:  C[i][j] *= beta;
    for (k=0; k<nk; k++)
T:    C[i][j] += alpha
      * A[i][k] * B[j][k];
  }}
```

Fig. 1. gemm using PLuTo (minimum reuse distance schedule) + manual best layout search (which resulted in transposing the dimensions of array B)

```
#pragma omp for ...
  for (i=0; i<ni; i++) {
    for (j=0; j<nj; j++)
S:  C[i][j] *= beta;
    for (k=0; k<nk; k++)
      for (j=0; j<nj; j++)
T:    C[i][j] += alpha
      * A[i][k] * B[k][j];
  }
```

Fig. 2. gemm using PolyAST + manual best layout search (which resulted in no change to the original data layout)

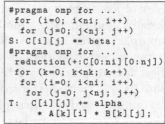

```
#pragma omp for ...
  for (i=0; i<ni; i++)
    for (j=0; j<nj; j++)
S:  C[i][j] *= beta;
#pragma omp for ... \
  reduction(+:C[0:ni][0:nj])
  for (k=0; k<nk; k++)
    for (i=0; i<ni; i++)
      for (j=0; j<nj; j++)
T:    C[i][j] += alpha
      * A[k][i] * B[k][j];
```

Fig. 3. gemm using our framework (which resulted in transposing the dimensions of array A, and also a different loop transformation)

- Analytical memory and computational cost models that can be used to evaluate the quality of pairs of data layout and loop transformations.
- A compile-time algorithm that can explore the broader optimization space and select the best combination of data layout and loop transformations based on the proposed cost models.
- Experimental results using 22 benchmarks from PolyBench 4.2 [20] on 12-core Intel Xeon and 24-core IBM POWER8 platforms, demonstrating that our proposed cost-based integration approach can respectively deliver $1.3\times$ and $1.6\times$ geometric mean improvements relative to PLuTo, a state-of-the-art loop optimizer, and a $1.2\times$ geometric mean improvement for both platforms over a phase-ordered approach, i.e., loop optimizations followed by the best layout selection.

The rest of the paper is organized as follows. Section 2 motivates the problem, and Sect. 3 contains background information on the polyhedral model. Section 3.3 introduces our extensions to model data layout transformations in an affine scheduling framework. Section 4 presents our affine scheduling framework for integrating data layout and loop transformations. Section 5 discusses the analytical cost models used to guide the loop and layout transformations. Section 6 presents experimental results to evaluate our approach on the three multicore systems. Finally, Sects. 7 and 8 summarize related work and our conclusions.

2 Motivating Example

We use the generalized matrix-multiply (gemm) from PolyBench 4.2 [20] as a motivating example. Figure 1 shows the output of the PLuTo [4,5] polyhedral compiler; its objective function is to minimize the temporal distance between two accesses to the same memory location, i.e., *minimum reuse distance*. This is also a core objective of many polyhedral optimizers to achieve maximal temporal data locality and outermost forall parallelism. As an example of the phase-ordered approach, after loop transformations we manually tried all possible ($2^3 = 8$) array dimensional permutation candidates on both platforms, and found the best layout: permuting 2-D array B so that the original B[k][j] was changed into B[j][k] with better spatial locality. As discussed later, the original B[k][j] layout was used when enabling intra-tile permutation by PLuTo, since PLuTo does not do any data layout transformations. We also applied PolyAST [24], a hybrid framework to integrate polyhedral and AST-based loop transformations, and obtained the output shown in Fig. 2. Due to PolyAST's cache-aware loop transformations, the original data layout was the best performant in the manually tested candidates.

Figure 3 is the output of our integrated data layout and loop transformations. Our framework selected very different loop transformations from past approaches, e.g., statements S and T are completely distributed and the k-loop is parallelized as an array reduction for statement T. Integrated with these loop transformations, the data layout selected by our framework includes permuting 2-D array A so that the original A[i][k] reference is changed to A[k][i]. Although the reduction parallelism incurs some overhead to compute the final values, our cost analysis detected that the overhead is sufficiently small and more than overcome by the benefits of reduced memory cost. The selected data layout minimizes the array read costs on A and B, while the partial sum of array reduction on C is accumulated into thread-local storage, thereby incurring no inter-thread communications except the final sum.

Table 1 clearly shows the effectiveness of the proposed approach over the phase-ordered strategies using the state-of-the-art polyhedral loop optimizers, on all three experimental platforms. Note that we omit loop tiling in Figs. 1, 2 and 3 for readability while tiling was performed when obtaining the results in Table 1. The 'PLuTo' and 'Min dist + layout' variants have the same inter-tile loop structures as shown in Fig. 1, while PLuTo additionally permutes intra-tile loops to enhance vectorization. To summarize, proper integration of data layout and loop transformations can find the optimal solution which may lie in a space not covered by phase-ordered approaches.

Table 1. Speedup over the original sequential code

	12-core westmere	12-core broadwell	POWER8 24-core
PLuTo	4.96×	4.44×	9.62×
Min dist + layout	5.09×	4.01×	8.62×
PolyAST + layout	5.72×	4.48×	11.58×
Our framework	7.50×	4.97×	14.96×

3 Background

The polyhedral model is a linear algebraic representation for collections of (imperfectly) nested loops in which loop bounds and branch conditions are affine functions of outer loop iterators and runtime constants, which are handled as global parameters [8]. Code regions amenable to this algebraic representation are called *Static Control Parts* and represented in the SCoP format [19]. In this model, a statement consists of three elements: iteration domain, access relation, and schedule. A dynamic instance of a statement is identified by its statement name S and loop iteration vector $\vec{i}$, as $S(\vec{i})$.

3.1 Basic Components

Iteration Domain, $\mathcal{D}_S$: The iteration domain of a statement S enclosed by m loops is represented by an m-dimensional polytope, where an element $S(\vec{i}) \in \mathcal{D}_S$ is an instance of statement S. As an example in Fig. 1, the iteration domain of statement S is:

$$\mathcal{D}_S = \{S(i,j) \mid 0 \leq i < \text{ni} \land 0 \leq j < \text{nj}\}$$

Access Relation, $\mathcal{A}_{S \to A}$: The array reference(s) to A by statement S is abstracted as an access relation, which maps a statement instance $S(\vec{i})$ to one or more array elements $A(\vec{e})$ to be read/written[1], typically as affine functions [34]. In Fig. 1, the write access relation for statement S to array C is:

$$\mathcal{A}_{S \to C}^{write} = \{S(i,j) \to C(e_1, e_2) \mid i = e_1 \land j = e_2\}$$

Schedule, Θ_S: The sequential execution order of a program is captured by the schedule, which maps a statement instance $S(\vec{i})$ to a logical time-stamp vector, expressed as a multidimensional (quasi-)affine function of $\vec{i}$. Statement instances are executed according to an increasing lexicographic order of their time-stamps. Dimensions of schedule may contain loop iterators. A dimension is called a *loop dimension* if it contains one or more iterators; otherwise it is called *scalar dimension*. Schedules to represent the sequential execution order of statements S and T in Fig. 1 are:

$$\Theta_S = \{S(i,j) \to (i,j,0)\}, \quad \Theta_T = \{T(i,j,k) \to (i,j,1,k)\}$$

3.2 Legality and Loop Transformations

As with traditional compiler optimizations, the polyhedral compilation computes dependences based on the original schedule and memory accesses, summarized as dependence polyhedra [5]. Polyhedral loop transformations amount to computing new schedules under the legality constraints of dependence polyhedra. In general,

---

[1] A scalar variable is considered as a degenerate case of an array.

any composition of iteration- and statement- reordering loop transformations (e.g., permutation, skewing, distribution, fusion, and tiling) can be specified by schedules. To compute new schedules, polyhedral optimizers rely on integer linear programming where dependence polyhedra are used as legality constraints and their optimization goals are formulated as objectives and/or constraints.

3.3   Affine Scheduling for Data Layout Transformations

In our previous work[2] [25], we presented two type of affine representations for data layout transformations, *array-based* and *value-based* representations that respectively map *array element* and *statement instance* into the transformed data layout. In this section, we summarize the array-based data layout representation that is main focus in this paper. Full details including value-based representation and code generation for the transformed data layouts are shown in [25].

Array Domain, $\mathcal{D}_A$: As with statements, let $A(\vec{e})$ denote an element of array A and $\mathcal{D}_A$ as the array domain of array A. Given SCoP region, the upper/lower bound of each dimension of A is an affine function of global parameters, and hence invariant. Therefore, array domain $\mathcal{D}_A$ of m-dimensional array A is a m-dimensional rectangular solid whose dimension sizes are fixed at the beginning of the SCoP region at runtime. In Figs. 1, 2 and 3, the array domain of array C is:

$$\mathcal{D}_C = \{C(e_1, e_2) \mid 0 \le e_1 < \text{ni} \wedge 0 \le e_2 < \text{nj}\}$$

Layout Mapping, Φ_A: Just as schedule Θ specifies the relative order of statement instances in time, let layout mapping Φ denote the relative order of array elements in the transformed memory space. Φ_A is the data layout of array A and maps each element $A(\vec{e})$ to a logical address vector, expressed as a multidimensional (quasi-)affine function [27] of $\vec{e}$. In this paper, we assume that layout Φ is a one-to-one mapping, i.e., each array element $A(\vec{e})$ has a unique location in the memory space and thereby no impact on legality constraints. The layout mapping in Fig. 3 are as follow, where array A's dimensions are interchanged. More layout transformations including SoA/AoS conversion, data skewing, and data tiling are discussed in [25].

$$\{C(e_1, e_2) \to (0, e_1, e_2)\}, \ \{A(e_1, e_2) \to (1, e_2, e_1)\}, \ \{B(e_1, e_2) \to (2, e_1, e_2)\}$$

4   Transformation Algorithms

4.1   Overall Framework

Algorithm 1 shows the overview of our end-to-end optimization framework, developed as an extension to the PolyAST hybrid compilation framework for combining polyhedral and AST-based transformations [24]. The input to our

---

[2] Note that [25] was presented in the IMPACT workshop, which does not have a formal· published proceedings.

Algorithm 1: End-to-end data layout and loop transformations

    Input   : Program $P := (scop,\ dependence\ polyhedra)$

1 **begin**

2     $\Phi_{best},\ \Theta_{best},\ cost_{min} := \varnothing,\ \varnothing,\ \infty$

3   **for** each $\Phi \in \{$ set of candidate layouts $\}$ **do**

4         $DL := \text{DL\_model\_creation}(P, \Phi)$

5         $\Theta := \text{PolyAST}(P, DL)$ # compute a new schedule guided by DL

6         $cost := \text{memory\_and\_computational\_cost\_estimation}(\Phi, \Theta)$

7   **if** $cost < cost_{min}$ **then**

8             $\Phi_{best},\ \Theta_{best},\ cost_{min} := \Phi,\ \Theta,\ cost$

9     $\text{codegen}(P, \Phi_{best}, \Theta_{best})$

    Output: Parallelized and optimized program

---

framework is the polyhedral representations of a source program and dependence information, in addition to the program features and runtime/architectural information (e.g., original layout, statement-level and synchronization costs).

Algorithm 1 is based on an iterative optimization process: 1) given candidate layout Φ, it builds the Distinct Lines (DL) model [9,22] for memory cost analysis; 2) guided by the DL model, the PolyAST algorithm computes schedule Θ to capture a composition of loop transformations and parallelization for given layout Φ; 3) based on program parameters, architectural features, and the DL model, the memory and computation costs for the current layout and schedule pair (Φ, Θ) is estimated; and 4) the best pair of (Φ, Θ) that minimizes the overall cost is selected as the output layout and schedule.

4.2 Candidate Layout Selection for Iterative Search

The iterative approach in Algorithm 1 computes schedule Θ for each candidate layout Φ and explores the best pair of Φ and Θ with minimum cost. While both Φ and Θ are affine functions, the legal space of Φ can be much larger than that of Θ due to the relaxed legality constraints – i.e., no ordering constraints posed on Φ while Θ must satisfy dependences described in Sect. 3. In this paper, we focus on array dimensional permutation. Although other layout transformations including AoS/SoA selection, data skewing, and data tiling can have a positive impact on performance (especially on GPUs), array dimensional permutation is a primary transformation to largely affect the best loop structures, i.e., the schedule. Let c_A denote a unique number among arrays and π denote an arbitrary permutation, this amounts to the following restricted form of candidate layout Φ_A for array A:

$$\Phi_A = \{A(e_1, e_2, ..., e_n) \rightarrow (c_A, e_{\pi(1)}, e_{\pi(2)}, ..., e_{\pi(n)})\}$$

5　Analytical Cost Model for Optimization Space Explorations

Cost estimation plays a key role in the proposed framework, which selects the best layout and schedule pair from the given candidate pairs. In this paper, we employ the static cost analyses discussed below. Given a candidate pair (Φ, Θ), per-iteration memory and computational costs of the innermost loop bodies (i.e., loop-free regions) are computed by the approaches in Sects. 5.1 and 5.2, respectively. Finally, the overall cost is computed as the weighted sum of parallelized iteration counts with synchronization costs. For instance, the overall cost of statements S and T in Fig. 3 are computed as follows:

$$cost_S = sync_{forall}(P) + \text{ni}/P \times \text{nj} \times (mem_S + comp_S)$$

$$cost_T = sync_{reduce}(P) + \text{nk}/P \times \text{ni} \times \text{nj} \times (mem_T + comp_T)$$

Here, P is the # hardware threads, $sync_{forall}$ and $sync_{reduce}$ are respectively the forall and reduction synchronization overheads as functions of P, and mem_S & $comp_S$ are the per-iteration memory & computational cost for statement S.

5.1　Memory Cost

The per-iteration memory cost of each loop body is computed by two analytical models, DL and ML, as shown below.

DL (Distinct Lines) Model. The DL model was designed to estimate the number of distinct cache lines, or TLB entries, accessed in a loop nest [9,22]. Based on machine parameters, e.g., cache line size and TLB page size, and program parameters, e.g., array dimension size and access function, the DL model expresses the number of distinct lines on a given cache/TLB as a function of enclosing loop sizes [9,22]. In the following discussion, we assume loop tiling to be applied and DL is a function of tile sizes, $DL(t_1, t_2, \cdots, t_d)$.

The per-iteration memory cost of a given loop nest on a specific cache/TLB is defined as follow.

$$DL(t_1, \cdots, t_d) = DL_{read}(t_1, \cdots, t_d) + DL_{write}(t_1, \cdots, t_d)$$

$$mem\_cost(t_1, t_2, \cdots, t_d) = \frac{Cost \times DL(t_1, \cdots, t_d)}{t_1 \times t_2 \times \cdots \times t_d}$$

Cost represents the memory cost (miss penalty) per line on cache/TLB of interest. Assuming that the tile sizes are selected so that the cache/TLB keeps any data until the last reuse, $Cost \times DL$ represents the per-tile memory access cost. The DL model is conservative in that it provides a memory cost upper bound that does not depend on ordering of statement instances within a tile.

While *DL* and *mem_cost* are functions of tile sizes, we use the per-iteration memory cost for the overall cost estimation, which is mostly independent of tile sizes. The next section shows how this at compile-time.

ML (Minimum Working-Set Lines) Model. The ML model was designed to estimate the minimum number of cache lines, or TLB entries, needed to execute
a tile without incurring any capacity misses [26]. This model is mainly used to
compute theoretical upper bounds in the loop tile size selection problem, based
on cache or TLB capacity. Given inter-tile loop order and array references within
the tile, ML is computed by: 1) constructing a special sub-tile based on analysis
of reuse characteristics; and 2) computing the DL value for that sub-tile [26]. As
with the DL model, the ML value of a given tile is defined as the function of tile
sizes. Given cache/TLB capacity C, ML defines the tile size upper bounds as:

$$ML(t_1, \cdots, t_d) \leq C$$

To compute a constant per-iteration memory cost, the cost estimation phase
contains the best compile-time tile size search that employs the ML tile size
upper bounds and returns the minimum per-iteration memory cost, mem_cost,
within the bounds. The ML model is optimistic in that it provides a memory cost
lower bound that depends on a specific ordering of statement instances within a
tile.

5.2   Computation Cost

The synchronization costs, i.e., $sync_{forall}$, $sync_{reduce}$, and $sync_{doacross}$, and per-
iteration computational costs of each loop body are obtained by the following
microbenchmarking on each target platform.

Synchronizations. We employed the EPCC OpenMP micro-benchmarks [7] to
collect the synchronization costs for forall, reduction and doacross constructs[3].

Statements. To compute per-iteration computational costs, we also used the
mechanism of EPCC benchmarking. Because the innermost loop has dominant
effects on vectorization, we microbenchmarked each statement with different
innermost loops and summarized the results in a per-statement cost table. Since
the computational cost should be computed independently from memory cost
(i.e., cache/TLB misses), all arrays are replaced by small 1-dimensional arrays
such that the innermost loop always exploits either temporal or spatial locality
according to the original array access. Although the microbenchmarking code
was generated manually for each tested benchmarks, the automation of this
process should be straightforward and addressed in future work.

Data Redistribution for Layout Transformations. We also collected the cost for
data assignments and used it for cost estimation of data copy-in and copy-out
statements between the original and new layouts. The estimated data redistribution cost is included in the computation cost.

---

[3] We extended the existing `ordered` micro-benchmark to doacross.

6   Experimental Results

6.1   Experimental Setup

Machines: We used two Linux-based SMP systems to obtain experimental results for this paper: a 12-core (dual 6-core) 2.8 GHz Intel Xeon Westmere and a 24-core (dual 12-core) 3.0 GHz IBM POWER8. On Xeon, all experimental variants were compiled using the Intel C/C++ compiler v15.0 with the "-O3 -xHOST" options for sequential runs and the "-O3 -xHOST -openmp" options for the output from automatic parallelization by PLuTo, PolyAST, and our framework. On POWER8, all variants were compiled using the IBM XL C/C++ compiler 13.1 with the "xlc -O5" command for sequential runs and the "xlc_r -O5 -qsmp=omp" command for the output from automatic parallelization by PLuTo, PolyAST, and our framework.

Benchmarks: We used the PolyBench/C v4.2 benchmark suite [20] along with the default benchmark datasets. PolyBench is a collection of benchmarks from a wide range of applications, including BLAS kernels, linear algebraic solvers, data mining, and stencil algorithms. The complete PolyBench suite consists of 30 benchmarks. Of these, we first collected results for 22 benchmarks with higher computational intensity, i.e., benchmarks in which n-dimensional arrays were accessed in m-dimensional loop nests such that $n < m$. These results for the 22 high computational intensity benchmarks are reported in Sect. 6.3; these results include the cost of data redistribution which is negligible due to the high computational intensity. We also report results for the eight benchmarks with low computational intensity in Sect. 6.4. Since the relative overhead of data redistribution is more significant in these cases, we present timing results for these eight benchmarks that exclude data redistribution overhead. These results are therefore applicable to cases when the desired data distribution is applied to the entire program without any redistribution.

Experimental Variants: Each benchmark was evaluated with the following five variants. We ran each variant 10 times in exclusive use of the machines and reported the fastest run.

1. **PLuTo:** Automatically parallelized and optimized OpenMP C code generated by the PLuTo [4,5] loop parallelizer/optimizer.
2. **PolyAST:** Automatically parallelized and optimized OpenMP C code generated by using the PolyAST [24] loop parallelizer/optimizer. As described in [24], the code generated by PolyAST assumes the availability of doacross support (as in OpenMP 4.5) and array reductions in the target system. Since our experimental systems do not as yet have support for OpenMP 4.5, we used the runtime support for doacross parallelism and array reductions that accompany the PolyAST framework.
3. **Loop-first (PolyAST + manual layout search):** After the PolyAST loop optimizations, possible array dimensional permutations are manually explored, and results are reported for the best layout for each data point.

Table 2. Speedup only by loop transformations on 12-core Intel Xeon Westmere (geometric mean speedup: 6.29× by PLuTo; and 7.05× by PolyAST)

	2 mm	3 mm	adi	cholesky	correlation	covariance	doitgen	fdtd-2d	floyd-warshall	gemm	gramschmidt
PLuTo	3.98	4.65	5.14	8.23	14.4	14.3	4.79	5.94	9.76	4.96	13.7
PolyAST	4.48	4.82	0.534	9.01	36.9	36.6	5.75	6.11	13.7	5.72	10.5
	heat-3d	jacobi-1d	jacobi-2d	ludcmp	lu		nussinov	seidel-2d	symm	syr2k	syrk	trmm
PLuTo	0.476	2.40	4.99	1.62	13.9		9.52	7.86	13.3	12.5	8.94	8.63
PolyAST	0.811	2.88	5.63	33.6	19.2		0.973	8.37	21.5	12.5	9.02	6.83

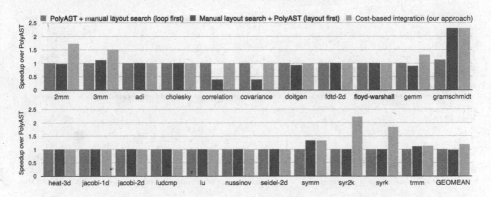

Fig. 4. Performance improvements by integrating loop and data layout transformations over PolyAST on 12-core Intel Xeon Westmere for the 22 computationally intensive benchmarks.

4. **Layout-first (manual layout search + PolyAST):** We manually explored the best array permutation for the original code, and then apply the PolyAST loop optimizations to the explored layout.
5. **Cost-based integration of data layout and loop transformations:** Our approach proposed in this paper.

6.2 Performance for Original Layout + Loop Transformations

We start with performance experiments for the PLuTo and PolyAST loop optimizers, where the original data layouts are used. Tables 2 and 3 show the speedups over sequential execution by PLuTo and PolyAST, on 12-core Intel Westmere and 24-core IBM POWER8, respectively. As shown in these results, PLuTo and PolyAST have different performance trends across benchmarks on all machines, which can be summarized by the following geometric mean speedups due to PLuTo and PolyAST: 6.29× and 7.05× on Westmere; and 7.61× and 9.71× on POWER8. Recall that PLuTo is a pure polyhedral optimizer that supports forall and wavefront parallelization, while PolyAST integrates the polyhedral and AST-based loop optimizations including forall, reduction, and doacross parallelization [24]. In the following section, we use PolyAST as the baseline to evaluate the effectiveness of integrating loop and data layout transformations,

Table 3. Speedup only by loop transformations on 24-core IBM POWER8 (geometric mean speedup: 7.61× by PLuTo; and 9.71× by PolyAST)

	2 mm	3 mm	adi	cholesky	correlation	covariance	doitgen	fdtd-2d	floyd-warshall	gemm	gramschmidt
PLuTo	17.7	18.1	11.8	13.6	33.1	32.9	7.70	5.40	0.513	9.62	19.1
PolyAST	19.9	22.7	0.917	13.3	59.5	59.2	7.60	6.93	8.74	11.6	13.0
	heat-3d	jacobi-1d	jacobi-2d	ludcmp	lu	nussinov	seidel-2d	symm	syr2k	syrk	trmm
PLuTo	1.08	0.194	5.57	1.03	60.9	2.08	5.33	16.5	12.1	9.49	74.1
PolyAST	0.932	1.83	6.40	19.6	64.1	0.994	5.53	17.4	12.1	9.57	27.1

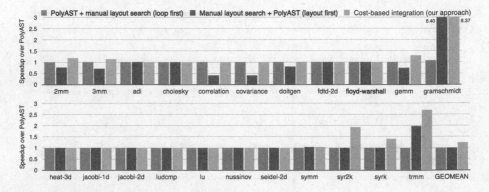

Fig. 5. Performance improvements by integrating loop and data layout transformations over PolyAST on 24-core IBM POWER8 for the 22 computationally intensive benchmarks.

since it has showed better overall performance than PLuTo for the benchmarks and platforms considered in this paper.

6.3 Performance for Loop and Data Layout Transformations

Figures 4 and 5 show improvement factors of the loop-first, layout-first, and cost-based integration approaches, relative to PolyAST respectively on the Westmere and POWER8 systems. Our proposed approach outperformed PolyAST by the geometric mean factors of 1.19× on Westmere and 1.24× on POWER8. Also, it achieved geometric mean improvements of 1.16× on Westmere and 1.21× on POWER8 over the loop-first approach; and 1.24× on Westmere and 1.24× on POWER8 over the layout-first approach. These results demonstrate the effectiveness of the proposed cost-based integration over both loop-first and layout-first approaches on all systems that we experimented with.

For the benchmarks where our proposed approach outperformed other variants, it generated output code with significantly different data layouts, loop structures, and/or parallelism from those generated by other experimental variants. On the other hand, the loop-first approach using PolyAST as the underlying loop optimizer showed nearly identical performance to PolyAST. The same trend was observed when using PLuTo instead of PolyAST. Since these loop optimizers compute the schedule based on the input data layout (e.g., cache-

Table 4. Speedup only by loop transformations on 12-core Intel Xeon Westmere (excluding data redistribution overhead)

	atax	bicg	deriche	durbin	gemver	gesummv	mvt	trisolv
PLuTo	2.58	5.39	5.63	0.87	7.52	2.41	4.36	1.03
PolyAST	3.46	6.69	4.42	0.90	9.04	4.71	4.71	2.33

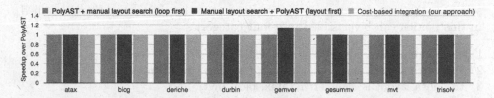

Fig. 6. Performance improvements by integrating loop and data layout transformations over PolyAST on 12-core Intel Xeon Westmere for the 8 benchmarks with low computational intensity (excluding data redistribution overhead)

aware affine scheduling by PolyAST and intra-tile loop permutation for vectorization enhancements by PLuTo), the manual best layout search selected the original layout for most benchmarks. The layout-first approach, i.e., manually select the best layout per the original code and apply PolyAST to the selected layout, showed different trends from the loop-first approach. It outperformed PolyAST for some benchmarks and underperformed for others, resulting in limited geometric mean improvements. In contrast, our proposed cost-based integration approach always showed the same or better performance than PolyAST, with certain geometric mean improvements. These results indicate that our proposed approach can guide integrated layout and loop transformations towards optimized combinations that are never considered in phase-ordered approaches, while never degrading performance.

6.4 Study of Low Computational Intensity Benchmarks

The 22 benchmarks studied in Sect. 6.3 contain kernel computations of m-dimensional loop nests accessing n-dimensional arrays such that $m > n$, and thereby the n-dimensional data redistribution cost is easily justified by the benefit of data layout transformations for m-dimensional loops. However, it's still worth studying the potential impact of data layout transformations on the remaining eight benchmarks for which the computational (i.e., loop nest level) and data (i.e., array rank) dimensionalities are the same. In this section, we report experimental results for the eight benchmarks, where the data redistribution overhead of layout transformations is excluded from the overall timing measurements. Thus, our results will be applicable to cases when the data distribution proposed by our optimization is implemented as the default data distribution for the entire program, without requiring any data redistribution.

Table 4 shows the speedups over sequential execution by PLuTo and PolyAST; and Fig. 6 shows the improvement factors over PolyAST by the loop-first, layout-first, and cost-based integration approaches on the Westmere system. As shown in the figure, our integration approach and the layout-first approach improved the performance of gemver by factor of 1.14× when ignoring the data distribution overhead. However, our approach selected the original data layout as the best candidate layout in all cases except for gemver. When manually selecting the best data layout, we observed that the eight benchmarks studied in this section can be classified into four categories:

1) the original data layout is suboptimal (gemver);
2) the original data layout is optimal (gesummv, trisolv, deriche);
3) the data layout is *symmetric* (atax, bicg, mvt); and
4) multi-dimensional arrays are not used (durbin).

Here, *symmetric* means that the data layout transformations result in the equivalent program to the original in terms of computational behavior, for instance: "x1[i] += A[i][j] * y_1[j]; x2[i] += A[j][i] * y_2[j]" as observed in mvt.

In summary, the proposed cost-based approach properly selected the best data layout combined with loop transformations for all of the eight benchmarks, and showed a certain performance improvement for gemver benchmark when assuming the data redistribution (i.e., matrix transpose) is performed at the data initialization step preceding the kernel computation. Perhaps the most important conclusion of this subsection is that our approach does not select a suboptimal data layout when the original layout performs the best.

7 Related Work

There is an extensive body of literature on loop and data layout transformations. We focus on past contributions that are most closely related to this paper.

[15] proposed a combined loop and data layout transformation framework for improving the cache performance of sequential codes. They first apply loop transformations to optimize the locality of a given loop nest, and then apply data transformations for arrays for which the array references do not exhibit good spatial locality after the loop transformations, i.e., loop-first approach. [28,29] was the first to address the unification of affine scheduling and storage optimization with consideration for the optimal tradeoff between parallelism and storage space. They proposed a mathematical framework that unifies the techniques of one-dimensional affine scheduling and occupancy vector analysis, which determines a good storage mapping for a given schedule, a good schedule for a given storage mapping, and a good storage mapping that is valid across a range of schedules. [30] extended the optimization algorithms of the R-Stream polyhedral compiler to enable array dimension permutations, thereby improving spatial locality for better vectorization efficiency. This extension introduces additional flexibility of permuting arrays per statement, on top of the existing optimization algorithm. As in [15], this raises the questions of how data layouts

should be managed across statements. [23] proposed an automatic data lay-out selection algorithm built on a source-to-source layout transformation tool. Given an input program and target machine specification, this approach rec-ommend a good SoA/AoS data layout. [6] introduced selection of optimized SoA/AoS generation for CPU+GPU hybrid architectures. Neither [23] nor [6] included loop transformations in the scope of their work. [14] presented the design and evaluation of Brainy, a program analysis tool for optimized data structure selection based on dynamic profiling. Given program, inputs, and tar-get architecture, it generates machine-learning based models to predict the best data structure implementation. Loop transformations were not included in the scope of this work. [21] addressed the minimization of inter-node communications on distributed-memory clusters by combining data tiling transformations with loop tiling. On top of polyhedral loop transformations to enable locality opti-mizations (including tiling), they successfully introduced additional constraints for data tiling to minimize communications.

These past contributions can fall into two categories: 1) the input programs are assumed to have good loop structures; or 2) loop transformations played the dominant role in the optimization problem. Further, in cases when both loop and data layout transformations were applied in a single framework, there wasn't the use of a cost function to select the best pair of loop and data layout transformations. To the best of our knowledge, our approach explores a broader space of combined loop and data layout transformations than in past work with a cost-based focus on multicore parallelism and cache locality, and thereby results in considerable performance gains over existing approaches.

8   Conclusions

In this paper, we introduced an affine scheduling framework for integrating data layout and loop transformations, using the polyhedral model as a foundation for our approach. With our extensions, data layout transformations are seam-lessly integrated with polyhedral loop transformations. Our approach is based on an iterative algorithm across candidate data layouts, and an exploration of loop transformations for each such layout. A key part of our contribution is the use of analytical DL/ML memory cost models, as well as computational cost models derived from micro-benchmarks, to select the best combinations of data layouts and loop transformations. Our experimental results on two SMP sys-tems demonstrated the effectiveness of our proposed integration framework over phase-ordered approaches using state-of-the-art loop optimizers.

Our future work includes: evaluations of layout manipulation phase to cover SoA/AoS conversion, data tiling, and data skewing, extension to GPU platforms, automation of cost-related microbenchmarking on target platforms, and search space pruning when high-dimensional arrays and array dimension fusion lead to large numbers of candidate data layouts.

References

1. The Polyhedral Compiler Collection. http://www.cs.ucla.edu/~pouchet/software/pocc/
2. Allen, J.R., Kennedy, K.: Automatic loop interchange. In: Proceedings of the 1984 SIGPLAN Symposium on Compiler Construction, SIGPLAN 1984, pp. 233–246. ACM, New York (1984)
3. Bacon, D.F., Chow, J.-H., Ju, D.-C.R., Muthukumar, K., Sarkar, V.: A compiler framework for restructuring data declarations to enhance cache and TLB effectiveness. In: CASCON First Decade High Impact Papers, CASCON 2010, pp. 146–158. IBM Corp, USA (1994)
4. Bondhugula, U., Acharya, A., Cohen, A.: The pluto+ algorithm: a practical approach for parallelization and locality optimization of affine loop nests. ACM Trans. Program. Lang. Syst. **38**(3), 12:1–12:32 (2016)
5. Bondhugula, U., Hartono, A., Ramanujam, J., Sadayappan, P.: A practical automatic polyhedral parallelizer and locality optimizer. In: Proceedings of PLDI 2008. ACM, New York (2008)
6. Barik, R., Majeti, D., Meel, K.S., Sarkar, V.: Automatic data layout generation and kernel mapping for CPU+GPU architectures. In: 25th International Conference on Compiler Construction, March 2016
7. EPCC OpenMP micro-benchmarks. https://www.epcc.ed.ac.uk/research/computing/performance-characterisation-and-benchmarking/epcc-openmp-micro-benchmark-suite
8. Feautrier, P., Lengauer, C.: Polyhedron model. In: Padua, D. (ed.) Encyclopedia of Parallel Computing, pp. 1581–1592. Springer, US (2011)
9. Ferrante, J., Sarkar, V., Thrash, W.: On estimating and enhancing cache effectiveness. In: Banerjee, U., Gelernter, D., Nicolau, A., Padua, D. (eds.) LCPC 1991. LNCS, vol. 589, pp. 328–343. Springer, Heidelberg (1992). https://doi.org/10.1007/BFb0038674
10. Grosser, T., Größlinger, A., Lengauer, C.: Polly - performing polyhedral optimizations on a low-level intermediate representation. Parallel Process. Lett. **22**(4), 1250010 (2012)
11. Henretty, T., Stock, K., Pouchet, L.-N., Franchetti, F., Ramanujam, J., Sadayappan, P.: Data layout transformation for stencil computations on short-vector SIMD architectures. In: Knoop, J. (ed.) CC 2011. LNCS, vol. 6601, pp. 225–245. Springer, Heidelberg (2011). https://doi.org/10.1007/978-3-642-19861-8_13
12. Irigoin, F., Triolet, R.: Supernode Partitioning. In: Proceedings of the 15th ACM SIGPLAN-SIGACT Symposium on Principles of Programming Languages, POPL 1988, pp. 319–329. ACM, New York (1988)
13. Integer set library. http://isl.gforge.inria.fr
14. Jung, C., Rus, S., Railing, B.P., Clark, N., Pande, S.: Brainy: effective selection of data structures. In: Proceedings of the 32Nd ACM SIGPLAN Conference on Programming Language Design and Implementation, PLDI 2011, pp. 86–97. ACM, New York (2011)
15. Kandemir, M., Choudhary, A., Ramanujam, J., Banerjee, P.: Improving locality using loop and data transformations in an integrated framework. In: Proceedings of the 31st Annual ACM/IEEE International Symposium on Microarchitecture, MICRO 31, pp. 285–297. IEEE Computer Society Press, Los Alamitos (1998)
16. Kennedy, K., McKinley, K.S.: Maximizing loop parallelism and improving data locality via loop fusion and distribution. In: Banerjee, U., Gelernter, D., Nicolau,

A., Padua, D. (eds.) LCPC 1993. LNCS, vol. 768, pp. 301–320. Springer, Heidelberg (1994). https://doi.org/10.1007/3-540-57659-2_18

17. Kong, M., Veras, R., Stock, K., Franchetti, F., Pouchet, L.-N., Sadayappan, P.: When polyhedral transformations meet SIMD code generation, vol. 48, pp. 127–138. ACM, New York, June 2013

18. McKinley, K.S., Carr, S., Tseng, C.-W.: Improving data locality with loop transformations. ACM Trans. Program. Lang. Syst. (TOPLAS) 18(4), 424–453 (1996)

19. Openscop specification and library. http://icps.u-strasbg.fr/bastoul/development/openscop/

20. PolyBench. The polyhedral benchmark suite. http://www.cse.ohio-state.edu/~pouchet/software/polybench/

21. Reddy, C., Bondhugula, U.: Effective automatic computation placement and data allocation for parallelization of regular programs. In: Proceedings of the 28th ACM International Conference on Supercomputing, ICS 2014, pp. 13–22. ACM, New York (2014)

22. Sarkar, V.: Automatic Selection of high order transformations in the IBM XL Fortran compilers. IBM J. Res. Dev. 41(3), 233–264 (1997)

23. Sharma, K., Karlin, I., Keasler, J., McGraw, J.R., Sarkar, V.: Data layout optimization for portable performance. In: Träff, J.L., Hunold, S., Versaci, F. (eds.) Euro-Par 2015. LNCS, vol. 9233, pp. 250–262. Springer, Heidelberg (2015). https://doi.org/10.1007/978-3-662-48096-0_20

24. Shirako, J., Pouchet, L.-N., Sarkar, V.: Oil and water can mix: an integration of polyhedral and ast-based transformations. In: Proceedings of the International Conference for High Performance Computing, Networking, Storage and Analysis, SC 2014, pp. 287–298. IEEE Press, Piscataway (2014)

25. Shirako, J., Sarkar, V.: Integrating data layout transformations with the polyhedral model. In: Proceedings of IMPACT 2019, Valencia, Spain, January 2019

26. Shirako, J., et al.: Expressing DOACROSS loop dependencies in OpenMP. In: Proceedings of the 2012 SIGPLAN Symposium on Compiler Construction (2012)

27. Verdoolaege, S., Grosser, T.: Polyhedral extraction tool. In: Proceedings of IMPACT 2012, Paris, France, January 2012

28. Thies, W., Vivien, F., Amarasinghe, S.P.: A step towards unifying schedule and storage optimization. ACM Trans. Program. Lang. Syst. 29(6), 34 (2007)

29. Thies, W., Vivien, F., Sheldon, J., Amarasinghe, S.P.: A unified framework for schedule and storage optimization. In: Proceedings of the 2001 ACM SIGPLAN Conference on Programming Language Design and Implementation (PLDI), Snowbird, Utah, USA, 20–22 June 2001, pp. 232–242 (2001)

30. Vasilache, N., Meister, B., Baskaran, M., Lethin, R.: Joint scheduling and layout optimization to enable multi-level vectorization. In: IMPACT-2: 2nd International Workshop on Polyhedral Compilation Techniques, Paris, France, January, Paris, France, January 2012

31. Wolf, M., Maydan, D., Chen, D.-K.: Combining loop transformations considering caches and scheduling. In: MICRO 29: Proceedings of the 29th Annual ACM/IEEE International Symposium on Microarchitecture, pp. 274–286 (1996)

32. Wolfe, M.: Loop skewing: the wavefront method revisited. Int. J. Parallel Program. 15(4), 279–293 (1986)

33. Wolfe, M.: Iteration space tiling for memory hierarchies. In: Proceedings of the Third SIAM Conference on Parallel Processing for Scientific Computing, pp. 357–361. Society for Industrial and Applied Mathematics, Philadelphia (1989)

34. Wonnacott, D.G.: Constraint-based array dependence analysis. Ph.D. thesis. UMI Order No. GAX96-22167, College Park, MD, USA (1995)

Guiding Code Optimizations with Deep Learning-Based Code Matching

Kewen Meng[(✉)] and Boyana Norris

Department of Computer and Information Science, University of Oregon,
Eugene, OR 97405, USA
{kewen,norris}@cs.uoregon.edu

Abstract. Performance models can be very useful for understanding the behavior of applications and guide design and optimization decisions. Unfortunately, performance modeling of nontrivial computations typically requires significant expertise and human effort. Moreover, even when performed by experts, it is necessarily limited in scope, accuracy, or both. In this paper, we are building the Meliora framework for machine learning-based performance model generation of arbitrary codes based on static analysis of intermediate language representations. We demonstrate good accuracy in matching known codes and show how Meliora can be used to optimize new codes though reusing optimization knowledge, either manually or in conjunction with an autotuner. When autotuning, Meliora eliminates or dramatically reduces the empirical search space, while generally achieving competitive performance.

1 Introduction

Performance models can be used to describe and possibly predict application performance on one or more architectures. Such models provide software developers with useful information about potential bottlenecks and help guide them in identifying optimization opportunities. Models can also improve the quality of compiler optimizations or accelerate the process of empirical autotuning.

Our primary objective is to accelerate the code optimization process by using a deep learning technique to match a target code to similar computations that have been optimized previously. To accomplish this, we define a new graph-based code representation and combine it with a code generation framework to enable the automated creation of a deep learning model for matching loop-based computations. The approach is based on learning accurate graph embeddings of a set of computational kernels $K_0, K_1, ..., K_N$ that have been autotuned or manually optimized on the target architecture. When a new code C_{new} must be considered, we apply the model to identify which optimized kernel, K_i, is the closest match. Based on that information and the autotuning results, we can select the best-performing version of K_i, $K_{i_{opt}}$, from our training set. This information can then be used by a human developer to manually optimize their implementation (which may involve significant refactoring), or it can be used by

© Springer Nature Switzerland AG 2022
B. Chapman and J. Moreira (Eds.): LCPC 2020, LNCS 13149, pp. 20–28, 2022.
https://doi.org/10.1007/978-3-030-95953-1_2

a compiler or an autotuner to automatically apply a small set of optimizations. The Meliora framework can thus greatly reduce or eliminate the exponential search space of potential optimizations.

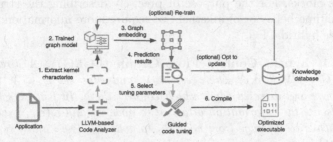

Fig. 1. Meliora workflow for model generation and use.

The two principal components of the Meliora approach are an LLVM-based frontend for extracting code features and an ML-based graph embedding component for learning code representations. The overall workflow of feature extraction, model generation, and subsequent code optimization is illustrated in Fig. 1.

2   Methodology

Meliora is a novel framework for characterizing computation, whose goal is to dramatically reduce the time and effort required for optimizing performance. The primary objective is to accelerate the process of searching the space of optimizations by using a CNN-based technique to identify previously optimized similar codes. When used in conjunction with an autotuner, Meliora can greatly reduce or eliminate the exponential search space of parameterized code versions. Here we refer to a *kernel* as any small to medium-sized computation consisting primarily of loops. The performance of many HPC applications is heavily dependent on the performance of a few key kernels, which would be the target for our analysis and optimization efforts. Unlike a library, Meliora does not aim to create a repository of ready-to-use functions optimized for particular architectures; rather, it provides a mechanism to *discover* successful optimization of *similar* (but rarely identical) computations.

The Meliora framework consists of two major components: front end for data collection and back end for data analysis. Figure 1 shows the overall process of performing the front-end analysis to extract the code representation and the data analysis in the backend.

2.1   The Hybrid Control Flow Graph Code Representation

The first step in extracting a code representation in Meliora is based on the traditional control-flow graph analysis. A control flow graph (CFG) consists of nodes and edges describing all the possible execution paths of a program.

The traditional CFG only contains nodes and edges that can provide limited information, such as the number of basic blocks and their connectivity. We can easily envision two codes with identical CFGs, but vastly different computations within basic blocks. For the purpose of precisely describing the structure and potential runtime behavior of a kernel, we require more information; hence, we introduce the hybrid CFG.

Definition 1 (hybrid Control Flow Graph (hCFG)). *A directed graph denoted as $G = \langle V, E, \delta, \epsilon \rangle$ where vertex V and edge set $E \subseteq V \times V$ stand for basic blocks and directed edges which connect them. In feature sets δ and ϵ, $\delta_i(v_n)$ represents the information attached to node v_n and $\epsilon_j(e_{mn})$ indicates the features attached to the edge from node v_m to node v_n. The i and j represent the id of the feature set.*

The graph structure of the hCFG is the same as that of the regular CFG, in which each vertex represents a basic block including a sequence of operations, and each edge indicates the direction of execution flow. To describe each node, we employ an instruction mix that consists of aggregated instruction counts of four major groups: floating-point, integer, memory access, and control operations. In addition to the instruction mix, Meliora also generates reuse distance histograms to abstract the pattern of memory access within a basic block [3,4]. Next, we compute the transition probabilities of each node by using the method described in [8], and attach the probability as an edge attribute.

2.2   Static Analysis for Metric Extraction

In the design of the analyzer, we focus on efficiency and usability. Users are able to obtain all the hCFG features during compile time, while dynamic profiling is optionally available if more precise data is needed for specific codes. In the pure static mode, the analyzer collects both the hCFG node and edge features, which are described in detail below. We have implemented the static analyzer on top of the LLVM intermediate representation (IR), which is the bridge between lexer, parser (frontend), and code generation (backend). This enables support for multiple language front-ends.

Independent of the types of the target metrics, we must inevitably traverse the abstract syntax tree (AST) or similar wrapped structure in LLVM IR one or more times, while keeping track of several values in order to summarize the corresponding metrics correctly. However, we can minimize the repeated process by adjusting the entry point of the analysis and also by aligning with the analysis granularity. Specifically, we consider loops, especially nested loops, as a whole graph so that we can flatten them from the outermost loop. After locating the top-level loop, we treat each basic block the same, independent of its type (e.g., loop SCoP) and traverse once to collect necessary data from basic blocks. Each basic block is examined to retrieve and categorize the parsed instructions. For coarser-grained results, we want to collect kernel-level information which might comprise several loops at the same level. To address this problem, we first identify and locate the first and last loops then generate a fake loop body to enclose them. After that, we can reuse the same method to process the fake loop and generate a kernel graph. This approach also allows finer control over granularity within each kernel that falls between kernel-level and single-loop.

The edge features can be extracted either statically or dynamically. The dynamic method requires source code instrumentation followed by execution to generate the hCFG transition probability edge attributes. By contrast, in the pure static approach, we provide an LLVM component for obtaining the edge data by using heuristics to compute the edge probability based on the weights produced by the DAG analysis. Both the static and dynamic approaches occur before the loop traversal pass, and the edge data are collected at the same time as node attributes. However, due to the extra steps of instrumentation and execution, the runtime of the dynamic approach is substantially higher than that of the static method.

Representing the memory access pattern without profiling data is a nontrivial task. Moreover, the enforcement of the static single assignment (SSA) form in LLVM IR complicates the implementation at the symbolic level. To address the challenges, Meliora uses the symbols extracted from the IR to estimate the bounds of the reuse distance in bytes. This is to say that we might not be able to obtain the precise memory references of an array, yet we can deduce the maximum and the minimum number of access of the same array by appropriate assumptions to compute reuse distance bounds.

2.3   Graph Representation Learning

Graph representation learning is at the heart of the Meliora workflow. The framework relies on machine learning techniques to train the model for unseen graph prediction in order to assist the selection of the tuning parameters for code optimization. In addition to the model, it converts the raw hCFGs generated in the front end into a vector while preserving significant graph properties. The embedded form reduces the costs of storage and computation on the original graphs, which is crucial for scaling up this approach to a large number of computational patterns. We build the component for graph representation learning on top of PSCN [10] proposed by Niepert et al. This approach is based on the convolutional neural network (CNNs) [6,7] aiming to learn the arbitrary graph with node and edge attributes for prediction.

2.4   Using the Model

Given a previously created model, users can apply Meliora to key loops in their code to locate the best match for an arbitrary graph with the kernels in the model. To achieve that, first Meliora compiles the source code in any language supported by LLVM into bitcode and then performs the static analysis described in Sect. 2.2 on the bitcode to collect the hCFGs representing the loops of the target kernel. Meliora supports two levels of granularity: full kernel and loop-level. One graph is created for each loop in the loop-level mode, otherwise a single graph for the entire kernel is generated. Subsequently, Meliora applies the model to the input graph data for prediction. As a result of prediction, it generates a coefficient vector with the same size as the number of neurons in the output layers of the neural network. Since we use *Sigmoid function* as the activation function for the output layer, so each value in the generated vector ranges between 0 and 1 representing the *activation* (probability) for each of the output class. We then choose from this vector the loop or kernel with the largest coefficient, i.e., the best match. At present, this is where Meliora stops, but in the future, we plan to integrate it more closely into the autotuning process. We note that this approach can be used for manual optimization, not just autotuning.

3 Evaluation

In this section, we evaluate the accuracy of the model, the performance of model generation, and the performance of model-based optimizations.

3.1 Dataset Generation

Manually creating a large-enough training dataset is a formidable task. Hence, we employed the Orio autotuning framework [5,11] to assist with this task. When Orio is applied to code, Meliora serves as a post-processor invoked by the autotuner to perform the static analysis on the various versions of the tuned code generated by Orio. No modifications to Orio were necessary; we believe integration with other autotuners is possible, too.

The dataset we used for training is a portion of the SPAPT benchmark suite [1,13], which contains four types of selected kernels. We chose SPAPT because it has a variety of computations (linear algebra, stencil, statistical) and it is already integrated with an autotuner, unlike most other available benchmarks. Each SPAPT kernel has several versions, which are first split into two groups for training (5201 graphs) and self-validation (1498 graphs), both in loop-level. In addition, a set of SPAPT kernels never used in training are used for validation (Sect. 3.3).

3.2 Model Validation

Figure 2 shows the self-validation results on the five-kernel dataset used for training. By self-validation, we mean selecting a transformed (by Orio) kernel version that was not used in training, and computing its match; for example, we expect that most versions of GEMVER would be matched with other versions of GEMVER. This is not a completely trivial validation since many of the transformations impact the hCFG and to a lesser

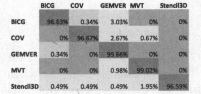

	BICG	COV	GEMVER	MVT	Stencil3D
BICG	96.63%	0.34%	3.03%	0%	0%
COV	0%	96.67%	2.67%	0.67%	0%
GEMVER	0.34%	0%	99.66%	0%	0%
MVT	0%	0%	0.98%	99.02%	0%
Stencil3D	0.49%	0.49%	0.49%	1.95%	96.59%

Fig. 2. Model self-validation at kernel-level granularity.

extent, the instruction mix. The labels on the X-axis and Y-axis are the same as the kernel names where the X-axis represents all the available classes in the training set corresponding to each of the selected kernels, and the Y-axis indicates the percentage of the graphs in the validation set predicted as the training kernels. The color of the tiles reflects the degree of similarity, from not similar at all in red (coefficient close to 0) to very similar in dark green (coefficient close to 1). The dark green diagonal indicates that self-similarity was successfully detected.

3.3 Evaluation on New Kernels

Most real-world use cases of Meliora would utilize the model to find the best match between unknown, arbitrary kernels and those in the model so that we can apply existing optimization knowledge to avoid the time-consuming search on the large variant spaces of performance optimizations. To demonstrate the application of Meliora to new codes, we present results of using it on a subset of the SPAPT benchmarks that *were not* used at all for building the model.

The evaluation procedure consists of the following steps. First, we apply Meliora to the subset of SPAPT codes that were not used for training. The accuracy of the match is shown in Table 1. These C codes typically contain several loops with various nesting depths and range in size from a tens to hundreds of lines.

Table 1. Meliora's matches for a set of new codes' loops.

New code and loop line number	Matched kernel and match coeff. (≤ 1)
adi: @132, @137	gemver (0.99), gemver(0.99)
correlation: @166, @177, @180, @185	covariance (0.99), mvt (0.99), mvt (0.85), covariance (1.00)
fdtd: @152, @154, @157, @160	bicgkernel (0.99), mvt (0.88), mvt (0.88), mvt (0.83)
jacobi: @76	gemver (0.99)
tensor: @130	stencil3d (1.00)
trmm: @124, @130	covariance (0.99), stencil3d (1.00)
dgemv: @255, @258, @260, @263, @265, @268, @270, @276, @278, @280	bicgkernel (0.83), gemver (1.00), bicgkernel (0.83), gemver (1.00), bicgkernel (0.91), gemver (1.00), bicgkernel (0.99), gemver (1.00), gemver (1.00), gemver (1.00)

Once the model returns a match, we compute the cosine similarity between the loops in the new kernel and those in the matched kernel to further refine the mapping. For example, the first loop in adi (adi@132) is matched with the gemver kernel, which has four loops. The cosine similarity between the embeddings of the adi@132 and the gemver@134 loops is the highest, hence we finalize the match to be adi@132-gemver@134.

The next step is to copy (manually) the tuning spec from the autotuned version of the matched kernel into the new code, adjusting variable names as needed.

For example, the **correlation** code has four loops, two of which were matched with **covariance**, and two with **mvt**. In the future, we will automate this step, while still allowing the user to customize the inserted tuning annotations.

Performance Improvement. The speedups obtained by modifying the new codes as described above are shown in Fig. 3a. The baseline is the original, unoptimized version, compiled with a recent GCC compiler using the -O3 optimization level. All optimization options in the matched kernels can be seen in the SPAPT benchmark repository [1, 13] and include loop unrolling, cache tiling, register tiling, SIMD pragma insertion, OpenMP parallelization, and scalar replacement. While we used an autotuner to enable rapid application of these optimizations, one could also apply them manually, albeit at a dramatically increased effort (the size of the tuned code is typically much larger than the original, especially when combining multiple transformations).

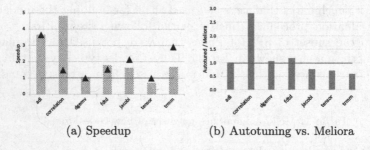

(a) Speedup   (b) Autotuning vs. Meliora

Fig. 3. Evaluation on new kernels: (a) Speedup over the unoptimized (base) versions: bars for Meliora-matched optimizations, black triangles for empirical autotuning results, and a red line for the baseline performance; and (b) Comparison with empirically tuned performance. Values greater than one indicate that Meliora-based optimizations outperformed the empirical autotuner.

We completely eliminated the empirical search *and* produced a better-performing version for some of the new codes (**adi** (1.78x[1]), **correlation** (4.2x), and **trmm** (1.12x)). In addition, we were able to improve performance further by applying limited autotuning for **adi** (3.7x), **dgemv** (1.1x), **fdtd** (1.8x), **jacobi** (1.6x) and **correlation** (4.8x); this required minimal extra effort to modify the parameter space to include the default options. In summary, we reduced the autotuning search time by 2x to 1,126x for the test kernels.

Figure 3b shows a comparison between Meliora-based optimized codes and empirically autotuned versions using a machine-learning-based search strategy capped at 1000 runs (the same as was used to generate the model, although in most cases, fewer than 100 runs were performed per kernel by the search method). Such capping is necessary because the size of the parameter search spaces (ranging from 10^4 to 10^24 for these codes) is too large to allow the exhaustive search. The only code for which the autotuner significantly outperformed

---

[1] Speedup with respect to the original code version.

the Meliora-based version is **trmm**. For **correlation**, using the tuning specification from the matched kernels significantly outperformed the result from autotuning the original by providing a better starting point for the search, as well as a slightly different set of optimizations.

Autotuning Search Performance. We evaluated the autotuning performance both on a single set of parameters and with limited autotuning on a small parameter space based on the matched loops. The post-match autotuning also benefits from the use of local optimization methods because we know that the starting point is likely to close to the optimum.

For the **correlation** benchmark, the Meliora-based optimization through a match with loops from the autotuned **covariance** and **mvt** kernels), we were able to actually outperform previous empirical tuning without any empirical testing. The results for **tensor** indicate that this specific benchmark is not optimizable via the kinds of optimizations we attempted (as indicated by the fact that both the Meliora and autotune results are close to the original performance). In part this is due to the fact that it contains a five-level loop; there is nothing similar among the other kernels in SPAPT. To use Meliora for such cases, a model should be trained with a greater number of representative kernels, including tensor contractions.

4   Related Work

Wen et al. [15] and Luk [9] use regression to predict application speedup and running time. Others use classification [2,14,16] or clustering [12] to obtain optimal parameters. Unlike most existing works, our approach focuses on defining an effective graph-based code representation and uses its embedding to estimate the similarity of loop-based computations to previously optimized codes. We also leverage an autotuner for training set generation in a manner that reduces the chance of overtraining.

5   Conclusions and Future Work

In this paper, we introduced Meliora, a framework for extracting code representations that can be used to find potential optimizations for new codes more easily, enabling reuse of optimization knowledge and reducing the human and autotuner search times. Our future work includes identifying more low-cost features on which to base metrics that represent other relevant code characteristics that affect performance in different settings, e.g., shared-memory parallel regions. We also plan to extend Meliora with inter-procedural analysis to enable correct handling of code containing function calls. In addition, we plan to complete the integration of Meliora into the autotuning process for speeding up autotuning of new codes by reducing the search space.

References

1. Balaprakash, P., Wild, S.M., Norris, B.: SPAPT: search problems in automatic performance tuning. Proc. Comput. Sci. **9**, 1959–1968 (2012)
2. Beckingsäle, D., Pearce, O., Laguna, I., Gamblin, T.: Apollo: reusable models for fast, dynamic tuning of input-dependent code. In: 2017 IEEE International Parallel and Distributed Processing Symposium (IPDPS), pp. 307–316. IEEE (2017)
3. Beyls, K., D'Hollander, E.: Reuse distance as a metric for cache behavior. In: Proceedings of the IASTED Conference on Parallel and Distributed Computing and systems, vol. 14, pp. 350–360. Citeseer (2001)
4. Ding, C., Zhong, Y.: Predicting whole-program locality through reuse distance analysis. In: Proceedings of the ACM SIGPLAN 2003 Conference on Programming Language Design and Implementation, pp. 245–257 (2003)
5. Hartono, A., Norris, B., Sadayappan, P.: Annotation-based empirical performance tuning using Orio. In: 2009 IEEE International Symposium on Parallel & Distributed Processing, pp. 1–11. IEEE (2009)
6. LeCun, Y., Bengio, Y., Hinton, G.: Deep learning. Nature **521**(7553), 436–444 (2015)
7. LeCun, Y., Bottou, L., Bengio, Y., Haffner, P.: Gradient-based learning applied to document recognition. Proc. IEEE **86**(11), 2278–2324 (1998)
8. Lim, R., Norris, B., Malony, A.: A similarity measure for GPU kernel subgraph matching. In: 31st International Workshop on Languages and Compilers for Parallel Computing (LCPC), October 2018
9. Luk, C.K., Hong, S., Kim, H.: Qilin: exploiting parallelism on heterogeneous multiprocessors with adaptive mapping. In: 2009 42nd Annual IEEE/ACM International Symposium on Microarchitecture (MICRO), pp. 45–55. IEEE (2009)
10. Niepert, M., Ahmed, M., Kutzkov, K.: Learning convolutional neural networks for graphs. In: International Conference on Machine Learning, pp. 2014–2023 (2016)
11. Norris, B., Hartono, A., Gropp, W.: Annotations for productivity and performance portability. In: Petascale Computing: Algorithms and Applications, pp. 443–462. Computational Science, Chapman & Hall / CRC Press, Taylor and Francis Group (2007). http://www.mcs.anl.gov/uploads/cels/papers/P1392.pdf. Also available as Preprint ANL/MCS-P1392-0107
12. Perelman, E., Hamerly, G., Van Biesbrouck, M., Sherwood, T., Calder, B.: Using simpoint for accurate and efficient simulation. ACM SIGMETRICS Perform. Eval. Rev. **31**(1), 318–319 (2003)
13. SPAPT benchmark codes. https://github.com/brnorris03/Orio/tree/master/testsuite/SPAPT. Accessed 22 Apr 2020
14. Stephenson, M., Amarasinghe, S.: Predicting unroll factors using supervised classification. In: International Symposium on Code Generation and Optimization, pp. 123–134. IEEE (2005)
15. Wen, Y., Wang, Z., O'boyle, M.F.: Smart multi-task scheduling for OpenCL programs on CPU/GPU heterogeneous platforms. In: 2014 21st International Conference on High Performance Computing (HiPC), pp. 1–10. IEEE (2014)
16. Yuki, T., Renganarayanan, L., Rajopadhye, S., Anderson, C., Eichenberger, A.E., O'Brien, K.: Automatic creation of tile size selection models. In: Proceedings of the 8th Annual IEEE/ACM International Symposium on Code Generation and Optimization, pp. 190–199 (2010)

Expanding Opportunities for Array Privatization in Sparse Computations

Mahdi Soltan Mohammadi[1], Mary Hall[2], and Michelle Mills Strout[3(✉)]

[1] NVIDIA, Beaverton, USA
mahdisoltanm@nvidia.com
[2] University of Utah, Salt Lake City, USA
mhall@cs.utah.edu
[3] University of Arizona, Tucson, USA
mstrout@cs.arizona.edu

Abstract. Sparse computation, where sparse formats are used to compress nonzero values of big data, are commonly used in real world applications. However, the compiler-based data dependence analysis of sparse computations needed for automatic parallelization is difficult due to usage of indirect memory accesses through index arrays, e.g. `col` in $val[col[j]]$, in these computations. One use of such data dependence analysis is to find opportunities for array privatization, which is an approach to increase available parallelism in a loop by providing each parallel thread its own copy of arrays where in each iteration the array reads are dominated by array writes in the same iteration. In this paper, we expand opportunities for compile-time array privatization in sparse computations by using newly formulated index array properties and a novel concept we call content-based privatization. Furthermore, we discuss existing opportunities to use our approach for detecting private arrays in existing library implementations of sparse computations.

Keywords: Privatization · First private arrays · Dependence analysis · Sparse computation

1 Introduction

Sparse structures are commonly used to compress nonzero values of big data manipulated in applications such as big graph data analytics [7] and numerical methods [4]. Sparse computations such as sparse triangular solve, cholesky, and LU exhibit partial parallelism in their outer loop due to indirect memory access through index arrays, e.g. `col` in $val[col[j]]$. However, storage-reuse-related, loop-carried data dependencies can obfuscate such partial parallelism from program analysis. When storage-related dependences are such that each element in an array is written in a particular iteration before it is read in the same iteration, the storage-related write-after-read (WAR) dependence between iterations can

© Springer Nature Switzerland AG 2022
B. Chapman and J. Moreira (Eds.): LCPC 2020, LNCS 13149, pp. 29–37, 2022.
https://doi.org/10.1007/978-3-030-95953-1_3

```
1 for (i=1; i < n ; i++){
2   for(j=idx1[i]; j < idx1[i+1]; j++){
3     B[idx2[j]] = ...
4   }
5   A [i] = A [i-1] + B[i] ...
6 }
```

Fig. 1. A sample sparse code where the outermost loop is sequential due to flow dependence that cannot be removed.

be eliminated by providing each thread a private copy of the array [22]. Parallelization of sparse computations including finding arrays that can be privatized is often done by hand since the content of index arrays is only available at runtime making compile-time dependence analysis nontrivial [1,2,13,14,19,23]. In this paper, we present compile-time analysis methods for automatically finding privatizable arrays that previous analysis approaches are unable to identify.

Although, flow dependences like the one in Fig. 1 prevent us from extracting any parallelism, storage-related dependences in sparse computations can be removed using privatization. For instance, consider the pseudocode in Fig. 2. The reads and writes to array A are storage related since each iteration of the i-loop writes the entire range of this array in the k-loop before reading some of its values in the j-loop. Therefore, we can extract wavefront parallelism for the i-loop while privatizing the array A. We can privatize an array like A for a loop like L, if the following two conditions described by Peng and Padua [22] hold:

1. "Every fetch to an element of A in L must be preceded by a store to the element in the same iteration of L".
2. "Different iterations of L may access the same location of A".

```
1 for (i=1; i < n ; i++){
2   for(k=0; k < n ; k++){
3     A [k] = ...
4   }
5   for(j=idx1[i]; j < idx1[i+1]; j++){
6     B[idx2[j]] = A [idx2[j]] ...
7   }
8   ... = B[i] ...
9 }
```

Fig. 2. Example sparse code pattern with simple private array that can be analyzed by previous works.

Several previous works have presented compile time and runtime methods to detect private arrays [5,10,12,15–18,20–22]. These previous works can only handle detecting private arrays in restricted code patterns involving indirect memory accesses through index arrays. Nevertheless, a number of them do use index array properties in limited capicity for detecting privatization. Lin and Padua presented a method that could analyze code with irregular memory accesses and recognize whether an array has been used like a stack data structure, and hence can be privatized [5]. They also used the range of index arrays to approximate range of read and write accesses to an array to see whether range of reads are subset of range of writes. Hybrid Analysis (HA) works used a special data structure called USR to efficiently record what section of an array has been accessed while collecting flow information for detecting private arrays [10,20,21]. Constraint-based dependence analysis using uninterpreted functions by Pugh and Wonnacott [16] used functional consistency to detect some privatization possibilities in sparse codes.

Most previous work cannot do the analysis for detecting private arrays at compile time when there is more than one index arrays involved in indirect memory accesses through index arrays. For instance consider the code pattern in Fig. 3, where we have two different index arrays indexing into the A-array. This code pattern can be found in typical library implementation of some of the commonly used sparse computations such as sparse Left Cholesky, sparse Left LU, and sparse QR solver from CSparse library [4]. However, Mohammadi et al. [8] presented an approach that enables representing index-array properties involving more than one index array. In this paper, we use that approach to find first-private and other privatizable arrays.

This paper contributes the following: (1) shows how index-array properties can enable content-based privatization opportunities (akin to first private privatization where each thread's private array instances get initialized to content of the array before the parallel loop), (2) introduces new index-array properties relevant for computations with fill-in, (3) shows how those properties can lead to more privatization opportunities, and (4) describes the key barrier to such approaches being the use of dynamic index arrays.

```
1  for (i = 0 ; i < n ; i++){
2    for (j = idx1[i]; j < idx1[i+1]; j++){
3      // ...
4      A[ idx2[j] ] = ...
5    }
6    for (k = idx4[i]; k < idx4[i+1]; k++){
7      ... = A[ idx5[k] ];
8    }
9  }
```

Fig. 3. General irregular code pattern with private arrays that previous works cannot analyze at compile time.

2. Constraint-Based Dependence Analysis

The constraints for memory access function to an array inside a loop nest are defined as follow:

$$\{\overbrace{\vec{I_t} \to d}^{\text{Array Access Expression}} : \exists \vec{I_r} : \overbrace{F(\vec{I}) = d \wedge Constraints(\vec{I}) \wedge Constraints(\vec{I'})}^{\text{Loop Bounds and Conditional Constraints (if,...)}}\}$$

where $\vec{I_t}$ refers to iterators of the loop nest up to the target loop t, and $\vec{I_r}$ are remaining iterators in the loop nest. For instance, the write memory access function to x-array, $x[idx2[j]]$ in line 4 of Fig. 3 with respect to outer most loop is as follows:

$$\{\overbrace{[i] \to [d]}^{\text{Array Access Expression}} : \exists j : idx2(j) = d \wedge \overbrace{0 \leq i < n \wedge idx1(i) \leq j < idx1(i+1)}^{\text{Loop Bounds}}\}$$

Mohammadi et al. [8] show that general index array properties can be represented using universially quantified assertions. And, we can use original constraints from loop-carried data dependences to instantiate such assertions, and produce new constraints that can be used alongside original constraints. Following same scheme, we can use constraints from memory access functions to instantiate index array properties. For instance, following formulates functional consistency about `idx1` index array from example access function in previous paragraph:

$$(\forall x_1, x_2)(x_1 = x_2 \implies idx1(x_1) < idx1(x_2))$$

Now, we can instanciate this property with $idx2(j) = d$ from the original access function constraints, and obtain: $idx1(idx2(j)) = idx1(d)$. Since, the constraint fits to the left handside of the property, we can surmise the right handside of the property must also hold true about the original set of constraints. Therefore, original set of constraints can be extended with newly instantiated constraint:

$$\{\overbrace{[i] \to [d]}^{\text{Array Access Expression}} : \exists j : idx2(j) = d \wedge \overbrace{0 \leq i < n}^{\text{Loop Bounds}} \ldots \wedge \overbrace{idx1(idx2(j)) = idx1(d)}^{\text{Instantiated}}\}$$

3 First-Private Analysis

In this section, we introduce a new scheme for detecting private arrays, called content-private that expands the opportunities for detecting private arrays in sparse computations. Consider the code pattern in Fig. 4a. Based on the traditional definition of privatizable arrays, the array A in this code cannot be privatized, since there could be loop-carried flow dependences from write in line 13 to reads in lines 8 and 12. However, we claim array A is private in this pattern not based on whether we have cross iteration flow of data based on reads/writes

```
1  for(k=0; k < m ; k++){
2    A [ k ] = 0
3  }
4  for (i=0; i < n ; i++){
5    for(j=0; j < m ; j++){
6      A [idx1[j]] = XX;
7
8      ... = A[idx2[j]] ...
9    }
10   ... = A[i] ...
11   for(k=0; k < m ; k++){
12     ... = A [ idx3[k] ] ...
13     A [ idx3[k] ] = 0;
14   }
15 }
```

(a) Array A is a content-private array.

```
1  for (i = 0 ; i < n ; i++){
2    x[ i ] = P;
3  }
4  for (i = 0 ; i < n ; i++){
5    for(j = idx1[i]; j < idx1[i+1]; j
       ++){
6      x[ idx2[j] ] = ...
7    }
8    for(l = idx3[i]; l < idx3[i+1]; l
       ++){
9      x[ idx4[l] ] = ...
10   }
11   x[ i ] = P;
12   for(k = idx5[i]; k < idx5[i+1]; k
       ++){
13     x[ idx6[k] ] = P;
14   }
15 }
```

(b) General pattern for content private.

Fig. 4. Patterns for demonstrating content-private arrays. The private arrays in these patterns can be privatized using first private, however, they cannot be detected through an approach for detecting first private.

accesses to this array, rather because all content of array A start every iteration of the i-loop being 0.

There are similarities between such a private case and copy-in privatization introduced by Peng and Padua [22]. An array is copy-in private, also called first private, if one or more iterations of the parallel loop read from parts of the private array that never get written in the loop. In first private, compiler needs to copy initial values of the original array to all of its thread private copies. To privatize array A in Fig. 4a, we need to copy its initial values to its thread private copies similar to scheme for first private. However, it cannot be detected using an automated approach for detecting traditionally defined first private arrays due to loop-carried flow data dependences.

We define a new scheme for detecting private arrays, called content private, in general irregular code pattern in Fig. 4b. A content-private array is temporary storage that can be privatized similar to first private. However, there could be loop-carried dependencies based on resetting writes and reads to content-private arrays. The resetting writes are those that reset values of the array to their initial values in the same iteration of the parallel loop that they have been modified.

For an intuitive reason why we can privatize arrays like x-array in Fig. 4b, it is important to note how its content get modified during the parallelization target loop. First, its entire range get initialized to a specific value (P) before the i-loop targeted for parallelization. Next, parts of x's content change from the initial value to other values at some lines like 6 and 9 in the i-loop. Finally, towards the end of the parallelization target loop, those content of x that have been changed from the initial value get reseted back to initial value, line 11 and 13 in Fig. 4b. This pattern guarantees that all the values of content-private x-array start all iterations of the i-loop being initialized to P.

4   Privatization and Preliminary Evaluation

In this section, we introduce our privatization analysis method when there are index arrays. We also introduce formulation of an index-array properties that have not been used in previous works, and is particularly useful for privatization analysis. Next, we have a discussion on sparse codes that have opportunities for applying our analysis, and detect more private arrays than previous works. Lastly, we discuss dynamic index-array issue, a problematic code pattern that complicates dependence analysis in sparse codes.

Our privatization analysis approach that integrates using index arrays properties is as follow:

1. First, we extract the memory access functions for all the read and write accesses to an array.
2. Then, we use an extended version of the instantiation procedure from Mohammadi et al. [9] to instantiate index array properties. Out of instantiated constraints, we collect the constraints that satisfy following conditions: first, they do not exist in at least one of the sets, and second, they are relevant to both sets by including at least one index array from both of the sets. Then, we add those collected constraints to both sets.
3. Next, we use the subsetting algorithm introduced by Mohammadi et al. Section [9] to check to see if range memory accessed by read accesses are (the read access functions) subset of range of write accesses (the write access functions).

Note that: this approach can only be applied to code patterns where statement ordering determines whether read accesses are happening before write accesses.

Sub-set-of Index Array Property Definition: We are also introducing a new index array property in this section called sub-set-of that is not introduced in the related papers [6, 8–10, 16, 21]. The sub-set-of property is defines between two index arrays like $f1$ and $f2$, where content of $f1$ is subset of $f2$. This property usually happens in sparse computations where nonzeros of output data includes nonzeros in the same locations as the input data plus some added nonzeros. In this way content of the index array recording row (or column) locations of nonzeros for the input data will be sub-set-of the index array recording row (or column) locations of nonzeros for the output. The sub-set-of property is defined as follow:

Sub-set-of property $= \{\forall x_1 : \exists x2 : lb1 \le x1 < ub1 \wedge lb2 \le x2 < ub2 \rightarrow lb2 \le x2 < ub2 \wedge f1(x1) = f2(x2)\}$

Several popular implementation of sparse computations include private arrays that cannot be detected at compile time using previous methods. Table 1

Table 1. Some library implementations of commonly used sparse computations with private arrays that cannot be detected at compile time by previous methods. Note all these computations have similar implementations in the CSparse Library [4] and Eigen citeEigenLib.

Kernel	Source	General private arrays	First private arrays	Dynamic index array
Sparse Matrix-Matrix Multiply	CSparse [4]	Yes	Yes	Yes
Left Cholesky	CSparse [4]	Yes	Yes	Yes
Left LU	CSparse [4]	Yes	Yes	Yes
Left QR	CSparse [4]	Yes	Yes	Yes
Static Left Cholesky	Sympiler [3]	No	Yes	No

```
1  for (j = 0 ; j < n ; j++){
2    Cp [j] = nz;
3    for (p1 = Bp [j]; p1 < Bp [j+1]; p1++){
4      for (p2 = Ap [Bi[p1]]; p2 < Ap [Bi[p1]+1]; p2++){
5        if (w [Ai [p2]] == 0){
6          w [Ai [p2]] = 1;
7          Ci [nz] = Ai [p2];
8          nz++;
9          x [Ai [p2]] = Bx [p1] * Ax [p2];
10       }
11       else {
12         x [Ai [p2]] += Bx [p1] * Ax [p2];
13       }
14     }
15   }
16   for (p = Cp [j]; p < nz; p++){
17     Cx [p] = x [Ci [p]];
18     w[Ci[p]] = 0;
19   }
20 }
```

Fig. 5. Sparse matrix-matrix multiply from CSparse [4].

list number of such computations. Index array properties can be used to detect private arrays in the computations in the table. However, the constraint-based dependence analysis approach that we describe so far cannot be directly used to analyze the kernels in the Table 1 except for Static left Cholesky. The reason is these kernels include a problematic code pattern that we call dynamic index array problem.

A fundamental assumption for doing constraint-based loop-carried data dependence analysis that we are using is that the loop bounds and array index expressions must be constants or function of enclosing loop iterators [11]. Additionally, the inspector/executor strategy that we are using assumes we will have the content of index arrays before the main computation. The reason is runtime inspectors of sparse dependences get executed before the main computation. Consequently, the index arrays and variables that get manipulated during the computation in a way that we cannot define them as a closed-from expression of the loop iterators create a barrier for applying the dependence analysis approach we have been using. We call such index arrays and variables (zero-dimensional arrays), dynamic index arrays. Figure 5 shows the Sparse Matrix-Matrix Multiply kernel. In this code, Ci, Cp, nz are all dynamic index arrays. Notice for instance how Cp's content get assigned to a value that cannot be defined as closed form expression of loop iterators in line 2. Handling such dynamic index arrays is a possible direction for future research.

5   Conclusions

In this paper, we show how index-array properties involving more than one index array can be used to discover more first-private and privatizable arrays at compile time in sparse computations.

References

1. Bell, N., Garland, M.: Implementing sparse matrix-vector multiplication on throughput-oriented processors. In: SC 2009: Proceedings of the Conference on High Performance Computing Networking, Storage and Analysis, pp. 1–11. ACM, New York (2009)
2. Byun, J.H., Lin, R., Yelick, K.A., Demmel, J.: Autotuning sparse matrix-vector multiplication for multicore. Technical report, UCB/EECS-2012-215, November 2012
3. Cheshmi, K., Kamil, S., Strout, M.M., Dehnavi, M.M.: Sympiler: Transforming sparse matrix codes by decoupling symbolic analysis. In: Proceedings of the International Conference for High Performance Computing, Networking, Storage and Analysis, SC 2017, pp. 13:1–13:13. ACM, New York (2017). https://doi.org/10.1145/3126908.3126936, http://doi.acm.org/10.1145/3126908.3126936
4. Davis, T., Hager, W., Duff, I.: Suitesparse (2014). http://faculty.cse.tamu.edu/davis/suitesparse.html
5. Lin, Y., Padua, D.: Compiler analysis of irregular memory accesses. In: Proceedings of the 21st Conference on Programming Language Design and Implementation, PLDI 2000, pp. 157–168 (2000). https://doi.org/10.1145/349299.349322
6. Lin, Y., Padua, D.: Compiler analysis of irregular memory accesses. In: Proceedings of the ACM SIGPLAN Conference on Programming Language Design and Implementation, vol. 35, pp. 157–168. ACM, New York, May 2000
7. McAuley, J., Leskovec, J.: Hidden factors and hidden topics: understanding rating dimensions with review text. In: Proceedings of the 7th ACM Conference on Recommender Systems, RecSys 2013, pp. 165–172. ACM, New York (2013). https://doi.org/10.1145/2507157.2507163, http://doi.acm.org/10.1145/2507157.2507163

8. Mohammadi, M.S., Cheshmi, K., Dehnavi, M.M., Venkat, A., Yuki, T., Strout, M.M.: Extending Index-array properties for data dependence analysis. In: Hall, M., Sundar, H. (eds.) LCPC 2018. LNCS, vol. 11882, pp. 78–93. Springer, Cham (2019). https://doi.org/10.1007/978-3-030-34627-0_7

9. Mohammadi, M.S., et al.: Sparse computation data dependence simplification for efficient compiler-generated inspectors. In: Proceedings of the 40th ACM SIG-PLAN Conference on Programming Language Design and Implementation, PLDI 2019, pp. 594–609. Association for Computing Machinery, New York (2019). https://doi.org/10.1145/3314221.3314646

10. Oancea, C.E., Rauchwerger, L.: Logical inference techniques for loop paralleliza-tion. In: Proceedings of the 33rd ACM SIGPLAN Conference on Programming Language Design and Implementation, PLDI 2012, pp. 509–520. ACM, New York (2012)

11. Padua, D.A., Wolfe, M.J.: Advanced compiler optimizations for supercomputers. Commun. ACM **29**(12), 1184–1201 (1986)

12. Paek, Y., Hoeflinger, J., Padua, D.: Efficient and precise array access analysis. ACM Trans. Program. Lang. Syst. **24**(1), 65–109 (2002)

13. Park, J., Smelyanskiy, M., Sundaram, N., Dubey, P.: Sparsifying synchronization for high-performance shared-memory sparse triangular solver. In: Kunkel, J.M., Ludwig, T., Meuer, H.W. (eds.) ISC 2014. LNCS, vol. 8488, pp. 124–140. Springer, Cham (2014). https://doi.org/10.1007/978-3-319-07518-1_8

14. Park, J., et al.: Efficient shared-memory implementation of high-performance con-jugate gradient benchmark and its application to unstructured matrices. In: Pro-ceedings of International Conference for High Performance Computing, Network-ing, Storage and Analysis, SC 2014, pp. 945–955. IEEE Press, Piscataway (2014)

15. Pugh, B., Wonnacott, D.: Nonlinear array dependence analysis. Technical report CS-TR-3372, Department of Computer Science, University of Maryland, November 1994

16. Pugh, W., Wonnacott, D.: Constraint-based array dependence analysis. ACM Trans. Program. Lang. Syst. **20**(3), 635–678 (1998)

17. Rauchwerger, L., Padua, D.: The privatizing DOALL test: a run-time technique for DOALL loop identification and array privatization. In: Proceedings of the 8th International Conference on Supercomputing. ICS 1994, pp. 33–43. Association for Computing Machinery, New York (1994). https://doi.org/10.1145/181181.181254

18. Rauchwerger, L., Padua, D.A.: The LRPD test: speculative run-time paralleliza-tion of loops with privatization and reduction parallelization. IEEE Trans. Parallel Distrib. Syst. **10**(2), 160–180 (1999). https://doi.org/10.1109/71.752782

19. Rennich, S.C., Stosic, D., Davis, T.A.: Accelerating sparse Cholesky factorization on GPUs. Parallel Comput. **59**, 140–150 (2016)

20. Rus, S., Hoeflinger, J., Rauchwerger, L.: Hybrid analysis: static & dynamic memory reference analysis. Int. J. Parallel Program. **31**(4), 251–283 (2003)

21. Rus, S.V.: Hybrid analysis of memory references and its application to automatic parallelization. Ph.D. thesis, Texas A&M (2006)

22. Tu, P., Padua, D.: Automatic array privatization. In: Banerjee, U., Gelernter, D., Nicolau, A., Padua, D. (eds.) LCPC 1993. LNCS, vol. 768, pp. 500–521. Springer, Heidelberg (1994). https://doi.org/10.1007/3-540-57659-2_29

23. Wang, E., et al.: Intel math kernel library. In: Wang, E., et al. (eds.) High-Performance Computing on the Intel® Xeon Phi^{TM}, pp. 167–188. Springer, Cham (2014). https://doi.org/10.1007/978-3-319-06486-4_7

OpenMP and Fortran

Concurrent Execution of Deferred OpenMP Target Tasks with Hidden Helper Threads

Shilei Tian[1]([✉]) [iD], Johannes Doerfert[2] [iD], and Barbara Chapman[1] [iD]

[1] Department of Computer Science, Stony Brook University, Stony Brook, USA
{shilei.tian,barbara.chapman}@stonybrook.edu
[2] Argonne Leadership Computing Facility, Argonne National Laboratory,
Lemont, USA
jdoerfert@anl.gov

Abstract. In this paper, we introduce a novel approach to support concurrent offloading for OPENMP tasks based on hidden helper threads. We contrast our design to alternative implementations and explain why the approach we have chosen provides the most consistent performance across a wide range of use cases. In addition to a theoretical discussion of the trade-offs, we detail our implementation in the LLVM compiler infrastructure. Finally, we provide evaluation results of four extreme offloading situations on the SUMMIT supercomputer, showing that we achieve speedup of up to 6.7× over synchronous offloading, and provide comparable speedup to the commercial IBM XL C/C++ compiler.

1 Introduction

Parallel programming is here to stay. In fact, the number of compute cores configured per platform continues to grow, and many of them are in the form of accelerators. GPUs are the most common type of accelerator in modern supercomputers; on some recent systems, multiple GPUs are present on a single node. As most of the computational power is within them, it is imperative for performance (per watt) to keep the GPUs occupied with productive work at all times. A meaningful approach is to perform as many computations as possible simultaneously [10,12]. Even NVIDIA Fermi GPUs, which have been on the market for ten years, allow for concurrent execution of up to 16 GPU kernels on a single device. Asynchronous offloading is a promising technique to achieve such concurrency as it allows a single CPU thread to overlap memory movement, GPU computation, and the preparation of new GPU tasks on the CPU. Costly stalls between GPU computations, aka. *kernels*, are avoided and the hardware can start the execution of an already prepared kernel as soon as the ones currently executed stop utilizing the entire device.

The OPENMP standard supports asynchronous offloading since version 4.5, though compiler support still varies. In OPENMP, computations are mapped to

B. Chapman and J. Moreira (Eds.): LCPC 2020, LNCS 13149, pp. 41–56, 2022.
https://doi.org/10.1007/978-3-030-95953-1_4

```
#pragma omp target depend(...) map(...)... nowait
{ ... }
```

Fig. 1. Generic `target` directive with `task` parts, e.g., the `depend` and `nowait` clause, offloading parts, e.g., the `map` clause, and other clauses such as `shared`.

accelerators via `target` directives such as the one sketched in Fig. 1. The statement following the directive is called the *target region* and the task created by the directive is called a *deferred target task*. Similar to other tasks, dependences can be specified with the `depend` clause and asynchronous execution can be permitted with the `nowait` clause. The `map` clause can be used to ensure memory regions are mapped between the host and the device. Depending on the situation and the clause arguments this can result in memory allocation, copies, deallocation, or none of these. While we describe the necessary semantics, we refer to the OPENMP standard for details and additional information.

In this paper we propose, compare, and evaluate a new scheme to implement the `nowait` clause on `target` directives to achieve concurrent offloading. It is designed to provide good performance regardless of the context. Our approach utilizes otherwise "hidden" helper threads to provide consistent results across various use cases. In Sect. 2.2 we introduce several possible implementations and compare them from a theoretical perspective. We discuss the implementation of our *hidden-helper-thread* design as part of the LLVM compiler in Sect. 3, before providing an evaluation of its behavior for four extreme offloading cases in Sect. 4. Our results show the *hidden-helper-thread* design gains up to 6.7× improvement on SUMMIT supercomputer, and also provides comparable speedup to the commercial IBM XL C/C++ compiler. We discuss related work in Sect. 5 and conclude with ideas for improvement in Sect. 6.

2   Design Discussion

In order to discuss different implementation designs for *deferred target tasks*, we first dissect one and identify its semantic steps. As part of the overall strategy it is important to determine which thread will execute each step, as that is a fundamental property of the design. Based upon this mapping of responsibilities, it is possible to reason about the performance potential of a given scheme in various scenarios without implementing all schemes and evaluating all scenarios.

The steps taken to execute a *deferred target task* are shown in Fig. 2. The first step is to resolve outstanding dependences, that is, wait for completion of previously generated sibling tasks that the target task depends on. Next, the memory regions are copied from the current, or issuing, device to

1. wait for outstanding dependences
2. copy requested memory to the device
3. execute the target region on the device
4. copy requested memory from the device
5. resolve outgoing dependences

Fig. 2. Breakdown of the semantic parts, or sub-tasks, of a *deferred target task*.

the target device as specified by the `map` clauses. In step three, the associated target region is executed on the target device[1]. Afterwards, memory is copied back from the target device to the issuing device, again as specified by the `map` clauses. Finally, dependences are marked as resolved such that dependent tasks are now allowed to proceed. While these semantic steps could potentially be overlapped, they have to appear *as-if* they are performed in this order.

2.1 Considered Designs

We considered three designs that we describe here and compare in Sect. 2.2.

Regular Task. In the *regular-task* design, the "task part" of the `target` directive is executed as if it was a regular, *undeferred* OpenMP task. A potential lowering of the generic *deferred target task* from Fig. 1 is shown in Fig. 3. As with other regular OpenMP tasks there is a binding to the encountering team, so that a thread from the encountering team will eventually execute the task. That thread will execute all five of the steps listed in Fig. 2, thus allowing the encountering thread to continue execution immediately after creating the regular OpenMP task. The *regular task* design is the easiest to implement and understand. However, it may not yield the desired result, namely asynchronous offloading, if there is no surrounding parallel region, or if the threads in the surrounding parallel region are busy and not able to pick up additional tasks.

```
#pragma omp task shared(...) depend(...) ...
#pragma omp target map(...) ...
{ ... }
```

Fig. 3. The `target` directive from Fig. 1 implemented in the *regular-task* design. The "task part" of the *deferred target task* becomes a regular, *undeferred* task.

Detachable/Callback-Task. The *detachable-task* design exploits semantics similar to the `detach` clause in combination with asynchronous calls to the native device runtime. Figure 4 visualizes this approach using a custom *native_async* clause. The idea is that the native device runtime, e.g., the CUDA driver, allows the queuing of events, memory copies, and launch kernels. The encountering thread can therefore set the first four steps shown in Fig. 2 in motion without waiting for any of them to complete. In practice, the fifth step can also be scheduled by providing a callback function for the native runtime to invoke once all prior steps have completed. The callback will fulfill the event associated with the `detach` clause and thereby, most likely, also perform the work associated with resolving dependences. That means that the encountering thread issues the work, and a thread of the native runtime will handle everything else, especially

---

[1] The fallback case, execution on the issuing device, is sufficiently similar.

the last step. Consequently, if the native runtime is rich enough and has sufficient threads to perform the (last) step, concurrent offloading is possible regardless of the context.

```
#pragma omp target depend(...) map(...) ... \
                        detach(native_async_calls_done) native_async
{ ... }
```

Fig. 4. The `target` directive from Fig. 1 implemented in the *detachable-task* design. Asynchronous calls to the native device runtime are used to issue the sub-tasks (see Fig. 2) including a host callback that will fulfill the *allow-completion-event* associated with the `detach` clause.

Hidden Helper Task. In the *hidden-helper-task* design, a *deferred target task* is executed in its entirety by a thread that is not started by nor (in any language-defined way) visible to the user. These *hidden-helper-threads* form a team of threads that is implicitly created at program start and is only responsible for the execution of the special *hidden-helper-tasks*. We denote them in our code as `hht_task`. Such tasks are not too different from other *deferred* OPENMP tasks except that they are always executed by an implicit *hidden-helper-thread*. It is especially important that they participate in the dependence resolution like any other tasks generated by the encountering thread. Thus they are siblings to tasks generated by threads in the same team as the encountering thread. The `hht_task` concept is not tied to *deferred target tasks* but could help the definition or extention of the OPENMP specification (see Sect. 6). Figure 5 shows how the generic *deferred target task* from Fig. 1 is executed in this design.

```
#pragma omp hht_task shared(...) depend(...) ...
#pragma omp target map(...) ...
{ ... }
```

Fig. 5. Conceptual lowering of the `target` directive from Fig. 1 in the *hidden-helper-thread* design. A special `hht_task` is used and executed by an *hidden-helper-thread* while the offload part is made synchronous.

2.2 Design Comparison

While all three schemes can result in concurrent execution of asynchronous offloading regions, they differ in complexity, extensibility, requirements, and probably performance. The regular task design is easy to implement, potentially even without compiler support, but it will fail to achieve the goal if there are no threads available to perform the offloading concurrently. Under ideal circumstances it can be expected that this scheme is similar to the design of *hidden-helper-thread*, though the required setup, e.g., an explicit parallel region with idle threads, is unrealistic and restrictive. The detachable task design can be expected to provide consistently good results under most circumstances. It could potentially be worse than the hidden-helper task design if the time taken by the encountering thread to issue asynchronous calls becomes the bottleneck or if the native runtime thread is otherwise needed while it resolves the dependences. However, those situations would only occur if the tasks are very small or the number of native runtime threads is too low. Moreover, the setup of the hht_task is not free either and the use of additional threads and task incurs overhead as well. There are more likely problems with the detachable task design though. For one, the scheme can become complex when dependences between host and target tasks are present. While one could resolve host task dependences as part of the setup, thus stalling the encountering thread until they are resolved, it would defeat the purpose. Using artificial host tasks to do the setup introduces the same problems as the regular task design; using extra threads is not much different from our proposed third design, but more complex for yet-to-be-determined gains. Finally, only the hidden-helper task design is generic and reusable. It puts no requirements on the native runtime, nor is the scheme tied to target offloading. That said, it is very likely that our scheme would benefit from resolving dependences directly on the device.

3 Implementation

To ensure concurrent execution of target tasks in every situation we need to augment the LLVM OPENMP runtime in two places: (1) we added *hidden-helper-threads* to which the execution of *target tasks* can be deferred, and (2) we utilize native device runtime features to offload multiple target tasks at the same time. In this section, we first introduce the key implementation details for hidden helper tasks and the hidden helper task team, before we discuss the support for concurrent task execution using multiple streams. Finally, we present the new dependence process mechanism.

3.1 Hidden Helper Task

In our design, a `target nowait` directive will be wrapped into a *hidden-helper-task*, which is a special OPENMP task that can only be executed by a *hidden-helper-thread*. In this section, we will introduce the allocation and synchronization of a *hidden-helper-task*. The execution will be discussed in Sect. 3.2.

Allocation. When the *encountering thread* T_E reaches a hidden helper task t_h, it registers t_h as a child by incrementing the child task counter and it also increments the number of unfinished hidden helper tasks of its team. Then T_E enqueues t_h in the task queue of a hidden helper thread chosen based on T_E's global thread id. This selection ensures that hidden helper tasks are distributed evenly if they are encountered by multiple threads at the same time. Finally, T_E increases a semaphore S_H which we will discuss in Sect. 3.2. Once the task is finished, the children and unfinished task counters will be decreased by one.

Synchronization. The synchronization of hidden helper tasks follows the rules of regular OPENMP tasks. They can be synchronized explicitly via a `taskwait` directive or implicitly at the end of a parallel region. For the explicit synchronization, the encountering thread T_E waits until the number of unfinished child tasks is zero. The implicit synchronization happens before the master thread of the team spawned by the `parallel` directive leaves the parallel region and continues execution of the succeeding statement. The master thread will first wait for all unfinished hidden helper tasks created by its team to complete.

3.2   Hidden Helper Thread Team

The *hidden helper thread team* is a special OPENMP team that, similar to the implicit initial team, exists at program start. It is not connected to the implicit initial team. The size of the hidden helper thread team, denoted by N_H, defaults to 8 in our implementation. It can be configured via an environment variable. This might be necessary based on the kernel sizes and hardware capabilities, e.g., if $N_H = 8$ threads fail to offload sufficient work while there is more available, the size should be increased. Just as with a regular team, the hidden helper thread team is implemented using a fork-join model. To avoid overheads when the feature is not used, the team is only initialized when the first hidden helper task is encountered.

The encountering thread T_E first creates a new thread T_H using the native host threading API. Note that T_H is not related to any other regular OPENMP threads but is similar to the initial thread that exists at the start of program execution. We call thread T_H the *master thread* of the hidden helper thread team. This new thread creates $N_H - 1$ hidden helper threads using the same facilities that other newly created OPENMP teams would use. That means, the T_H is not connected to the existing team structure but the hidden helper thread team is itself a regular OPENMP team. T_E is allowed to proceed only after the new team has been initialized and is ready to accept tasks.

While the team behaves like a regular one, the hidden helper threads are set up slightly differently from regular OPENMP threads. A regular OPENMP worker thread (in the LLVM OPENMP runtime) keeps looping with the expectation that one hardware thread is allocated to it. It is optimized for fast reaction time, so once a regular OPENMP task is encountered by its team the worker thread can pick it up and execute it right away. In contrast, it is crucial that hidden helper threads do not occupy host resources if they are not used. Assuming the host is fully utilized by regular OPENMP threads, there are no CPU cycles left for the hidden helper threads to use. In order to avoid contention, the hidden helper threads immediately block on the semaphore S_H after their setup is complete. Whenever a new hidden helper task is enqueued, S_H is incremented and at least one hidden helper thread is woken up to execute the task. After the execution is finished, the thread will block itself on S_H and wait to be woken again.

Like regular OPENMP threads, hidden helper threads use a work-stealing strategy to find suitable tasks. A hidden helper thread first checks whether there are tasks in its own queue. If so, it will take one and execute it; otherwise, the thread will try to steal from other thread queues by sweeping over all others in its hidden helper thread team.

3.3 Stream Manager

Steps 2–4 in Fig. 2 show how the host interacts with a target device via the native device runtime. These runtimes usually accept a queue-like data structure that we call a *stream*[2] in this paper, as a parameter to which the corresponding operations are pushed. Operations in the same stream are executed in the issued order; operations in different streams can be executed concurrently if there are no synchronizing events. As a result, if we want to run multiple tasks concurrently, we must use *multiple streams*.

We implemented a *stream manager* which can efficiently arbitrate concurrent requests for streams. Initially, a stream pool containing K streams is created. The size K is configurable via an environment variable and defaults to 32. For each target device operation, e.g., a host to device memory copy or a kernel offload, a new stream is requested from the stream manager. On request, the last used available streams in the pool can be "borrowed". If all streams in the pool have been borrowed, the stream manager will double the pool size to create fresh streams that can be handed out. Once a user is finished with a stream, it returns it to the stream manager such that it can be reused.

Since the target region can be only executed after the required data is copied to the device, and outgoing dependence resolution can only be started after data is copied back to the issuing device, Steps 2–4 in Fig. 2 are in fact implicitly dependent. Given this fact, we optimize the target operations in the following way: all operations for the same target task use the same stream. In addition, all synchronous operations are replaced by their asynchronous counterparts, with a single synchronization performed at the end of Step 4. In this way, the OPENMP runtime library does not need to wait for an operation to finish before issuing the next one. But it will register them all directly with the native runtime, allowing for potential concurrency during memory transfers in the future. Even for non-detachable target tasks, this synchronization scheme can reduce overheads compared with the use of multiple synchronous operations. Finally, it is worth noting that the stream manager alone already allows multiple threads to concurrently offload independent operations.

3.4 Processing Dependences

The dependences of a regular OPENMP task are resolved and processed on the host side. If the dependences of a task are not fulfilled, the task will not be enqueued, which implies that a target task will also not be enqueued, dispatched and executed if the tasks it depends on are not finished, no matter whether they are regular tasks or target tasks. However, almost all device runtime libraries

---

[2] This is CUDA terminology, but almost all heterogeneous programming models have a similar concept, such as the *command queue* in OpenCL.

support a more efficient way to process dependences via device-dependent *events*. The host side no longer is involved, and all a target task's successors whose dependences have been resolved can be enqueued for dispatch and execution.

The native device dependence resolution works as follows. A *fulfill* operation is put into the stream S such that it is executed after all operations enqueued to S before. A *wait* operation is added to stream S', which can be S, to ensure operations enqueued into S' afterward are stalled until the matching fulfill operation in S was executed. It is worth noting that the fulfill and wait operations are put into the stream without blocking the issuing thread.

In our approach, we perform dependence processing on the target device. Assume a target task t depending on m tasks $\{t_{d_1}, \cdots, t_{d_m}\}$. For each task t_{d_i}:

- If t_{d_i} is a regular task: add t to t_{d_i}'s *successor* list, and increment t's counter of predecessors `npredecessors`. This is same as the existing mechanism.
- If t_{d_i} is a target task: add t_{d_i} to t's *predecessor* list.

In this way, if the `npredecessors` of a task is not zero, the task depends on unfinished regular tasks. All tasks in the predecessor list are target tasks and will be processed on the device side.

When t is started, it first checks whether its `npredecessors` is zero. If yes, the current task yields because target device events can not tackle dependences on regular tasks. After that, for each task t' in t's predecessor list, if t and t' are on the same *type* of devices, insert a wait for t''s event to t's stream. This approach does not work if t and t' are not on the same *type* of devices. Two target tasks are not on the same *type* of devices if they are not using the same set of device runtime interfaces. In that case, t will take a check-and-yield: check the status of t''s event; if the event is not fulfilled, t will yield its execution. After all dependences are processed, t proceeds to its remaining offloading work, such as data mapping and kernel launch.

The *hidden-helper-thread* executing *hidden-helper-tasks* will wait for the target parts (Step 2–4 in Fig. 2) before proceeding to Step 5 to make sure that this dependence process can also work when a host task depends on a target task.

4   Evaluation

We performed experiments with four synthetic benchmarks described in the following to show performance gained by asynchronous offloading with Hidden Helper Threads (HHT) over vanilla LLVM. We additionally compare the prototype to the implementation in the commercial IBM XL C/C++ compiler (XLC) by measuring the speedup of asynchronous offloading (with `nowait`) over synchronous offloading (without `nowait`).

4.1   Benchmarks

The benchmark functions B1, B2, B3, and B4 contain the timed code parts. B1, B2, and B3 each consists of a `target nowait` directive, and B4 consists of four target nowait directives with depend clauses. In the target region a *daxpy*-like computation is performed on vectors of length N, as shown below. Outer data mapping, which is not shown in the paper, is used such that data is transferred only once in each benchmark. The benchmarks are designed to be extreme instances of potential real world situations.

```
#define C(a, X, Y, N)                                    \
  for (int i = 0; i < N; ++i)                            \
    for (int j = 0; j <= i; ++j)                         \
      y[i] = y[i] + a * x[j];

inline void K(double a, double *X, double *Y, int N) {
#pragma omp target teams distribute parallel for simd nowait
  C(a, X, Y, N);
}
```

B1: Single-Threaded Asynchronous Offloading, No Parallel Region

In benchmark B1, a single thread issues the T asynchronous offloading requests before it waits for all of them to finish. A situation like this can arise if an application with independent parallel loops is ported to an accelerator. Existing omp parallel for simd are replaced with the omp target teams distribute parallel for simd nowait pragma.

```
void B1(double a, double *X, double *Y, int T, int N) {
  for (int t = 0; t < T; ++t)
    K(a, X, Y, N);
#pragma omp taskwait
}
```

B2: Multi-threaded Asynchronous Offloading Inside a Parallel Region

In benchmark B2, all threads created by an outer parallel region issue the T asynchronous offloading requests. Note that the encountering thread can only finish the parallel region once all offloading requests have completed. One can imagine an implicit omp taskwait at the end of the parallel region. A situation like this can arise if an application utilizes multiple host threads for offloading onto the same (set of) devices.

```
void B2(double a, double *X, double *Y, int T, int N) {
#pragma omp parallel for
  for (int t = 0; t < T; ++t)
    K(a, X, Y, N);
}
```

B3: Single-Threaded Asynchronous Offloading Inside a Parallel Region

In benchmark B3, the master thread of an outer parallel region issues the T asynchronous offloading requests. Note that the other threads created by the parallel region do not participate in the offloading and will be busy (waiting) until all offloading requests have finished. A situation like this can arise if an application utilizes some host threads for offloading while others perform unrelated tasks, e.g., work on the host or offloading to other devices.

```
void B3(double a, double *X, double *Y, int T, int N) {
  std::atomic_bool done(false);
#pragma omp parallel
  {
    if (omp_get_thread_num() == 0) {
      B1(a, X, Y, T, N);
      done.store(true);
    } else {
      while (!done.load())
        ;
    }
  }
}
```

B4: Single-Threaded Asynchronous Offloading with Dependences

In benchmark B4, a single thread issues four asynchronous offloading tasks in each loop iteration. Task 2 and 3 depend on task 1, and task 4 depends on task 2 and 3. Task 2 and 3 are mutually independent, therefore they can be running concurrently. A situation like this can arise if an application with parallel loops is ported to an accelerator and multiple such loops are offloaded concurrently to improve the overall performance.

```
#define TARGET_NOWAIT \
 #pragma omp target teams distribute parallel for simd nowait

void B4(double a, double *X, double *Y, int T, int N) {
  for (int t = 0; t < T; ++t) {
// Hidden helper task 1
TARGET_NOWAIT depend(in: x[0:N]) depend(inout: y[0:N])
    C(a, X, Y, N);
// Hidden helper task 2, depending on task 1
TARGET_NOWAIT depend(inout: x[0:N])
    C(a, X, X, N);
// Hidden helper task 3, depending on task 1
TARGET_NOWAIT depend(inout: y[0:N])
    C(a, Y, Y, N);
// Hidden helper task 4, depending on task 2 and 3
TARGET_NOWAIT depend(in: x[0:N]) depend(inout: y[0:N])
    C(a, X, Y, N);
  }
#pragma omp taskwait
}
```

4.2   Configurations

We run our experiments with 13 different vector sizes, and four different number of offloading jobs. The vector size, determined by N, is one of 2^4, $2^5 - 1$, 2^6, $2^7 - 1$, 2^8, $2^9 - 1$, 2^{10}, $2^{11} - 1$, 2^{12}, $2^{13} - 1$, 2^{14}, $2^{15} - 1$, and 2^{16}. We choose seven powers of two as well as six values between them. The number of offloading jobs, determined by T, is one of 2^4, 2^6, 2^8, and 2^{10}.

4.3   Systems and Versions

All experiments were executed on the SUMMIT supercomputer at Oak Ridge National Laboratory [2]. Each SUMMIT node contains two IBM POWER9 processors and six NVIDIA Volta V100 GPUs.

We implemented out prototype on top of LLVM d8c35031. Since parts of our work have already been merged into the trunk of LLVM, in order to demonstrate our complete approach, the vanilla LLVM was obtained by removing the related changes from d8c35031. All variants of LLVM were built with GCC 7.4.0. For comparison, we use IBM XL C/C++ V16.1.1 (5725-C73, 5765-J13) loaded by default on SUMMIT. CUDA 10.1.243 was used by all configurations.

All benchmarks were compiled with flags -std=c++14 -O2. We used one resource set, which has 42 CPU cores and one GPU, per execution. Each configuration was executed 30 times and the execution times were averaged. We ran the experiments using the following command:

```
jsrun --smpiargs="-disable_gpu_hooks" --nrs=1          \
      --tasks_per_rs=1 --cpu_per_rs=42 --gpu_per_rs=1 \
      --rs_per_host=1 --bind=rs PROGRAM
```

4.4   Results

Comparison with Vanilla LLVM. Figure 6 shows the speedup of concurrent execution with our implementation. We can see in all cases that speedup first increases with vector length N (kernel size), starts to decrease after a certain point, and finally levels off. This is to be expected, because at the beginning when N is small, multiple concurrent target tasks cannot fully utilize the GPU. The extra overhead of the target tasks cancels out the small improvement in execution time. As N grows, we start to observe the improvement in execution time resulting from overlapping execution. At the point when a single target tasks saturates the GPU alone, the speedup decreases with the ratio of the target task execution time that is executed concurrently with other target tasks. Given large enough target tasks a speedup of 1 is expected.

We also note that the maximum speedup increases with T (number of target tasks). With increasing values of T the amount of time spent in the less concurrent warm-up and tear-down stages of the pipeline decreases relatively to the overall execution time, thus allowing for larger speedups.

Both B1 and B3 show significant performance improvement (up to 6.7×) in all configurations, while B2 and B4 exhibit degradation for small tasks and minor

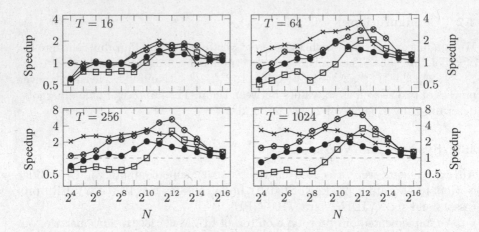

Fig. 6. Speedup of concurrent execution with *hidden-helper-threads* compared to vanilla LLVM for the benchmarks B1 (-⊕-), B2 (-⊟-), B3 (-⨯-) and B4 (-●-) described in Sect. 4.1

gains for larger values of N. This is to be expected, because B2 contains multithreaded offloading inside a parallel region. Even without the `nowait` clause, there are 168 threads (on SUMMIT, each physical core supports four hardware threads) issuing offload requests almost at the same time. The implementation of the `nowait` clause introduces indirection through the *hidden-helper-thread*, which increases host-side overheads (for task allocation, scheduling, and task yield) that are not incurred when issuing multiple tasks directly from different native OpenMP threads. Here, the performance gain from introducing multiple streams is offset by the extra overheads of using a deferred target task when the kernel size is very small. In this case, the modest amount of time spent in kernel execution does not allow us to benefit from dispatching them into multiple streams. For B4, there are at most two concurrent tasks (2 and 3), and they can finish before they get a chance to run at the same time when N is very small. As a result, similar to B2, the extra overheads degrade performance.

Comparison with IBM XL C/C++ Compiler. IBM XLC can generate very efficient kernels compared with LLVM (up to 50x performance gap with benchmarks in this paper), a lightweight configuration (smaller N) for XL can be heavy for LLVM. We are still exploring the reasons for this, but LLVM's register file usage on GPUs appears to be highly inefficient and could be a leading contributor. Since a direct comparison does not make sense given the above performance difference, we instead compare the speedup of pairs of kernels that have approximately the same average execution time.

Figure 7 shows the speedup of asynchronous offloading over synchronous offloading using our prototype (HHT) and IBM XLC in different benchmarks (B1-4) and for different T (number of offloading jobs). We see that our HHT outperforms XL in B2, although there is performance degradation from both HHT

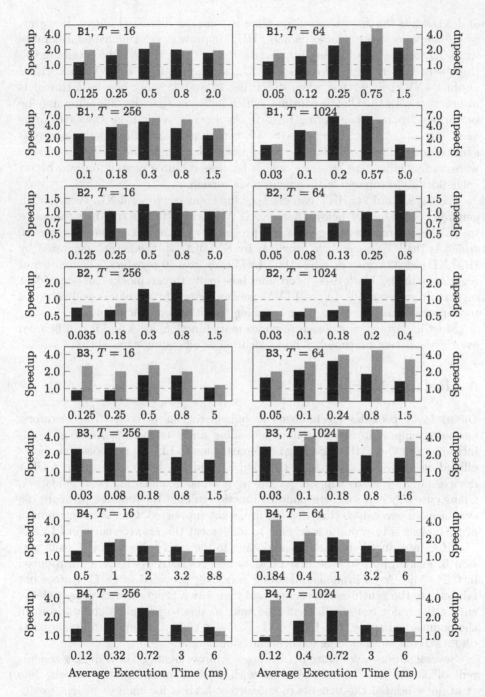

Fig. 7. Comparison between the speedup using our prototype (■) and IBM XLC (■) in different benchmarks (B1-4) and T (number of offloading jobs). The average execution time is the total time of T target tasks executing serially divided by T.

and XL when the kernel execution time is short, as discussed above. However, when the kernel size is large enough, HHT improves performance considerably while XL cannot provide any improvement. We think this can be attributed to the use of hidden helper threads. For XL, we observe from the NVIDIA Visual Profiler (NVVP) [8], that when executing B1 and B3, only one host thread is interacting with the CUDA runtime, which indicates that the offloading may be performed by the encountering threads. As a result, aside from the extra overhead introduced to support `nowait`, XL can at most get same performance as synchronous offloading in B2. In our approach, only eight *hidden-helper-threads* were issuing offloading requests, which has less resource contention and better cache locality compared with synchronous version.

For B1, B3, and B4, HHT can get speedup comparable with XL, even though generally it is slightly below that of XL. We expect this is due to weaknesses in LLVM's current kernel generation process. From the log shown from `ptxas`, which is the PTX assembler provided by NVIDIA [7], the kernel generated by IBM XL uses 32 registers, while the LLVM code uses 40 registers. The number of registers a thread block uses determines how many thread blocks can be resident on a multiprocessor [6]. In the LLVM version, fewer thread blocks will run on a multiprocessor at the same time, reducing the maximal concurrency.

Most important, our design provides more functionalities and it can be used even if the native runtime has no asynchronous offloading capabilities.

5   Related Work

OPENMP 4.0 provides mechanisms to offload regions of code to accelerators, and adds support for asynchronous offloading since version 4.5. Antao et al. [1] introduces an OPENMP offloading implementation to LLVM. For now it supports offloading to X86_64, AArch64, PPC64[LE], and has basic support for CUDA devices [3]. As regards support for the asynchronous offloading (`nowait` clause), Clang currently emits a corresponding function call but the function just calls the synchronous version, so that this feature is not supported. One key contribution of this paper is to propose a scheme to implement the `nowait` clause in LLVM.

GCC introduced support for offloading to the Intel® Xeon Phi™ from version 5, and support for the first GPU target, NVIDIA NVPTX, is introduced in GCC 7 [9]. Asynchronous offloading is not yet provided in GCC. It does not fall back to the synchronous version and therefore a program with `nowait` clause currently cannot run at all. Hence we were unable to provide a comparison. In the commercial space, the IBM® XL C/C++ V16.1.1 compiler fully supports OPENMP 4.5 [4], including asynchronous offloading.

Several papers investigate performance improvements by introducing concurrent offloading task/kernel execution with different programming models. Jiao et al. [5] validated the benefits of concurrent kernels for energy-efficient execution with CUDA. Wen et al. [11] proposed a graph-based algorithm to optimize OpenCL concurrent kernel execution. To the best our knowledge, this is the first paper investigating the concurrent execution of OPENMP target tasks.

6 Conclusions and Future Work

In this work we introduced support for concurrent execution of OPENMP target task, and discussed different designs for asynchronous offloading and evaluated our implementation on four extreme offloading situations against vanilla LLVM and IBM XL C/C++ compiler on the SUMMIT supercomputer. Our results show that the *hidden-helper-thread* design can provide low-overhead, concurrent offloading of OPENMP target regions without support from the underlying native runtime. In addition, the proposed design can be a stepping stone towards other "free", "unshackled", or "non-team-bound" tasks, both in terms of implementation as well as design. Our next step is to improve the execution efficiency of kernels. A promising candidate approach is to reduce register usage in LLVM (see Sect. 4.4) by optimizing the device runtime library such that it can drop some parts if the kernel does not require those features.

Acknowledgments. This research was supported by the Exascale Computing Project (17-SC-20-SC), a collaborative effort of two U.S. Department of Energy organizations (Office of Science and the National Nuclear Security Administration) responsible for the planning and preparation of a capable exascale ecosystem, including software, applications, hardware, advanced system engineering, and early testbed platforms, in support of the nation's exascale computing imperative.

References

1. Antao, S.F., et al.: Offloading support for OpenMP in clang and LLVM. In: The Workshop on the LLVM Compiler Infrastructure in HPC (LLVM-HPC), Salt Lake City, UT, USA, pp. 1–11 (2016)
2. Oak Ridge Leadership Computing Facility: Summit - oak ridge leadership computing facility. https://www.olcf.ornl.gov/summit/
3. Group, L.D.: OpenMP support – clang 11 documentation - LLVM. https://clang.llvm.org/docs/OpenMPSupport.html
4. IBM: OpenMP support in XL C/C++. https://www.ibm.com/support/knowledgecenter/SSXVZZ_16.1.1/com.ibm.xlcpp1611.lelinux.doc/getstart/omp_v1611.html
5. Jiao, Q., Lu, M., Huynh, H.P., Mitra, T.: Improving GPGPU energy-efficiency through concurrent kernel execution and DVFS. In: IEEE/ACM International Symposium on Code Generation and Optimization (CGO), pp. 1–11. IEEE, San Francisco (2015)
6. NVIDIA: CUDA C best practices guide. https://docs.nvidia.com/cuda/cuda-c-best-practices-guide/index.html
7. NVIDIA: Nvidia PTX optimizing assembler. https://docs.nvidia.com/cuda/cuda-compiler-driver-nvcc/index.html
8. NVIDIA: Nvidia visual profiler. https://developer.nvidia.com/nvidia-visual-profiler
9. Project, G.: Offloading support in GCC. https://gcc.gnu.org/wiki/Offloading
10. Wang, L., Huang, M., El-Ghazawi, T.: Exploiting concurrent kernel execution on graphic processing units. In: International Conference on High Performance Computing & Simulation, pp. 24–32. IEEE, Istanbul, July 2011

11. Wen, Y., O'Boyle, M.F., Fensch, C.: MaxPair: enhance OpenCL concurrent kernel execution by weighted maximum matching. In: Workshop on General Purpose GPUs, pp. 40–49. ACM, Vienna (2018)
12. Wende, F., Cordes, F., Steinke, T.: On improving the performance of multi-threaded CUDA applications with concurrent kernel execution by kernel reordering. In: Symposium on Application Accelerators in High Performance Computing, pp. 74–83. IEEE, Chicago (2012)

Using Hardware Transactional Memory to Implement Speculative Privatization in OpenMP

Juan Salamanca$^{(\boxtimes)}$ and Alexandro Baldassin

São Paulo State University, Rio Claro, SP, Brazil
{juan,alex}@rc.unesp.br

Abstract. Loop Thread-Level Speculation on Hardware Transactional Memories is a promising strategy to improve application performance in the multicore era. However, the reuse of shared scalar or array variables introduces constraints (false dependences or false sharing) that obstruct efficient speculative parallelization. Speculative privatization relieves these constraints by creating speculatively private data copies for each transaction thus enabling scalable parallelization. To support it, this paper proposes two new OpenMP clauses to `parallel for` that enable speculative privatization of scalar or arrays in *may* DOACROSS loops: `spec_private` and `spec_reduction`. We also present an evaluation that reveals that, for certain loops, speed-ups of up to 3.24× can be obtained by applying speculative privatization in TLS.

Keywords: Privatization · Reduction · Thread-level speculation

1 Introduction

Using Hardware Transactional Memory to implement Thread-Level Speculation (TLS) is a promising strategy to accelerate hard-to-parallelize loops [12]. Programmers can use powerful OpenMP constructs to write parallel code such as `parallel for tls` when parallelizing loops with a low *Loop-carried Dependence Probability* (LCP) [11]. However, prior work showed that well-known performance issues to loop parallelization (false dependences and false sharing) are exacerbated in the presence of HTM [10]. To overcome these issues, this paper proposes two new clauses to `for tls`, `spec_private` and `spec_reduction`, that enable speculative privatizations of scalar or arrays in *may* DOACROSS loops—loops that may have loop-carried dependences. Thus, programmers can mark variables as: (i) speculative private, when he/she suspects that: (a) a scalar variable is private in all or some iterations (*partial private*) of the loop but it cannot be showed statically—failure to take advantage of this property in some loops leads to false dependences (WAR or WAW) at runtime and, even worse, in conflict aborts in TLS-HTM; (b) an array has false sharing thus degrading the performance in any

Supported by FAPESP, grants 18/07446-8 and 18/15519-5.

B. Chapman and J. Moreira (Eds.): LCPC 2020, LNCS 13149, pp. 57–73, 2022.
https://doi.org/10.1007/978-3-030-95953-1_5

```
1  #pragma omp parallel for tls(SS)
       shared(n)...
2  for (j=0; j<iterations; j++){
3    ...
4      n += pBitCntFunc[...](...);
5  }
```

Fig. 1. Fragment of `bitcount`'s loop using `for tls`

```
1  #pragma omp parallel for tls(SS)
       spec_reduction(+:n)...
2  for (j=0; j<iterations; j++){
3    ...
4      n += pBitCntFunc[...](...);
5  }
```

Fig. 2. The same loop using `tls` clause and `spec_reduction`

```
1  #pragma omp parallel for schedule(static,1)
       shared(n)...
2  for (j=0; j<iterations; j+=SS){
3    ...
4      long nL=0;
5      BEGIN(...);
6      for(jj=j; jj<iterations && jj-j<SS; jj++){
7        nL += pBitCntFunc[...](...);
8      }
9      END(...)
10     n+=nL;
11     next+=SS;
12 }
```

Fig. 3. `spec_reduction` in the code of Fig. 2 converted to standard OpenMP

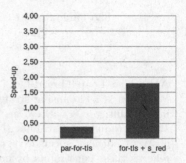

Fig. 4. Performance of `loopA` using: (a) `for-tls`; and (b) `for-tls` plus speculative privatizations

parallelization—particularly in TLS, it results in a excessive number of conflict aborts. Or (ii) speculative reduction, when the loop has a reduction pattern, but it is hard to prove that the reduction variable is free of another loop-carried dependence.

A reduction is a computation that repeatedly applies the same reduction operator (e.g., addition) to a sequence of operands (e.g., the results of the function calls `pBitCntFunc[...]()` of Fig. 1) to get a single result stored in the reduction `shared` variable (e.g., n). To use the clause `reduction` in a loop parallelized through the `parallel for` construct, the loop has to be conforming, that is, it has to be DOALL except in the reduction pattern. Then, OpenMP creates a private variable of the reduction variable for each thread, and the runtime system stores each thread's result in this private variable. The reduction of the values produced by each thread can be done in linear time (using `critical`) or logarithmic time (using a tree-based approach).

For instance, the listing of Fig. 1 shows the code of `loopA` from `bitcount` benchmark where n accumulates the results of function calls using an array of pointers to functions `pBitCntFunc`. If it is possible to prove statically that in those functions n is not read, we could use the clause `reduction(+:n)` to parallelize this loop. However, one has to be conservative and assume that the loop has loop-carried dependences inside the function called, even though none of these dependences materialize at runtime. An attempt to parallelize this loop using TLS is shown in Fig. 1, but it yields slowdowns with respect to serial execution.

Similar to reductions, speculative reductions create local copies but for each transaction. A successful technique to parallelize this loop using TLS-HTM is to privatize the `shared` variable n within the transaction for each worker thread and to accumulate partially the results in the shared variable after each transaction commits thus respecting the order of execution of iterations (if a function reads n in a next iteration, the value will be correct). We propose `spec_reduction` clause as an extension to OpenMP `parallel for tls`, which can be used as shown in Fig. 2. Figure 3 shows the result of the code transformation behind `spec_reduction`.

Figure 4 shows the speed-ups (with respect to sequential execution) of `loopA` (compiled with Clang and linked against the Intel OpenMP runtime) for the following cases: (a) when using `parallel for tls` (left); and (b) when using `parallel for tls` and the proposed `spec_reduction` clause (right). Speed-up measurements were performed in a quad-core Intel Skylake machine with TSX-NI support. As shown, `parallel for tls` parallelization of `loopA` results in performance degradation with respect to serial execution because many transactions abort due to data conflicts when try read or write n in Line 4 of Fig. 1. Then, transactions have to retry thus serializing the execution of the iterations. In the case of `for tls spec_reduction`, TLS-HTM is used to parallelize the loop and the `spec_reduction` clause privatizes the shared variable within the transaction thus reducing the number of conflict aborts and showing an improvement of almost 80% with respect to serial.

In this paper we make the following contributions:

- We propose a novel implementation of speculative privatization using HTM through two OpenMP clauses (Sect. 3) that extend the `parallel for tls` and enable the programmer to effectively parallelize (*may*) DOACROSS loops.
- A thorough experimental analysis (Sect. 6) shows the effectiveness of the code transformations, achieving speed-ups of up to 3.24× using a 4-core machine.

This paper is organized as follows. Section 2 describes the main concepts and related work to introduce our proposal. Section 3 presents our proposal and the design of the new clauses. Section 4 details the implementation of `tls spec_private`. Benchmarks, methodology and settings are described in Sect. 5. Section 6 evaluates the performance of the clause. Finally, Sect. 7 concludes the work.

2 Background

This section presents related works and the main concepts used in this paper: privatization and reductions, speculative parallelization of loops, and speculative privatizations.

2.1 Privatization and Reductions

False dependences (anti and output) can be removed through privatization. This technique creates, for each thread, private copies of variables that can produce anti or output dependences. This transformation can be applied to a loop variable if it can be proven that every read access to it is preceded by a write access to the same variable within the same iteration [3]. Reductions are operations of the form $x = x \otimes exp$, where $\otimes$ is an associative and commutative operator, and no operation (in exp or anywhere else in the loop) reads an intermediate value from x. The values of variable x can be accumulated in private storage for each thread followed by a global reduction operation. The difficulty encountered by compilers in parallelizing loops with reductions arises not from the transformation of the loop but from correctly identifying and validating reduction patterns [15].

2.2 Speculative Parallelization of Loops

If a loop is executed in parallel before data dependences are uncovered, it can produce out of order memory references, which may cause incorrect results. Such execution model is called *speculative execution*, or *optimistic execution*, because its performance is based on the optimistic assumption that the dependences do not materialize at runtime or are infrequent. If dependences do occur, the final computation must produce equivalent results of the sequential execution. To ensure this, the speculative execution model includes *checkpointing* (save safe state), *commit*, and *rollback* mechanisms [8,9]. When loop-carried dependences are expected (pessimistic case) the speculation should be verified frequently, so that iterations where a violation occurred can be restarted, thus reducing wasted computation. This approach is known as Speculative DOACROSS and can be quite expensive because it requires global synchronization. In addition, the commit phase is done in iteration order, which constitutes a serial bottleneck. Implementations of this approach are diverse, some of them include advanced features as forwarding, multiversioning, and ordered transactions [4].

2.3 Speculative Privatization

Speculative privatization is a technique that eliminates some false dependences at the cost of increased memory footprint and runtime checks that validate the safety of data accesses [1,6–8]. It involves costly instrumentation of all memory accesses of privatized objects for logging or communication. At commit, the private copies of each worker are merged according to a resolution policy.

2.4 TLS on Hardware Transactional Memories

Thread-Level Speculation (TLS) or Speculative DOACROSS has been widely studied [13,14]. For performance, TLS requires hardware mechanisms that support four primary features: conflict detection, speculative storage, in-order commit of transactions, and transaction roll-back. However, to this day, there is no off-the-shelf processor that provides direct support for TLS. Speculative execution is supported, however, in the form of Hardware Transactional Memory (HTM) available in processors such as the Intel Core and the IBM POWER [12]. HTM implements three out of the four key features required by TLS: conflict detection, speculative storage, and transaction roll-back. And thus these architectures have the potential to be used to implement TLS [10, 12]. Our proposal is based on this approach.

3 Our Proposal

This section presents the proposed extension to OpenMP that enables programmers to easily annotate scalar or array variables to be speculatively privatized. This extension allows programmers to successfully parallelize *may* DOACROSS loops using TLS and speculative privatization.

3.1 spec_private Clause

The use of the `spec_private` clause is possible in `parallel for` constructs when the clause `tls` is present. It is syntactically similar to the standard `private` clause. The syntax of *parallel for* is as follows:

```
#pragma omp parallel for tls(size) spec_private(list) [clause[[,]clause]...]
    for-loop
```

where:

– *size* is the number of iterations assigned to each speculative implicit task generated by the worksharing-loop construct. In compiler parlance, it is said that the loop is partitioned into strips, and thus this size is often called the strip *size* of the loop;
– *list* consists of a collection of one or more *list items* separated by commas;
– *list item* is a scalar variable or an array; *clause* can be any clause allowed for `parallel for` except `schedule`, `ordered`, and `collapse`.

3.2 tls Construct

`tls` construct is a stand-alone directive that specifies if a variable is written or first read in all or some iterations of the loop. Thus, it can be used to specify transient *may*-RAW-dependence or false-sharing patterns in loops. The use of this directive is possible only when `spec_private` is present. The syntax of the directive is as follows:

```
#pragma omp tls [clause[[,]clause]...]
```

where:

– *clause* is one of the following: (a) `read(scalar)`, which specifies that *scalar* is read before any write to *scalar* for each loop iteration; (b) `write(item)`: *item* is written for each loop iteration; (c) `if_read(scalar)`: *scalar* can be read before any write to *scalar* for some loop iterations depending on the `if` control

```
1  #pragma omp parallel num_threads(N_CORES)
2  #pragma omp for tls(S_SIZE) shared(A)
       firstprivate(n) spec_private(glob)
3  for (i = INI; i < n; i++){
4    ...
5    #pragma omp tls write(glob)
6    glob = f(&ptr,..);
7    A[i] = glob*i;
8    ...
9  }
```

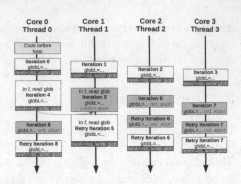

Fig. 5. Code using using the `tls` and `spec_private` clauses, and the `tls` directive

Fig. 6. Possible execution flow of Fig. 5 with S_SIZE=1 and N_CORES=4

flow; and (d) `if_write(`*item*`)`: *item* can be written for some loop iterations depending on the `if` control flow. *item* is a scalar variable or an array; *scalar* is a scalar variable.

3.3 `spec_private` in Scalar Variables

This clause can be used when the loop has *may* loop-carried dependences in `shared` variables that are not privatizable at compile time because of the complexity of the analysis (e.g. pointers) or the nondeterminism of the control flow of the program. For example, in the loop of Fig. 5, `glob` could have been declared as `shared` because function `f` manipulates pointers and it is not possible to determine if `glob` is privatizable. However, `glob` is marked as `spec_private`, thus a copy (`globL`) is created for each implicit task such that it can replace `glob` within the transaction. Moreover, the `tls write(glob)` directive indicates that the variable `glob` is actually written in all iterations of the loop (Line 6) and could generate a loop-carried dependence. Thereby, the `globL` has to be non-speculatively copied back to `glob` after committing.

At runtime, if a read memory reference to `glob` is performed in function `f` within a transaction T executing iteration i and, at the same time, another thread executing iteration $i - 1$ within a transaction T' writes `globL`, after T' commits and the corresponding thread non-speculatively modifies `glob`, a conflict is detected between the read of transaction T and the non-speculative write, causing the abortion of T. As explained in [10], the speculative privatization of scalar variables enables:

a) A conflict resolution policy: As explained earlier for the example of Fig. 5, the non-speculative write of `glob` after committing T' forces the abortion of transaction T when it reads `glob` (e.g., in Fig. 6, Iteration 4 would be T', and Iteration 5, T). Without speculative privatization, T', which executes iteration $i - 1$, could abort many times due to memory conflicts (with T)

```
1  #pragma omp parallel num_threads(N_CORES)
2  #pragma omp for tls(S_SIZE) shared(A,B)
        firstprivate(n) spec_private(glob)
3  for (i = INI; i < n; i++) {
4    #pragma omp tls write(glob)
5    if (/*cond*/){
6      #pragma omp tls if_read(glob)
7      glob++;
8    }else
9      glob=i;
10   A[i]= glob*i;
11   if (/*cond2*/){
12     B[i]=glob*glob;
13   }
14 }
```

```
1  #pragma omp parallel num_threads(N_CORES)
2  #pragma omp for tls(S_SIZE)
        firstprivate(n) spec_private(glob,A,B)
3  for (i = INI; i < n; i++) {
4    #pragma omp tls write(glob)
5    if (/*cond*/){
6      #pragma omp tls if_read(glob)
7      glob++;
8    }else
9      glob=i;
10   #pragma omp tls write(A)
11   A[i]= glob*i;
12   if (/*cond2*/){
13     #pragma omp tls if_write(B)
14     B[i]=glob*glob;
15   }
16 }
```

Fig. 7. Code using speculative privatization for scalar variable `glob` (`tls if_read`). `cond` and `cond2` depend on the input.

Fig. 8. Another version of Fig. 7's code using speculative privatization for array variables A and B (`tls if_write`).

before committing, since HTMs available in commodity hardware do not have a conflict resolution policy between transactions;

b) Elimination of memory conflicts caused by WAR and WAW loop-carried dependences: Without speculative privatization, T and T' write shared variable `glob`, and hence a conflict is always detected even though `glob` could be actually private at runtime. In the example of Fig. 6, Iterations 0–3 write their private copy `globL` without aborts due to conflict. Similarly, without privatization, if T' (executing iteration $i-1$) reads `glob` in f and T (executing iteration i) writes `glob`, a conflict due to a WAR dependence is detected and one of the two transactions has to abort. With speculative privatization, both transactions can commit since false dependences are removed and no RAW dependence is present (i.e. f does not read `glob` in T). For instance, in Fig. 6, Iteration 5 would be T' and Iteration 6, T.

On the other hand, static analysis fails when the loop has *may* loop-carried dependences that arise only when a certain flow of a program is taken at runtime. For instance, the code of Fig. 7 shows the parallelization of a loop using `parallel for tls`; `glob` could have been declared as `shared` because, in a conservative way, it is necessary to assume that the RAW loop-carried dependence in `glob` exists. However, if the condition `cond` evaluates to false in all iterations, `glob` will be loop private.

When the *may* loop-carried dependence is within conditional statements (e.g., Fig. 7's loop) and the programmer knows the possible sinks of this dependence (Line 7), he/she can annotate the scalar variable to be speculatively privatized (using `spec_private`) and to be speculatively read when the conditional statements are true at runtime (using `tls if_read`). If the conditions are false, the variable is not speculatively read within the transaction and does not cause conflict aborts. Otherwise, in the example of Fig. 7, if `spec_private` is not used and `glob` is `shared`, transactions will abort every time that they are concurrently executed; even a transaction, which is about to commit, can abort because of the lack of a conflict resolution policy that can give preference to lower iterations.

However, it is still possible to use spec_private for glob without the directive tls if_read and to have a correct execution through the directive tls read(glob), which means that variable glob is actually first read in all iterations of the loop. In this case, concurrent transactions will also abort every time due to conflicts, but the speculative privatization emulates a conflict resolution policy that will give preference to lower iterations. Moreover, tls read can also be used instead of firstprivate when it is not possible to show that a variable is just read and not written in the loop. At runtime, this variable will be speculatively read for each implicit task within a transaction, however, if a write to the variable occurs, the transaction will abort.

3.4 spec_private in Arrays

Previous work showed that false sharing issues are exacerbated in TLS parallelization on top of HTM [10]. False sharing can be overcome with strip mining in some cases. For instance, in the loop of Fig. 7 (Line 10), consecutive iterations write to consecutive memory positions of array A leading to false sharing when the loop is parallelized in a round-robin fashion. Since A is an array of int and assuming a cache-line size of 64 bytes, setting S_SIZE to sixteen and aligning the accesses to the start of a cache line eliminates false sharing. However, previous studies [10] about false sharing in TLS showed that: (a) there is a trade-off between the size of strip and the capacity of transactions, thus to eliminate false sharing increasing the strip size can originate capacity aborts; (b) when false sharing is originated by non-consecutive writes to arrays, strip mining cannot remove it (e.g. lbm hottest loop case explained in [10]). (c) Intel prefetcher can cause false sharing in transactions because adjacent memory locations are fetched and tracked as reads. To overcome these limitations, we propose to create thread-local arrays which work as a buffer within the transactions, and then after committing, their content is copied back to the original shared arrays. This technique is known as speculative array privatization and yields performance improvement in TLS on HTM even with the additional copies.

Because of these issues and previous results [12], in general, speculative array privatization is a more performant solution than only using strip mining, and thereby we propose the clause spec_private to enable programmers to mark arrays to be speculatively privatized. For example, Fig. 8 shows the use of the clause spec_private and the directive tls write(A). spec_private(A) transforms the loop in Fig. 8, creating thread-local arrays (e.g., AL) to perform writes within the transaction and then non-speculatively copying back to the original array A after committing. The write clause means that every loop iteration writes array A, thereby the non-speculative writes from AL to A are also performed for every iteration.

On the other hand, if_write(B), shown in Line 13 of Fig. 8, analogously to the case of scalars, indicates that the writes to the array are conditioned to the control flow of the program (in the example, the result of cond2 in each iteration). Therefore, array B is speculatively privatized (spec_private(b)) and, only when the conditional statement is true at runtime, non-speculatively written after committing.

3.5 spec_reduction Clause

The use of the spec_reduction clause is possible in parallel for constructs when the clause tls is present. It is syntactically similar to the standard reduction clause. The syntax of *parallel for* is as follows:

```
#pragma omp parallel for tls(size) spec_reduction(op: list) [clause[[,]clause]...]
    for-loop
```

where:

- *op* is one of the following operators: +, -, *, &, |, ˆ, && and ||;
- *list* consists of a collection of one or more *scalar* separated by commas;
- *clause* can be any clause allowed for parallel for except schedule, ordered, and collapse.

This clause can be used when the loop has *may* loop-carried dependences in shared variables that have a pattern of reduction in the loop; however, it is not conservative to use standard OpenMP reduction clause because of uncertainty of having cross-iteration dependences at runtime. In the previous example, the loop of Fig. 1, n is declared as shared because it is not possible to prove that n is not read in functions being pointed by pBitCntFunc[...]. Nevertheless, the reduction pattern of n can be speculated using spec_reduction clause. As shown in Fig. 3, the code transformation involves creating a private copy of n for each implicit task and replacing n with the private copy (nL). Hence, each thread accumulates its result and, after committing, updates the shared variable n.

At runtime, in the case that, within transaction T executing iteration i, n is actually read in some function pointed by an element of pBitCntFunc before transaction T' (executing iteration $i-1$) commits, T will abort and retry to read the correct value of n. Otherwise, if n is read in all iterations, transactions will always abort and the execution will be serialized (the same effect with n as shared in TLS but still the results will be correct). On the other hand, the use of the OpenMP reduction clause results in wrong results for any of the two previous cases.

4 Implementation of the Clauses

Clang 4.0 was adapted to generate the AST (*Abstract Syntax Tree*) to support the new clauses. For the following discussion, consider Fig. 9, which shows the OpenMP translated code from Fig. 8. The translation mechanism for the clause tls(*strip_size*) is listed in Algorithm 1.

```
1   int next_strip_to_commit=INI ;
2   #pragma omp parallel num_threads(N_CORES)
3   #pragma omp for schedule(static,1)
        firstprivate(n) shared(glob,A,B)
4   for (i = INI; i < n; i+=S_SIZE) {
5     int globL,flag_r_glob=0,count_1=-1;
6     int AL_1_1[S_SIZE],BL_1_2[S_SIZE];
7     char pred_B_2[S_SIZE]={0};
8     int speculative=
        BEGIN(&next_strip_to_commit,i);
9     for (int ii=i; ii < n && ii - i <
        S_SIZE; ii++){
10       count_1++;
11       if (/*cond*/){
12         if (!flag_r_glob){
13           flag_r_glob=1;
14           globL=glob;
15         }
16         globL++;
17       }else
18         globL=ii;
19
20       AL_1_1[count_1]= globL*ii;
21       if (/*cond2*/){
22         pred_B_2[count_1]=1;
23         BL_1_2[count_1]=globL*globL;
24       }
25     }
26     END(speculative,&next_strip_to_commit,i);
27     glob=globL;
28     count_1=-1;
29     for (int ii=i; ii < n && ii - i <
        S_SIZE; ii++){
30       count_1++;
31       A[ii]=AL_1_1[count_1];
32       if (pred_B[cont1]);
33         B[ii]=BL_1_2[count_1];
34     }
35     next_strip_to_commit+=S_SIZE;
36   }
```

Fig. 9. Code converted to standard OpenMP

Algorithm 1: Mechanism for `tls` (*strip_size*)

Data: parallel_for construct (directive D and for-loop L) and *strip_size*
Result: Transformed code to be parallelized with TLS on HTM

1 Create BEGIN and END functions;
2 Outside of the construct, create a new variable *next* whose identifier is next_strip_to_commit of the same type of the induction variable;
3 Initialize *next* to the initial value of the induction variable;
4 Set schedule to (static,1) in D;
5 Apply strip mining transformation to the loop L using loop-local variable *ii* and a size of strips equal to *strip_size* (induction variable is replaced by *ii* in he inner loop L');
6 Insert a call to the BEGIN function before L';
7 Insert a call to the END function after L';
8 **if** $D.list\_spec\_private \neq$ NULL **then**
9 $\quad$ $flag\_array\_nspec\_w \leftarrow 0$;
10 $\quad$ **foreach** $var \in D.list\_spec\_private$ **do**
11 $\quad\quad$ **if** var is scalar **then** Run Algorithm 2
12 $\quad\quad$ **else if** var is array **then**
13 $\quad\quad\quad$ Run Algorithm 3;
14 $\quad\quad\quad$ **if** $flag\_array\_nspec\_w = 0$ **then**
15 $\quad\quad\quad\quad$ $flag\_array\_nspec\_w \leftarrow 1$
16 $\quad$ **if** $flag\_array\_nspec\_w = 1$ **then** Run copy_back_arrays_algorithm
17 **if** $D.list\_spec\_reductions \neq$ NULL **then**
18 $\quad$ **foreach** scalar $var \in$ $D.list\_spec\_reduction$ **do** Run spec_reduction_algorithm
19 At the end of L, insert a statement to increment the value of *next* by *strip_size*;

BEGIN function creates a transaction T that encapsulates S_SIZE speculative iterations. The size of the strip is specified as a parameter of the clause. At runtime, each implicit task created by `parallel for` will execute the BEGIN function. On the other hand, END function will try to commit the transaction T if all previous strips have already committed and no conflict is detected; otherwise, the implicit task will abort and re-start T.

When spec_private(*list*) clause is present in the directive and depending on the type of each variable in the *list*, Algorithm 2 or Algorithm 3 can be executed. All variables in spec_private are set as shared. Algorithm 2 creates a private copy for glob called globL in the example of Fig. 9, which replaces glob in the inner loop after applying strip mining. Then, it creates the mechanism specified by the directive if_read(glob) to read glob within the transaction only when it is actually read in the if statement (Lines 12–15 in Fig. 9). Because of the variable glob is written in every iteration, which is specified by write(glob), globL is copied to glob after committing (Line 27).

Algorithm 2: Mechanism for `spec_private(var)` when *var* is scalar

Data: parallel_for construct, *var*, *list_ir* of if_read, *list_r* of read, *list_iw* of if_write, and *list_w* of write

Result: Transformed code with variable *var* speculatively privatized

1 Set *var* as shared;
2 Create a variable *varL* of the same type of *var* (with identifier "<*var.id*>" plus "L");
3 Replace *var* with *varL* in the inner loop *L'*;
4 **if** *list_ir[var.id]* ≠ NULL **then**
5   Create a variable *flag_r* (with identifier "flag_r" plus "_<*var.id*>") and initialize it to 0;
6   **foreach** *loc_var* ∈ *list_ir[var.id]* **do**
7   Create a statement *s1* to assign 1 to *flag_r*;
8   Create a statement *s2* to assign the value of *var* to *varL*;
9   Create an if statement *if_st_r* with condition (!<*flag_r.id*>), and set *s1* and *s2* as the then-part;
10   At *loc_var*, insert *if_st_r*;

11 **else if** *list_r[var.id]* ≠ NULL **then**
12   After the BEGIN function call and before *L'*, insert a statement to assign the value of *var* to *varL*;

13 **if** *list_iw[var.id]* ≠ NULL **then**
14   Create a variable *flag_w* (identifier "flag_w" plus "_<*var.id*>") and initialize it to 0;
15   **foreach** *loc_var* ∈ *list_iw[var.id]* **do**
16   Create a statement *s3* to assign 1 to *flag_w*;
17   At *loc_var*, insert *s3*;
18   Create a statement *s4* to assign the value of *varL* to *var*;
19   Create an if statement *if_st_w* with condition (<*flag_w.id*>), and set *s4* as the then-part;
20   After the END function call, insert *if_st_w*;

21 **else if** *list_w[var.id]* ≠ NULL **then**
22   After the END function call, insert a statement to assign the value of *varL* to *var*;

Overall, Algorithm 3 goes through the structure that groups array writes by indexes, to these indexes by array variables, and finally these variables by fors. For each *for* where *var* writes, it creates a counter if this does not exist and a statement to update the counter in each iteration of that *for*. In each *write* using *index*, the algorithm creates a mechanism to replace *var* with the private copy of this. In the case of `if_write`, it creates predicates to know if the copy back for a determined position of *array var* must be performed. In the example of Fig. 9, the algorithm creates a private copy for A of size S_SIZE (AL_1_1), then it replaces A with its copy in the inner loop (Line 20), and it finally copies back the private array to the **shared** array A after committing. Analogously, the algorithm proceeds for B (Lines 22–23), but because it is within an `if` statement, it creates an array of predicates to determine if a position of the array is written or not. Then, these predicates are used to copy back the private array to B.

`spec_reduction_algorithm` takes as input the construct, the scalar *var*, *op_red*, and *statement_red*. The algorithm sets *var* to **shared**. Then, it creates a local copy of *var* and initialize its value to the identity value of operator *op_red*. This local copy replaces *var* in the reduction pattern (*statement_red*). Finally, after committing, it accumulates the partial results in the **shared** *var* using *op_red*.

Algorithm 3: Mechanism for `spec_private`(*var*) when *var* is array

    Data: `parallel_for` construct, *var*, and *list_for*
    Result: Transformed code with variable *var* speculatively privatized
1 Set *var* as shared;
2 **foreach** *for* ∈ *list_for* **do**
3   **if** *for.list_aw[var.id]* ≠ NULL **then**
4   **if** *for.count* = NULL **then**
5   Create a variable *count* ot type int (with identifier "count" plus "_<*for.id*>")
             and initialize it to -1;
6   Create a statement *s_inc* to increment the value of *count* by 1;
7   Create a statement *s_init* to assign -1 to *count*;
8   After the *for.entry*, insert *s_inc*;
9   After the END function call, insert *s_init*;
10   *for.count* ← *count*;
11   **else** *count* ← *for.count*
12   **foreach** *index* ∈ *for.list_aw[var.id]* **do**
13   Create an array *varL* of the same type of *var* and size *for.size* (with identifier
             "<*var.id*>" plus "L" plus "_<*for.id*>" plus "_<*index.id*>");
14   **foreach** *write* ∈ *index.list_write* **do**
15   *write.var* ← *var*;
16   *write.varL* ← *varL*;
17   *write.index* ← *index*;
18   Create a statement *s1* to assign the right expression of *write.st* to array
                varL at the position *count.value*;
19   **if** *write.type* = IF_WRITE **then**
20   Create an array *pred* of type char (with identifier "pred" plus
                    "_<*var.id*>" plus "_<*write.id*>") and initialize it to {0};
21   Create a statement *s_pred* to assign 1 to array *pred* at the position
                    count.value;
22   Replace *write.st* with two statements: *s_pred* and *s1*;
23   **else if** *write.type* = WRITE **then**
24   Replace *write.st* with *s1*;

---

5   Benchmarks, Methodology and Experimental Setup

The performance assessment in this work reports speed-ups and abort/commit ratios (transaction outcome) for the `for-tls`, `for-tls+spec_private`, and `for-tls-all-spec_private` parallelizations of *may* DOACROSS loops from the Collective Benchmark [5] (`cBench`) and SPEC benchmark suites running on Intel Core. The `for-tls-all-spec_private` parallelization is the same `for-tls+s_priv` one, but with all `private` variables converted to `spec_private`, it is used to measure the overhead of actually using `spec_private` instead of `private` or `shared` clauses.

For all experiments, the default input is used for the `cBench` benchmarks and the reference input for `mcf`. The baseline for speed-up comparisons is the serial execution of the same benchmark program compiled at the same optimization level. Loop times are compared to calculate speed-ups. Each software thread is bounded to one hardware thread (core). Each benchmark was run twenty times and the average time is used. Runtime variations were negligible and are not presented.

Loops were annotated with the proposed clauses `spec_private` and `spec_reduction` as also with the `tls` directive, following the syntax described in Sect. 3.

Table 1. Characterization and TLS execution of loops.

Loop ID	Loop Information				Loop Characterization			for-tls		for-tls + s_priv			for-tls all s_priv		
	Benchmark	Location	%Cov	Invocations	N	%lc	Average Iteration Size	S_SIZE	Speed-up	Spec Priv	S_SIZE	Speed-up	# to Spec Priv	S_SIZE	Speed-up
A	automotive_bitcount	bitcnts.c,65	100%	560	1125000	100%	12 B	5020	0.37	spec_reduction	5020	1.79	1	5020	1.70
B	automotive_susan_c	susan.c,1458	83%	344080	590	0%	48 B	67	1.34	No	67	1.34	10	67	1.17
C	automotive_susan_e	susan.c,1118	18%	165308	592	0%	14 B	72	1.03	if_write	72	1.60	12	72	1.35
D	automotive_susan_e	susan.c,1057	56%	166056	594	0%	76 B	88	1.04	if_write	88	1.13	3	88	1.09
E	automotive_susan_s	susan.c,725	100%	22050	600	0%	14 B	45	0.89	if_write	150	1.66	10	150	1.50
H	automotive_susan_e	susan.c,1117	18%	374	442	0%	3 KB	1	2.20	if_write	1	3.24	13	1	2.97
I	automotive_susan_e	susan.c,1056	56%	374	444	0%	4 KB	2	1.52	if_write	2	2.05	4	2	1.87
J	automotive_susan_s	susan.c,723	100%	49	450	0%	3 KB	1	0.51	if_write	1	1.86	11	1	1.67
V	automotive_susan_c	susan.c,1614	7%	782	440	34%	1 KB	9	1.01	if_read, if_write	9	1.15	2	9	1.10
mcf	429.mcf	pbeampp.c,165	40%	21854886	300	3.1%	300 B	40	1.26	if_read, if_write	40	1.31	1	40	1.29

They were then executed using an Intel Core i7-6700HQ machine, and their speed-ups measured with respect to sequential execution. Table 1 lists the loops used in the study.

This study uses an Intel Core i7-6700HQ processor with 4 cores with 2-way SMT, running at 2.6 GHz, with 16 GB of memory on Ubuntu 18.04.4 LTS (GNU/Linux 4.15.0-112-generic x86_64). The cache-line prefetcher is enabled by default. Each core has a 32 KB L1 data cache and a 256 KB L2 unified cache. The four cores share an 6144KB L3 cache. The benchmarks are compiled with customized Clang 4.0[1] at optimization level -O3 and with the set of flags specified in each benchmark program. Code compiled by clang -fopenmp was linked against the Intel OpenMP Runtime Library. To guarantee that each software thread is bound to one hardware thread (core), the environment variable KMP_AFFINITY is set to granularity=fine,scatter.

6   Experimental Results

This section presents results and analysis. The first part of the Table 1 shows the information of loops: (1) the ID of the loop in this study; (2) the benchmark of the loop; (3) the file/line of the target loop in the source code; (4) %Cov, the fraction of the total execution time spent in the loop; and (5) the number of invocations of the loop in the whole program. The features used to characterize the loops are shown in the second part of Table 1: (1) N, the average number of loop iterations; (2) %lc, the percentage of iterations that have actual RAW loop-carried dependences for the default input of cBench loops and the reference input of mcf; and (3) the average size in bytes read/written by an iteration. The parameters in the third part of Table 1 describe: (1) S_SIZE, the *strip size* used for the experimental evaluation of for tls, for-tls+s_priv, and for-tls-all-s_priv; (2) the average speed-ups with four threads for for-tls, for-tls+s_priv, and for-tls-all-s_priv; (3) the kind of speculative privatizations (and the clause of tls directive) used in the for-tls+s_priv implementation of the loops; and (4) the number of variables that were converted from private to spec_private in the for-tls-all-s_priv implementation.

---

[1] Clang 4.0 was adapted to generate AST to support the new clauses as explained in Sect. 4.

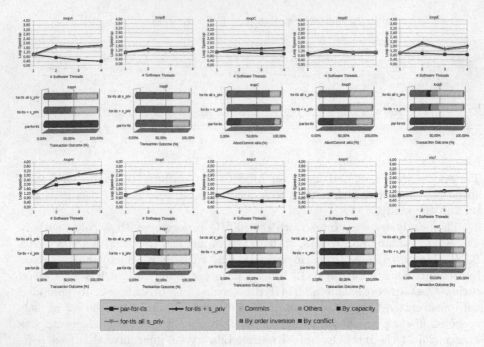

Fig. 10. Speed-ups and Abort ratios for `taskloop-tls` and `parallel-for-tls` execution on Intel Core (TSX-NI)

6.1 Loops with `if`-Writes Pattern in Arrays

As shown in Fig. 10, there is a class of loops, which write to arrays inside one or several `if` statements, being performant with speculative privatization (loops C, D, E, H, I and J). These often write to non-consecutive positions in consecutive iterations, thus they may have a variable pattern that makes difficult to remove false sharing. The evaluation shows that the use of the proposed directive `tls if_write` can be very effective to overcome this issue and to result in speed-ups from 1.13× in `loopD` up to 3.24× in `loopH` using four threads on TLS-HTM. As shown in Fig. 10, the abort ratios due to conflicts are almost completely removed in these loops by using the code transformations behind `spec_private`.

6.2 Scalar Variables with Transient Loop-Carried Dependences

There are some loops with transient dependencies generated by the nondeterminism of the control flow, that is, scalar variables within `if` statements that are only updated in some iterations. For instance, loops V and `mcf` have an `if` statement whose condition depends on the benchmark input and generates a *may* loop-carried dependence when the `then` path is taken. In the case of `loopV`, the variable n is updated inside of the `if` and then used as the index of an array. A `par-for-tls` parallelization of this loop results in a modest speed-up of 1%; however, when `spec_private(n)` clause joint the `tls if_read(n)` if_write(n) directive are used to identify the pattern, the conflict-abort ratio in TLS decreases and thus the loop performance improves up to 15%. As the dependencies in these loops, despite being transient, are actual (RAW), the code transformations cannot remove them; nevertheless, it removes data conflicts caused by false dependencies and the lack of resolution policy. This kind of loops is difficult to parallelize using DOACROSS techniques because the components with dependences are serialized.

6.3   Loops with Speculative Reductions in Scalars

The case of loopA, shown in Fig. 2 and explained in Sect. 1, exemplifies this type of loops. Using spec_reduction(n) in this loop yields performance improvements of 79%, as shown in Fig. 10. In the case where the reduction pattern is not correct, that is, n is read in the loop, the transformation behind does not alter the behaviour of the program, of course, paying an overhead. The standard reduction would lead to incorrect results.

6.4   The Increase of Capacity and Interrupt Aborts Results in Non-significant Overhead in par-for-all-s_priv Parallelization

Depending on the number of variables converted to spec_private, the *strip size*, and the speculative size of the loop, the presence of a higher number of aborts due to capacity overflow can be noticed in par-for-all-s_priv parallelization. Specifically, in cases that already had this issue in TLS (loops E, H, I, and J), it worsened. Although there is, in all cases, an overhead of tracking additional memory addresses of the local copies in addition to the shared ones, using spec_private instead of private as data-sharing attribute clause for the variables in the studied loops does not significantly hurt the performance. As shown in Fig. 10, there is a performance degradation for all loops parallelized using par-for-tls-all-s_priv with respect to par-for-tls+s_priv parallelization; however, this is not so serious to yield slowdowns. Similar to capacity aborts, the abort ratio due to other reasons (OS interrupts) increases in the par-for-all-s_priv parallelization of some loops that already had this problem due to the long loop-iteration time and the strip size used.

6.5   Difficulty to Find Patterns and the Effectiveness of spec_private

If it is very difficult to detect patterns in a loop, it is possible to use the tls clause only and have correct results, and even some speed-ups as in loopB. On the other hand, notice the effectiveness of spec_private in removing false dependences and false sharing, in the drastic reduction of the abort ratio due to conflicts of all loops (except B), even those with actual loop-carried dependences that will still have a high ratio.

6.6   Order-Inversion Aborts

In almost all loops, there is a considerable abort ratio due to order inversion caused by the lack of ordered transactions. A system with support for suspending and resuming transactions would solve the problem. This ratio decreases as the number of software threads decrease; for that reason loops, such as D and E, have speed-ups with 2 threads even better than with 3 or 4 threads. For these two loops, this ratio decreases to almost 0% with 2 threads (in loop E falls from 34% with 4 threads to 0.69% with 2 threads), thus overweighting the parallelization work with 3 or 4 threads (each abort can cost 150 cycles).

7   Conclusions

This paper shows that `spec_private` is a simple yet powerful code transformation that allows programmers to get rid of cumbersome profilers and static analysis to find out if a variable is private in a possible TLS-HTM loop parallelization, and simply to mark it as speculative as well as a write or read depending on how much information one has of the variable, all of this using off-the-shelf hardware available anywhere today. Besides, the patterns in the loops studied are very common, proof of this is that of the 22 cBench loops studied, in only two it was not possible to identify any of the patterns. Finally, until today TLS is still studied in hardware simulations with results, when tested on real machines (such as Blue Gene/Q), often times did not give the expected results [2]. This work is a clear contribution to implement the ideas behind TLS on commodity hardware at once and can be truly used.

References

1. Apostolakis, S., Xu, Z., Chan, G., Campanoni, S., August, D.I.: Perspective: a sensible approach to speculative automatic parallelization. In: International Conference on Architectural Support for Programming Languages and Operating Systems (ASPLOS), Lausanne, Switzerland, pp. 351–367 (2020)
2. Bhattacharyya, A., Amaral, J.N., Finkel, H.: Data-dependence profiling to enable safe thread level speculation. In: International Conference on Computer Science and Software Engineering, Markham, Canada, pp. 91–100 (2015)
3. Burke, M.G., Cytron, R., Ferrante, J., Hsieh, W.C.: Automatic generation of nested, fork-join parallelism. J. Supercomput. **3**(2), 71–88 (1989)
4. Cintra, M., Llanos, D.R.: Toward efficient and robust software speculative parallelization on multiprocessors. In: ACM SIGPLAN Symposium on Principles and Practice of Parallel Programming (PPoPP), San Diego, USA, pp. 13–24 (2003)
5. cTuning Foundation: cbench: Collective benchmarks (2016). http://ctuning.org/cbench
6. Gupta, M., Nim, R.: Techniques for speculative run-time parallelization of loops. In: International Conference on High Performance Computing, Networking, Storage and Analysis (SC), Orlando, USA, p. 12 (1998)

7. Johnson, N.P., Kim, H., Prabhu, P., Zaks, A., August, D.I.: Speculative separation for privatization and reductions. In: ACM SIGPLAN Conference on Programming Language Design and Implementation (PLDI), Beijing, China, pp. 359–370 (2012)
8. Rauchwerger, L., Padua, D.A.: The LRPD test: speculative run-time parallelization of loops with privatization and reduction parallelization. IEEE Trans. Parallel Distrib. Syst. (TPDS) **10**(2), 160–180 (1999)
9. Rauchwerger, L.: Speculative Parallelization of Loops, pp. 1901–1912. Springer, Boston (2011). https://doi.org/10.1007/978-0-387-09766-4_35
10. Salamanca, J., Amaral, J.N., Araujo, G.: Evaluating and improving thread-level speculation in hardware transactional memories. In: IEEE International Parallel and Distributed Processing Symposium (IPDPS), Chicago, USA, pp. 586–595 (2016)
11. Salamanca, J., Amaral, J.N., Araujo, G.: Using hardware-transactional-memory support to implement thread-level speculation. IEEE Trans. Parallel Distrib. Syst. (TPDS) **29**(2), 466–480 (2018)
12. Salamanca, J., Amaral, J.N., Araujo, G.: Performance evaluation of thread-level speculation in off-the-shelf hardware transactional memories. In: Rivera, F.F., Pena, T.F., Cabaleiro, J.C. (eds.) Euro-Par 2017. LNCS, vol. 10417, pp. 607–621. Springer, Cham (2017). https://doi.org/10.1007/978-3-319-64203-1_44
13. Sohi, G.S., Breach, S.E., Vijaykumar, T.N.: Multiscalar processors. In: International Symposium on Computer Architecture (ISCA), S. Margherita Ligure, Italy, pp. 414–425 (1995)
14. Steffan, J.G., Colohan, C.B., Zhai, A., Mowry, T.C.: A scalable approach to thread-level speculation. In: International Conference on Computer Architecture (ISCA), Vancouver, Canada, pp. 1–12 (2000)
15. Zima, H., Chapman, B.: Supercompilers for Parallel and Vector Computers. Association for Computing Machinery, New York (1990)

Improving Fortran Performance Portability

Jacob Marks[1,2], Eric Medwedeff[1,3,4], Ondřej Čertík[1], Robert Bird[1],
and Robert W. Robey[1(✉)]

[1] Los Alamos National Laboratory, Los Alamos, NM, USA
brobey@lanl.gov
[2] New Mexico Tech, Socorro, NM, USA
[3] San Diego State University, San Diego, CA, USA
[4] University California Irvine, Irvine, CA, USA

Abstract. We present a new Fortran source-to-source tool that helps to bridge the gap in the current Fortran tooling ecosystem. The goal of this tool is to translate standard Fortran code to various parallel programming languages in Fortran and C/C++ to enable running on a wide variety of GPUs and CPUs. The translation is performed using the full syntax parsing capabilities of the LFortran compiler, a research compiler currently in development. Using the Abstract Semantic Representation intermediate output of the compiler in this new work has made the translation simpler to accomplish. We also develop a map of the needed parallel constructs for a complete parallel language and begin to identify possible extensions to the existing Fortran language.

Keywords: Parallel Fortran · Performance portability · GPU programming

1 Introduction

We demonstrate a tool to improve the Fortran ecosystem for parallel code generation for various hardware devices, including all types of CPUs and GPUs. According to a survey by Willard and Segervall [14], Fortran is being used in seven out of the top ten high-performance computing applications. Good performance and support for multi-dimensional arrays and complex numbers has led Fortran to its widespread use in large-scale High Performance Computing applications.

But to deliver on the full power of the Fortran language, the toolchain should be improved to deliver the full advantage of the Fortran language potential and the existing code-base, both in Fortran-only and mixed-language implementations. Due to a variety of circumstances, the development of tooling for Fortran

Work was performed under U.S. Government contract 89233218CNA000001, managed by Triad National Security, LLC.; LA-UR-20-26284.

B. Chapman and J. Moreira (Eds.): LCPC 2020, LNCS 13149, pp. 74–83, 2022.
https://doi.org/10.1007/978-3-030-95953-1_6

has been neglected in comparison to some other languages. The Fortran language itself must be extended to encompass all the requirements of a complete parallel definition. As we identify needed language constructs, we plan on submitting them as formal proposals to the Fortran Standards Committee.

2   Background

Fortran is one of a few languages suitable for high-performance computing. Performance has always been a key design factor for the language. Many parallel language concepts were first prototyped in Fortran and as a result it has many of the necessary features for a complete parallel language. This innovation continues to occur.

The *do concurrent* syntax was added in Fortran 2008 [7]. It enables fine-grained parallelism using threads or vector lanes to parallelize loops. For distributed memory parallelism, co-arrays provide a more natural way within the language to handle inter-process communication [4,9,10]. Co-arrays are supported in recent Intel, GNU, Cray and NAG Fortran compilers [3].

Despite the targeting of Fortran for high-performance computing it is still lacking some tooling and a few language features that would complete the necessary ecosystem to generate parallel code for the increasingly wide variety of computer hardware ranging from CPUs to GPUs. Fortran compilers do not take full advantage of a lot of parallel features of the Fortran language. The *do concurrent* syntax has only been exploited in limited circumstances by a few compilers such as Cray and PGI.

A recent survey of the available parallel Fortran compilers by Hsu et al. [6] examined the support for generating code from each language to hardware platforms. We have updated the survey and at first glance, it looks like there is a lot of support for Fortran applications. Taking a closer look at the available parallel languages for Fortran, we see that some of them are incomplete or are not being actively developed. If we remove these from the picture, we get the map to hardware platforms shown in Fig. 1.

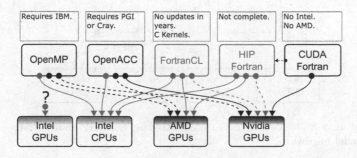

Fig. 1. Map for operational parallel Fortran languages to hardware platforms.

A deeper examination of the mapping to hardware platform reveals that even these parallel language implementations are limited to one or two compilers and generate code for only a single type of GPU. For some GPUs, there is no existing pathway for Fortran applications to generate code for emerging vendor GPUs. We must conclude that at present there is no easy way to write performance portable code that runs on both multi-core CPUs and GPUs.

3   Methodology

Source-to-source translation of Fortran to a few key parallel languages with good portability can quickly fix the gaps in the current language map. In order to do robust source-to-source translations, we need a compiler that understands the language. We have implemented our translation tool with the LFortran [15] compiler and have implemented a prototype Fortran to C++ backend.

Our prototype source-to-source translator will translate a simple set of parallel constructs, including a *parallel for*, a *parallel reduction*, and have recently started working on a *parallel scan*. The eventual goal is to translate representative kernels from production codes at LANL and elsewhere and publish research results so that other Fortran compilers can provide similar extensions.

In order to provide semantically equivalent features as Kokkos [2] in the Fortran language, we concentrate on translating the *do concurrent* loops for both CPUs and GPUs by targeting our chosen GPU languages. Using the proposed *reduce* keyword with *do concurrent* loops, we are also able to translate reductions to Kokkos and OpenMP.

We have just begun looking at the memory layout of arrays (with the same kernel) and possibly a few other extensions to the language, and we are exploring the most natural syntax (such as adding a keyword at an array declaration [13]).

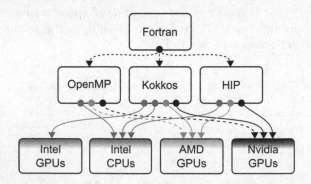

Fig. 2. Our map from Fortran to OpenMP, Kokkos, and HIP shows that we can map to any parallel hardware.

The choice of the target languages covers the three types of GPU languages available (Fig. 2). These are:

1. **OpenMP** using a Fortran-to-Fortran translation
2. **Kokkos** using a Fortran-to-C++ translation
3. **HIP** using a Fortran-to-C++ translation.

By translating to these three GPU languages the same Fortran code can be run on all current GPUs and Intel CPUs. If we can generate OpenMP code, we can generate other directive-based languages. Similarly for the native language representative, HIP, which is similar to CUDA and OpenCL. Our Kokkos target was chosen for the group of C++ GPU languages that use the lambda construct.

3.1 LFortran Architecture (AST, ASR)

We are using the LFortran [15] compiler to explore how to do the translation. Figure 3 describes the architecture of the compiler. The process starts with Fortran source code. See Listing 1.1 for the example source code being used. The parser parses it into an Abstract Syntax Tree (AST)

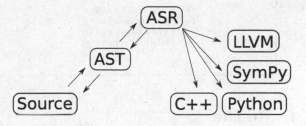

Fig. 3. LFortran architecture.

as shown in Listing 1.2. The AST has a node for each syntactic element of the Fortran language, but the semantic information is not readily available in the AST representation. The AST then gets transformed into an Abstract Semantic Representation (ASR), which is a standalone non-redundant representation that contains all the semantics such as types and a symbol table. The ASR representation is shown in Listing 1.3. ASR can then be used by backends to transform it to various other representations, such as an LLVM Intermediate Representation (IR) or C++. In this work we are mostly leveraging the C++ backend to build our source-to-source translator.

Listing 1.1. Fortran source for add subroutine.

```
1  subroutine add(a, b, c)
2      real, intent(in) :: a, b
3      real, intent(out) :: c
4      c = a + b
5  end subroutine
```

Listing 1.2. LFortran (0.4.0) AST for add subroutine.

```
1  (TranslationUnit [
2      (Subroutine add [(a) (b) (c)] [] [
3          (Declaration [
4              (a "real" [] [(Attribute intent [(in)] [])] ())
5              (b "real" [] [(Attribute intent [(in)] [])] ())
6          ])
7          (Declaration [
8              (c "real" [] [(Attribute intent [(out)] [])] ())
```

```
 9                      ])
10            ] [(= c (+ a b))] [])
11    ])
```

Listing 1.3. LFortran (0.4.0) ASR for add subroutine.

```
 1  (TranslationUnit (SymbolTable a8aa5374 {
 2      add: (Subroutine (SymbolTable 0038e214 {
 3              a: (Variable 0038e214 a 1 (Real 4 [])),
 4              b: (Variable 0038e214 b 1 (Real 4 [])),
 5              c: (Variable 0038e214 c 2 (Real 4 []))
 6          }) add [
 7              (Var 0038e214 a)
 8              (Var 0038e214 b)
 9              (Var 0038e214 c)
10          ] [
11              (= (Var 0038e214 c)
12              (+ (Var 0038e214 a)
13                 (Var 0038e214 b)
14                 (Real 4 [])))
15          ] ())
16  }) [])
```

4   Results

We have demonstrated the source-to-source translation of a Fortran stream triad kernel, and a reduction kernel, into OpenMP, Kokkos, and HIP. Both kernels are written in standard Fortran code. Listing 1.4 shows the source for the stream triad kernel, while Listing 1.5 shows the source for the reduction kernel. Currently these translations only function on simple kernels and have some aspects that cannot be translated automatically yet.

Listing 1.4. Fortran Stream Triad Kernel

```
1  subroutine triad(a, b, scalar, c)
2      real, intent(in) :: a(:), b(:), scalar
3      real, intent(out) :: c(:)
4      integer :: N, i
5      N = size(a)
6      do concurrent (i = 1:N)
7          c(i) = a(i) + scalar * b(i)
8      end do
9  end subroutine
```

Listing 1.5. Fortran Reduction Kernel

```
 1  subroutine sum_reduce(a, s)
 2      real, intent(in) :: a(:)
 3      real, intent(out) :: s
 4      integer :: N, i
 5      N = size(a)
 6      s = 0
 7      do concurrent (i = 1:N) reduce(+: s)
 8          s = s + a(i)
 9      end do
10  end subroutine
```

We started with simple kernels so that the accuracy of translation is easier to check. Our first step is to test a simple *do concurrent* loop to establish the translating process for *parallel for* constructs before moving on to other parallel constructs. Translating serial Fortran to Fortran with OpenMP is straightforward. This currently involves converting a *do concurrent* loop to a *do* loop and adding the necessary *!$OMP PARALLEL DO* directive. When the *reduce* keyword in Listing 1.5 we instead add the *!$OMP PARALLEL DO REDUCTION* directive while specifying the reduction operation and the variable being reduced. The OpenMP translation with the reduction kernel can be seen in Listing 1.6.

Listing 1.6. Translated Fortran Reduction Kernel using OpenMP

```
 1  subroutine sum_reduce(a, s)
 2  real, intent(in) :: a(:)
 3  real, intent(out) :: s
 4  integer :: N
 5  integer :: i
 6  N = size(a)
 7  s = 0
 8  !$OMP PARALLEL DO REDUCTION(+:s)
 9  do i = 1:N
10      s = (s) + (a(i))
11  end do
12  !$OMP END PARALLEL DO
13  end subroutine sum_reduce
```

While the translation to OpenMP is relatively simple, requiring only added pragmas, both Kokkos and HIP are more complicated translation targets because of the conversion to C++. Using the ASR we have enough syntactic and semantic information to translate simple kernels to Kokkos. The stream triad kernel is translated in Listing 1.7 and the reduction kernel is translated in Listing 1.8. Currently we make some assumptions about types. For example Fortran arrays are always translated to a *Kokkos::View* type even if that array is not used in a parallel segment. *Do concurrent* loops are translated to a *Kokkos::parallel_for*. If the *do concurrent* loop has a *reduce* keyword, it is instead translated to a *Kokkos::parallel_reduce*. Currently the reduction kernel is translated using only the AST so it lacks the semantic information. This results in some unnecessary code generated. For example line 4 in Listing 1.8.

Listing 1.7. Translated C++ Stream Triad using Kokkos

```
 1  void triad(const Kokkos::View<const float*> &a,
 2             const Kokkos::View<const float*> &b,
 3             float scalar,
 4             const Kokkos::View<float*> &c)
 5  {
 6      int N;
 7      N = a.extent(0);
 8      Kokkos::parallel_for(N, KOKKOS_LAMBDA(const long i) {
 9          c[i] = a[i] + scalar*b[i];
10      });
11  }
```

Listing 1.8. Translated C++ Reduction Kernel using Kokkos

```
1   void sum_reduce(const Kokkos::View<const float*> & a, float *s)
2   {
3       size_t N;
4       size_t i;
5       N = a.extent(0);
6       *s = 0;
7       Kokkos::parallel_reduce(N, KOKKOS_LAMBDA(const long i, float &
            updatevar_0) {
8           updatevar_0 = (updatevar_0) + (a[i]);
9       }, *s);
10  }
```

When using HIP as a translation target the kernel must be implemented separately and called using *hipLaunchKernelGGL*. The two parts of the generated HIP implementation are shown in Listing 1.9. HIP also requires additional copies of arrays for placing into device memory. The additional variables and kernels all need to be implemented so they do not conflict with names in scope. Currently the HIP translation uses only the AST and not the ASR. Using the symbol table that is part of the ASR, we will be able to more efficiently create readable variables that do not conflict.

Listing 1.9. Translated C++ Stream Triad using HIP

```
1   #define blocksize 128
2
3   __global__ void Tempkernelname(int N, float scalar, float *b, float
            *a, float *c){
4       int i = blockIDx.x*blockDim.x+threadIdx.x;
5       if (i >= N) return;
6       c[i] = (a[i]) + ((scalar)*(b[i]));
7   }
8
9   void triad(float *a, size_t a_size, float *b, size_t b_size, float
            scalar, float *c, size_t c_size)
10  {
11      size_t N;
12      size_t i;
13      N = a_size;
14      int gridsize = (N + blocksize - 1)/blocksize;
15      float *b_d;
16      hipMalloc(&b_d, N*sizeof(float));
17      hipMemcpy(b_d, b, N*sizeof(float), hipMemcpyHostToDevice);
18      float *a_d;
19      hipMalloc(&a_d, N*sizeof(float));
20      hipMemcpy(a_d, a, N*sizeof(float), hipMemcpyHostToDevice);
21      float *c_d;
22      hipMalloc(&c_d, N*sizeof(float));
23      hipMemcpy(c_d, c, N*sizeof(float), hipMemcpyHostToDevice);
24      hipLaunchKernelGGL(Tempkernelname, dim3(gridsize), dim3(
            blocksize), 0, 0, N, scalar, b_d, a_d, c_d);
25  }
```

In this demonstration, we have focused on the code generation to run on the GPU. To be complete, we still need a way to call the generated code. This could be accomplished by either translating the full source code instead of just kernels, or this could be done with a Fortran-to-C wrapper using *ISO_C_Bindings* that were added to the 2003 Fortran standard [11]. Some tools already exist to automatically generate the interface code [12].

5   Parallel Constructs

A fully featured parallel machine model needs to not only cover *how* the code executed and in what *order*, but also needs to include a specification for *where* both the data and code are executed. To uncover a mapping of common parallel language constructs, we look to the Kokkos programming model and VPIC [1], [5] to capture these ideas of *how*, *where*, and *order*.

We have mapped the *how* to *Execution Patterns* and the *where* to *Execution Spaces* and *Memory Spaces*. *Order* can be mapped to *Concurrency* or lack there of - represented by synchronous and asynchronous, accordingly. Test functions written in Kokkos were extracted from VPIC and studied to uncover the mapping. The aforementioned mapping is presented in more detail in another work [8], and thus is not fully discussed here. We present a summary of candidate language features that could be represented in an extension to Fortran in Table 1. We also list their current support in Kokkos, OpenMP, HIP and Fortran.

Table 1. Parallel constructs found in Kokkos and Fortran

Parallel constructs		Currently supported			
		Kokkos	OpenMP	HIP	Fortran
Execution patterns	**parallel_for**	*yes*	*yes*	*yes*	*yes*
	parallel_reduce	*yes*	*yes*	*no*	*no*
	parallel_scan	*yes*	*no*	*no*	*no*
Memory/Execution spaces	**CPU**	*yes*	*yes*	*yes*	*yes*
	GPU	*yes*	*yes*	*yes*	*no*
Concurrency	**Asynchronous**	*yes*[*]	*yes*	*yes*[*]	*no*
	Synchronous	*yes*	*yes*[*]	*yes*	*no*

[*]default

6   Conclusion

The original mission of Fortran should still be the mission today: enable scientists, engineers, and other domain experts to write programs that naturally express the mathematics and algorithms employed, are portable across HPC systems, remain viable over decades of use, and extract a high percentage of performance from the underlying hardware. To fulfill the Fortran promise, the Fortran toolchain needs some additions to fill the current gaps.

Our current status is that we have a source-to-source translator that can handle most Fortran syntax. We have an intermediate representation that has the necessary information to generate source code for GPU languages. We have prototyped the generation of common computational loop constructs for different GPU languages. There is no reason to expect large performance differences between our generated loops and those from a manual process. The next step is to develop a design for the handling of the data movement between CPU and GPU. Having the semantic representation in the intermediate language should allow the kind of analysis and code generation that will minimize the costs of data transfer and lead to well-performing applications. But much remains to be done before we can show the actual performance and claim success.

This demonstration project has shown the viability of translating Fortran source code to the major classes of parallel languages for CPUs and GPUs. Using a Abstract Syntax Tree (AST) and Abstract Semantic Representation (ASR) generated from the Fortran source code we have enough information to create accurate translations. Though the ASR is currently only used for translating to Kokkos, we will be able to use it to improve all of our translations. In the process, we have identified some helpful extensions to the Fortran standard that would give a more complete language to map to the full set of required parallel constructs outlined in Sect. 5.

References

1. Bowers, K., Albright, B., Bergen, B., Yin, L., Barker, K., Kerbyson, D.: 0.374 Pflop/s trillion-particle kinetic modeling of laser plasma interaction on Roadrunner. In: 2008 SC - International Conference for High Performance Computing, Networking, Storage and Analysis, SC 2008, pp. 1–11, November 2008. https://doi.org/10.1109/SC.2008.5222734. Paper 63
2. Edwards, H.C., Trott, C.R., Sunderland, D.: Kokkos: enabling manycore performance portability through polymorphic memory access patterns. J. Parallel Distrib. Comput. **74**(12), 3202–3216 (2014)
3. Fanfarillo, A., Burnus, T., Cardellini, V., Filippone, S., Nagle, D., Rouson, D.: OpenCoarrays: open-source transport layers supporting coarray Fortran compilers. In: Proceedings of the 8th International Conference on Partitioned Global Address Space Programming Models, 6 October 2014, pp. 1–11 (2014). https://doi.org/10.1145/2676870.2676876
4. Garain, S., Balsara, D.S., Reid, J.: Comparing Coarray Fortran (CAF) with MPI for several structured mesh PDE applications. J. Comput. Phys. **297**, 237–253 (2015). https://doi.org/10.1016/j.jcp.2015.05.020
5. Harrell, S.L., et al.: Effective performance portability. In: 2018 IEEE/ACM International Workshop on Performance, Portability and Productivity in HPC (P3HPC), pp. 24–36. IEEE (2018). https://doi.org/10.1109/P3HPC.2018.00006
6. Hsu, A., Asanza, D.N., Schoonover, J.A., Jibben, Z., Carlson, N.N., Robey, R.: Performance portability challenges for Fortran applications. In: 2018 IEEE/ACM International Workshop on Performance, Portability and Productivity in HPC (P3HPC), pp. 47–58. IEEE (2018). https://doi.org/10.1109/P3HPC.2018.00008
7. IEC/ISO JTC1/SC22/WG5: ISO/IEC 1539 Fortran 2018 Standard (2018)
8. Marks, J., Medwedeff, E., Čertík, O., Bird, R., Robey, R.: Making Fortran performance portable. Technical report LA-UR-20-25755, Los Alamos National Laboratory (2020)
9. Numrich, R.W., Reid, J.: Co-array Fortran for parallel programming. In: ACM SIGPLAN Fortran Forum, vol. 17, pp. 1–31. ACM New York (1998). https://doi.org/10.1145/289918.289920

10. Numrich, R.W., Reid, J.: Co-arrays in the next Fortran standard. In: ACM SIG-PLAN Fortran Forum, vol. 24, pp. 4–17. ACM New York (2005). https://doi.org/10.1145/1080399.1080400

11. Rasmussen, C.E., Squyres, J.M.: A case for new MPI Fortran bindings. In: Di Martino, B., Kranzlmüller, D., Dongarra, J. (eds.) EuroPVM/MPI 2005. LNCS, vol. 3666, pp. 183–190. Springer, Heidelberg (2005). https://doi.org/10.1007/11557265_26

12. Rasmussen, C.E., Sottile, M.J., Shende, S.S., Malony, A.D.: Bridging the language gap in scientific computing: the Chasm approach. Concurr. Comput.: Pract. Exp. 18(2), 151–162 (2006). https://doi.org/10.1002/cpe.909

13. Rouson, D.: Hybrid coarrays: a PGAS feature for many-core architectures. Parallel Comput.: Road Exascale 27, 175 (2016). https://doi.org/10.3233/978-1-61499-621-7-175

14. Willard, C.G., Snell, A., Segervall, L.: HPC user site census: systems. Intersect360 Reports, 9 March 2015

15. Čertík, O., et al.: LFortran: modern Fortran compiler and interpreter. Los Alamos National Laboratory (2020). https://lfortran.org

Domain Specific Compilation

COMET: A Domain-Specific Compilation of High-Performance Computational Chemistry

Erdal Mutlu[1], Ruiqin Tian[1,2], Bin Ren[2], Sriram Krishnamoorthy[1], Roberto Gioiosa[1], Jacques Pienaar[3], and Gokcen Kestor[1(✉)]

[1] Pacific Northwest National Laboratory, Richland, USA
gokcen.kestor@pnnl.gov
[2] The College of William & Mary, Williamsburg, USA
[3] Google, Boulder, USA

Abstract. The computational power increases over the past decades have greatly enhanced the ability to simulate chemical reactions and understand ever more complex transformations. Tensor contractions are the fundamental computational building block of these simulations. These simulations have often been tied to one platform and restricted in generality by the interface provided to the user. The expanding prevalence of accelerators and researcher demands necessitate a more general approach which is not tied to specific hardware or requires contortion of algorithms to specific hardware platforms. In this paper we present COMET, a domain-specific programming language and compiler infrastructure for tensor contractions targeting heterogeneous accelerators. We present a system of progressive lowering through multiple layers of abstraction and optimization that achieves up to 1.98× speedup for 30 tensor contractions commonly used in computational chemistry and beyond.

1 Introduction

The recent slowdown of growth in realized multi-core performance of commodity microprocessors has pushed vendors and users to consider more specialized architectures, including GPGPUs, FPGAs, and system-on-chip. Several domains, such as artificial intelligence, have experienced an explosion of highly-specialized heterogeneous architectures, including Google TPUs [10], NVIDIA DLA, and Intel Nirvana. With such a large variety of architectures, performance portability and productivity have become as important as peak performance, if not more. On one side, scientists and engineers have moved towards high-level, domain-specific (DSL) languages that facilitate implementing complex algorithms and allow them to focus on the algorithm's details rather than the specific idiosyncrasies of the underlying architectures. On the other side, to achieve optimal performance on modern architectures, it is imperative to exploit hardware features by writing highly-specialized, low-level, architecture-dependent kernels.

B. Chapman and J. Moreira (Eds.): LCPC 2020, LNCS 13149, pp. 87–103, 2022.
https://doi.org/10.1007/978-3-030-95953-1_7

This struggle for balance is not a simple one to solve. A one-to-one mapping between each DSL and each architecture is impractical and expensive to maintain. Instead, researchers have looked into ways to abstract the domain-specific aspects of an implementation from the architecture-specific ones and identify intermediate representations (IRs) to realize such abstractions. For example, LLVM [11] maps multiple front-end programming languages (e.g., C, C++, and Fortran) to LLVM IR, and then maps this IR to various target architectures. On the other hand, a generalized IR also means that domain-specific information and semantics are lost while lowering the code. For example, there is no simple way to express in LLVM IR common operations such as generic matrix-matrix multiplication (GEMM) or 2D convolution. It follows that domain-specific optimizations are impractical to be performed at such low-level IR, which could introduce performance loss. To overcome this limitation, modern systems (e.g., TensorFlow [1], Rust, and Halide [14]) propose high-level IRs where domain-specific optimizations are performed before lowering the code to the lower IRs.

In this work, we introduce COMET, a novel compiler infrastructure and programming language for tensor algebra targeting high-performance computational chemistry. COMET increases productivity by providing very high-level programming abstractions that resemble Einstein notations [3], performs sophisticated domain-specific code optimizations and rewriting, and generates code amenable to be executed on heterogeneous architectures. COMET is based on the Multi-Level Intermediate Representation (MLIR) recently introduced by Google to simplify writing new compiler infrastructures. In the COMET multi-level IR, domain-specific, application-dependent optimizations are performed at higher levels of the IR stack where operations resemble programming languages' abstractions and can be optimized based on the operations semantics. Generic, architecture-specific optimizations are, instead, performed at lower-levels, where simpler operations are mapped to the memory hierarchy and to processor's registers. A distinct advantage of a compiler-based approach compared to library-based solutions [9,21,22] is that COMET can handle arbitrary multi-operand tensor expressions and perform state-of-the-art algorithmic and code optimizations. Our performance results indicate that the code automatically generated by COMET is on par or better than manually-optimized tensor contractions from TCCG [20] that leverage state-of-the-art computational libraries, such as BLIS [22] and HPTT [21], and achieves up to 1.98× speedup over a set of 30 contractions. COMET provides enough expressiveness and completeness to implement two complex methods (coupled-cluster **singles** and **doubles** excitation equations) from the NorthWest Chemistry (NWChem) [2] computational chemistry package, which consists of 154 expressions and a total of 417 tensor contractions, and achieves up to 23.9× speedup over executing tensor contraction in the natural order of the expression. Additionally, by pairing our compiler to hardware accelerator simulators, COMET can be used to study novel data-parallel hardware designs and their impact on the entire chemistry methods. To the best of our knowledge, COMET is the first modular compiler framework that allows researchers to express complex tensor expressions, perform domain-

and architecture-specific code optimizations and transformations outperforming hand-tuned solutions, and can be used for hardware-software co-design. In summary, we make the following contributions:

- COMET, a novel compiler and DSL for tensor algebra that specifically targets chemistry applications with support for multi-operand expressions;
- a multi-level IR, a set of progressive lowering steps, and a series of domain- and architecture-specific optimizations to generate efficient code;
- a new co-design methodology to study custom accelerators;
- a comparison with state-of-the-art, manually-implemented tensor contraction benchmarks that leverage highly-optimized computational libraries.

2 Tensor Contractions

Tensor contractions are high-dimension analogs of matrix multiplications widely used in many scientific and engineering domains, including deep learning, quantum chemistry, and finite-element methods. For example, the perturbative triples correction in couple cluster CCSD(T) [15] methods used in the NWChem computational chemistry framework [2] originates a 6D output tensor from two 4D inputs tensors. Tensor contractions are computationally intensive and dominate the execution time of many computational applications.

Because of their wide applications in many fields, tensor contractions have been widely studied and optimized. Consider the following tensor contraction, expressed using Einstein notation [3], where two 4D tensors, A and B, are contracted to produce a 4D tensor C:

$$C[a, b, c, d] = A[a, e, b, f] * B[d, f, c, e] \tag{1}$$

In this contraction, the indices e, f appear in both right-hand tensors but not in the left-hand tensor C (*summation* or *contraction* indices). The indices a, b, c, d appear in exactly one of the two input tensors and the output tensor (*external* or *free* indices). A tensor contraction is, thus, the contraction of the two input tensors A and B over the contraction indices e, f:

$$C[a, b, c, d] = \sum_{e,f} A[a, e, b, f] * B[d, f, c, e] \tag{2}$$

A naïve way to perform the above computation is to directly lower to a nested-loop implementation of the problem. Such implementations have been shown to be inefficient due to poor data locality. A more efficient approach, commonly used in modern high-performance tensor libraries, leverages highly optimized GEMM engines. This approach, often referred as transpose-transpose-GEMM-transpose (TTGT), performs the permutations of the input tensors followed by a high-performance matrix-matrix multiplication and a final permutation to reconstruct the output tensor. The first two transposes "flatten" a multi-dimensional tensor into a 2D matrix by first permuting the indices so that they are contiguous

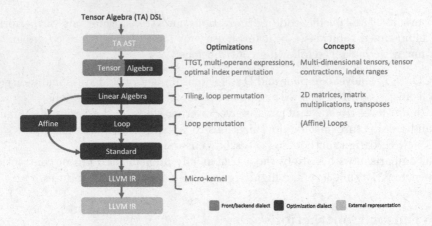

Fig. 1. COMET execution flow and compilation pipeline

in memory $(A \rightarrow TA)$ and then merging pairs of consecutive indices to form lower-dimensional tensors $((a,b) \rightarrow i, (e,f) \rightarrow j, (d,c) \rightarrow k)$:

$$A[a,e,b,f] \rightarrow TA[a,b,e,f] = A_p[i,j]; \quad B[d,f,c,e] \rightarrow TB[e,f,d,c] = B_p[j,k]$$

The tensor contraction expressed in Eq. 1 can then be expressed as

$$C_p[i,k] = A_p[i,j] * B_p[j,k] \tag{3}$$

where $C_p[i,k] = TC[a,b,d,c] \rightarrow C[a,b,c,d]$. The TTGT method is effective to perform high-efficient tensor contractions despite the overhead of potentially performing three additional permutations. In fact, highly-optimized GEMM operations perform considerably better than nested loop implementations on modern architectures and exploit high data locality (see Sect. 6). In this work, we consider employing custom accelerators to perform even more efficient GEMM operations, thus our compiler produces target code that is optimized and amenable to such accelerators (Sects. 6 and 7).

3   The COMET Compiler Infrastructure

Our proposed compiler infrastructure consists of a DSL language for tensor algebra computations, a progressive lowering process to map high-level operations to low-level architectural resources, a series of optimizations performed at each step in the lowering process, and various IR dialects to represent key concepts, operations, and types at each level of the multi-level IR. COMET is based on the MLIR framework [12], a compiler infrastructure to build reusable and extensible compilers. MLIR supports the compilation high-level abstraction and domain-specific constructs and provides a disciplined, extensible compiler pipeline with gradual and partial lowering. Users can build domain-specific compilers and customized IRs, as well as combining existing IRs, opting in to optimizations and analysis.

⟨ilabel⟩ ::= **IndexLabel**
              ⟨id-list⟩ = ⟨range⟩ ;
⟨range⟩ ::= [*int*]
          | [*int* : *int* : *int*]
⟨tensor⟩ ::= **Tensor**
              < ⟨element-type⟩ > ⟨id-list⟩ ;
⟨id-list⟩ ::= ⟨id⟩ | [⟨id⟩ , ⟨id-list⟩]
⟨id-list⟩ ::= *int* | *double* | *float*
  ⟨id⟩ ::= *any object identifier*

(a) Tensor label grammar

⟨tensor-op⟩ ::= ⟨op-lhs⟩ = ⟨op-rhs⟩
            | ⟨op-lhs⟩ += ⟨op-rhs⟩
            | ⟨op-lhs⟩ -= ⟨op-rhs⟩
⟨op-lhs⟩ ::= ⟨label-tensor⟩
⟨op-rhs⟩ ::= ⟨alpha⟩ | ⟨label-tensor⟩
         | ⟨alpha⟩ * ⟨label-tensor⟩
         | ⟨alpha⟩ * ⟨label-tensor⟩ * ⟨label-tensor⟩
         | ⟨op-rhs⟩ * ⟨label-tensor⟩
⟨label-tensor⟩ ::= ⟨tensor-id⟩ (⟨label-list⟩)
⟨alpha⟩ ::= *tensor value type*

(b) Tensor operations grammar

Fig. 2. Tensor label and operation grammar.

Figure 1 shows the compilation pipeline of COMET. Users express their computation using a high-level tensor algebra language (Sect. 4). The language operators, types, and structures are first mapped to an abstract syntax tree and then to the tensor algebra (TA) *dialect*, the first dialect in the COMET IR stack. The TA dialect contains domain-specific concepts, such as multi-dimensional tensors, contractions, and tensor expressions. Here, several domain-specific optimizations are performed, such as reformulating tensor contractions using the TTGT method. Next, COMET lowers the TA dialect representation of the computation to a mixed dialect based on the linear algebra (LinAlg) and Affine loop dialects. High-level concepts, such as tensor contractions, are replaced with more general operations (transpose, matrix multiplication, affine maps, etc.). At this stage, there is a departure from domain-specific concepts but the operations are still architecture-independent. The next step consists of further lowering of LinAlg operations to the (Affine) Loop dialect: at this stage, COMET performs architecture-specific optimizations and requires information for the specific target. GEMMs are tiled to fit matrix slices in the processor's data caches as well as to map computation to the processor's registers. The innermost GEMM computation is performed using an architecture-specific, highly-optimized micro-kernel (Sect. 6) or (simulated) custom accelerators (Sect. 7). Finally, COMET lowers the program to standard dialect and then to the LLVM dialect, which is then mapped to LLVM IR and lowered to machine instructions for execution.

4 Tensor Algebra Language

We developed a high-level Tensor Algebra (TA) DSL for tensor algebra computation. As for any DSL, the goal of the COMET language is to allow scientists 1) to express concepts and operations in a form that closely resembles familiar notations and 2) to convey domain-specific information to the compiler for better program optimization. Our language represents Einstein mathematical notation and provides users with an interface to express tensor algebra semantics.

Figure 2a describes the tensor structures and how they are represented and constructed in our DSL. A tensor object refers to a multi-dimensional array

```
#map0 = affine_map<(d0, d1, d2, d3, d4, d5) -> (d0, d4, d1, d5)>
#map1 = affine_map<(d0, d1, d2, d3, d4, d5) -> (d3, d5, d2, d4)>
#map2 = affine_map<(d0, d1, d2, d3, d4, d5) -> (d0, d1, d2, d3)>

module {
  func @main() {
    %c0 = constant 0 : index
    %c72 = constant 72 : index
    %c1 = constant 1 : index
    %0 = "ta.index_label"(%c0, %c72, %c1) : (index, index, index) -> !ta.range
    %1 = "ta.index_label"(%c0, %c72, %c1) : (index, index, index) -> !ta.range
    %2 = "ta.index_label"(%c0, %c72, %c1) : (index, index, index) -> !ta.range
    %3 = "ta.index_label"(%c0, %c72, %c1) : (index, index, index) -> !ta.range
    %4 = "ta.index_label"(%c0, %c72, %c1) : (index, index, index) -> !ta.range
    %5 = "ta.index_label"(%c0, %c72, %c1) : (index, index, index) -> !ta.range
    %6 = "ta.tensor_decl"(%0, %4, %1, %5) : (!ta.range, !ta.range, !ta.range, !ta.range)
                                            -> tensor<72x72x72x72xf64>
    %7 = "ta.tensor_decl"(%3, %5, %2, %4) : (!ta.range, !ta.range, !ta.range, !ta.range)
                                            -> tensor<72x72x72x72xf64>
    %8 = "ta.tensor_decl"(%0, %1, %2, %3) : (!ta.range, !ta.range, !ta.range, !ta.range)
                                            -> tensor<72x72x72x72xf64>
    "ta.fill"(%6) {value = 1.000000e+00 : f64} : (tensor<72x72x72x72xf64>) -> ()
    "ta.fill"(%7) {value = 1.000000e+00 : f64} : (tensor<72x72x72x72xf64>) -> ()
    "ta.fill"(%8) {value = 0.000000e+00 : f64} : (tensor<72x72x72x72xf64>) -> ()
    "ta.tc"(%6, %7, %8) {indexing_maps = [#map0, #map1, #map2]} :
                                (tensor<72x72x72x72xf64>, tensor<72x72x72x72xf64>,
                                tensor<72x72x72x72xf64>) -> ()
    "ta.return"() : () -> ()
  }
}
```

```
1   def main(){
2       #IndexLabel Declarations
3       IndexLabel [a, b, c, d, e, f] = [72];
4
5       #Tensor Declarations
6       Tensor<double> A[a, e, b, f];
7       Tensor<double> B[d, f, c, e];
8       Tensor<double> C[a, b, c, d];
9
10      #Tensor Fill Operation
11      A[a, e, b, f] = 1.0;
12      B[d, f, c, e] = 1.0;
13      C[a, b, c, d] = 0.0;
14
15      #Tensor Contraction
16      C[a, b, c, d] = A[a, e, b, f] * B[d, f, c, e];
17  }
```

(a) DSL TA language

(b) TA dialect

Fig. 3. Example tensor contraction in COMET DSL and its relative TA dialect.

of arithmetic values that can be accessed by using indexing values. Range-based index label constructs (⟨ilabel⟩) represent the range of indices expressed through a scalar, a range, or a range with increment. Index labels can be used both for constructing a tensor (⟨tensor⟩) or for representing a tensor operation (⟨label-tensor⟩). In a tensor construction, index labels are used to represent each dimension size. In the context of a tensor operation, they represent slicing information of the tensor object where the operation will be applied. Figure 2b shows the grammar for supported tensor operations. Similar to the tensor construction, index labels are used as the main construct for representing the operations on the tensors. Each tensor operation production rule (⟨tensor-op⟩) is composed of a left-hand side (lhs) and a right-hand side (rhs) operation. While lhs can only be a labeled tensor construct, rhs can be of different types:

- alpha value (`A[i,j] = <const>`), which corresponds to a tensor fill operation where all the elements in the tensor are set to a scalar value.
- labeled tensors (`A[i,j] = alpha * D[j,i]`) correspond to a tensor copy operation (with respect to the label permutation). If the index label used in the rhs tensor is different from the one using during the tensor construction, the lhs tensor will represent a *view*. Following tensor operations that employ this lhs tensor will operate on a slice of the original tensor.
- multiplication of two labeled tensors (`C[i,k,l] = alpha * A[i,j] * B[j,k,l]`) updates the lhs with the tensor contraction results.
- multi-operand expressions (`D[i,l] = alpha * A[i,j] * B[j,k] * C[k,l]`) computes the whole pipeline of tensor contractions and updates the lhs.

The COMET TA language simplifies writing tensor algebra program by supporting common programming paradigms and enables users to express high-level concepts with familiar notations. Figure 3a shows a general tensor contraction implementation using COMET TA language. Line 3 describes an index label representing the size of each tensor dimension and the operation labels for describing the tensor fill and tensor contraction. Our TA language supports defining multiple `IndexLabel` variables (similar to structured bindings in C++-17) in a single statement. Tensors are then constructed using the `IndexLabel`s and the element type (lines 6–8). and contracted over indices `[e,f]` (line 16).

5   The Tensor Algebra Dialect

The Tensor Algebra dialect is the first dialect in the COMET compiler stack (Fig. 1). The main goal of this dialect is to represent basic building blocks of the tensor algebra computation, describe tensor algebra specific types and operations, and represent semantics information expressed through the TA DSL.

Figure 3b shows the TA dialect representation of the tensor contraction example shown in Fig. 3a. We define new operations in TA dialect that correspond to each tensor algebra DSL operation semantic. A `ta.index_label` corresponds to an `IndexLabel` construct in the TA language while a `ta.labeled_tensor` is for the `LabeledTensor` constructs. Figure 3b shows how an index label operation is constructed using a range (`!ta.range`) type. New tensors are declared with the `ta.tensor_decl` operation, which takes as input the index labels for each dimension and the data type. The `ta.labeled_tensor` operation represents a slice of a tensor that is being used in any operation that references it. This operation takes a tensor declaration and a set of index label references as inputs to construct a sliced version of the tensor.

Three classes of tensor operations are currently supported: unary (fill, copy, set), binary (contraction), and multi-operand expressions (contraction chains). `ta.fill` initializes a tensor object with a single value provided as an attribute to the operation. `ta.copy` performs an element-wise copy operation between two tensors scaling the output tensor by factor `alpha`. `ta.set` operates similarly to `ta.copy` but takes as input the result of a binary operation instead of a tensor. This operation is used to support multi-operand tensor contractions. Tensor contractions `ta.tc` take as input the input and output tensors, the scaling value `alpha`, and the indexing maps for the labels used in the contraction. For multi-operand expressions that involve several contractions, we introduce a utility operation (`ta.mult`) that represents a binary operation. The actual computation for a multi-operand expression includes calculation of intermediates and then the actual tensor contractions. We represent the order of binary operations with a binary tree and assign results to the output tensor using `ta.set`.

6   Optimizations and Transformations

The main advantage of a multi-level IR is that different kinds of optimizations can be applied at each level of the IR stack and optimizations can be shared and reused across different stacks. In the COMET compiler, we apply domain-specific optimizations at the TA dialect level, general optimizations at the LinAlg dialect

```
#map0 = affine_map<(d0, d1, d2, d3) -> (d0, d1, d2, d3)>            %4 = alloc() {alignment = 32 : i64} : memref<72x71x68x67xf64>
#map1 = affine_map<(d0, d1, d2, d3) -> (d0, d2, d1, d3)>            affine.for %arg0 = 0 to 72 {
#map2 = affine_map<(d0, d1, d2, d3) -> (d3, d1, d2, d0)>              affine.for %arg1 = 0 to 71 {
#map3 = affine_map<(d0, d1, d2, d3) -> (d0, d1)>                       affine.for %arg2 = 0 to 68 {
#map4 = affine_map<(d0, d1, d2, d3) -> (d2, d3)>                         affine.for %arg3 = 0 to 67 {
                                                                          %8 = affine.load %0[%arg0, %arg2, %arg1, %arg3] : memref<72x68x71x67xf64>
module {                                                                  affine.store %8, %4[%arg0, %arg1, %arg2, %arg3] : memref<72x71x68x67xf64>
  func @main() {                                                    } } } }
    // ..
    %4 = alloc() {alignment = 32 : i64} : memref<72x71x68x67xf64>
    linalg.copy %0, %4) {inputPermutation = #map0, outputPermutation = #map1} :
                        memref<72x68x71x67xf64>, memref<72x71x68x67xf64>
    %5 = alloc() {alignment = 32 : i64} : memref<68x67x70x69xf64>   scf.for %arg0 = %c0 to %c4830 step %WC {
    linalg.copy(%1, %5) {inputPermutation = #map0, outputPermutation = #map2} :   scf.for %arg1 = %c0 to %c4556 step %KC {
                        memref<69x67x70x68xf64>, memref<68x67x70x69xf64>       scf.for %arg2 = %c0 to %c5112 step %WC {
    %6 = linalg.reshape %4 [#map3, #map4] : memref<72x71x68x67xf64>              // ... affine.min
                        into memref<5112x4556xf64>                              %14 = subview %6[%arg2, %arg1] [%12, %13] [%c1, %c1] :
    %7 = linalg.reshape %5 [#map3, #map4] : memref<68x67x70x69xf64>                    memref<5112x4556xf64> to memref<?x?xf64, #map12>
                        into memref<4556x4830xf64>                              %16 = subview %7[%arg1, %arg0] [%13, %15] [%c1, %c1] :
    %8 = linalg.reshape %2 [#map3, #map4] : memref<72x71x68x69xf64>                    memref<4556x4830xf64> to memref<?x?xf64, #map12>
                        into memref<5112x4830xf64>                              %17 = subview %8[%arg2, %arg0] [%12, %15] [%c1, %c1] :
    linalg.matmul %6, %7, %8) {__internal_linalg_transform__ = "__tiling__"} :       memref<5112x4830xf64> to memref<?x?xf64, #map12>
                        memref<5112x4556xf64>,                                  scf.for %arg3 = %c0 to %15 step %MR {
                        memref<4556x4830xf64>,                                    scf.for %arg4 = %c0 to %12 step %NR {
                        memref<5112x4830xf64>                                      scf.for %arg5 = %c0 to %13 step %KC {
    // ..                                                                            // ... affine.min
    return                                                                          %20 = subview %14[%arg4, %arg5] [%18, %19] [%c1, %c1] :
                                                                                          memref<?x?xf64, #map12> to memref<?x?xf64, #map12>
                                                                                    %22 = subview %16[%arg5, %arg3] [%19, %21] [%c1, %c1] :
                                                                                          memref<?x?xf64, #map12> to memref<?x?xf64, #map12>
                                                                                    %23 = subview %17[%arg4, %arg3] [%18, %21] [%c1, %c1] :
                                                                                          memref<?x?xf64, #map12> to memref<?x?xf64, #map12>
                                                                                    linalg.matmul(%20, %22, %23) {__internal_linalg_transform__ = "__micro_kernel__"} :
                                                                                          memref<?x?xf64, #map12>, memref<?x?xf64, #map12>, memref<?x?xf64, #map12>
                                                                                  } } } } } }
```

Fig. 4. TA dialect after reformulation with a TTGT method (left panel). Lowering and optimization of transpose (right-top) and GEMM (right-bottom).

level, and architecture-specific optimizations at the lower levels. In the following, we explain our optimizations from the top IR level while lowering the code.

TTGT. As discussed in Sect. 2, tensor contractions can be reformulated by transposing multi-dimensional input tensors into 2D matrices, performing a GEMM operation, and unflatting the output tensor back to its original form. Although, this approach incurs the additional overhead of transpose operations, employing highly-optimized GEMM kernels outweighs this overhead. The left panel in Fig. 4 shows the TTGT reformulation of the `ta.tc` operation: transpose of input tensors (`linalg.copy`) and a GEMM operation (`linalg.matmul`).

Optimal Permutation for TTGT. The permutation chosen to reformulate a tensor contraction using the TTGT method has a considerable impact on performance. The cost of transposing a high-dimension tensor into a 2D tensor depends on which indices are transposed and the storage format. For row-major format, transposing the first indices is more expensive than transposing the latest ones, especially for the output tensor. In order to select the best permutation, we use a cost model based on a heuristic that assigns higher costs to permutations that move the outermost dimensions. Additionally, some permutation naturally results in a reduction of the number of transpose operations. We compute the cost of each valid transposition of input and output tensors, including the position swap for the input tensors, and select the permutation with the lowest cost.

Multi-Operand Expression. Given the associative property of tensor contractions, the order in which contractions are computed in a multi-operand expression produces the same results. However, the *number of operations* performed may vary depending on the grouping order of the contractions. Performance variation may be significant, especially if some of the tensors involved have low cardinality in some dimensions (e.g., "skinny matrices"). We explore all possible ordering of a multi-operand expression and identify the one that minimizes the overall number of operations. We then organize the sequence of operations in a binary tree and lower the multi-operand expression to a sequence of tensor contractions. Note that because the shape of the intermediate tensors is different from the original one, some tensor contractions may degenerate to simpler lower-dimension operations, such as GEMM or tensor-vector multiplications, which are further optimized (e.g., removing additional transpose).

Transpose Optimization. Our transpose optimization consists of two steps: loop permutation and tiling. The main rational of the cost model is that the loops corresponding to the innermost indices should be at the innermost level. We assign a weight to each loop index according to its position in the input and output tensor (the weight is higher if an inner index does not correspond to an inner loop) and compute the overall cost of the permutation by summing these weights. The right-top panel in Fig. 4 shows the IR after the selected loop permutation $(i, j, k, l \rightarrow i, k, j, l)$. Next, we employ tiling to improve locality.

GEMM Optimizations. GEMM plays a paramount role in a broad range of domains such as deep learning, scientific computing, and image processing. Tiling and blocking are effective methods to improve data locality and overlap computation and memory access. We employ the same tiling strategy used [9,22]: given $C[M, N] = A[M, K] * B[K, N]$, the C matrix is partitioned into multiple tiles with size $M_c \times N_c$. Each tile of C needs to access to A matrix with size $M_c \times K$ and a whole column of B matrix with size of $K \times N_c$. Since the whole row band of A and column of B are still large to be accommodated in the processor's cache, the K-dimension has to be partitioned into smaller tiles of A ($M_c \times K_c$) and B ($K_c \times N_c$). M_c, K_c and N_c are carefully selected so that the sub-matrix of B ($K_c \times N_c$) fits into the L3 cache and the A sub-matrix ($M_c \times K_c$) fits into the L2 cache. The N_c and M_c dimensions are further tiled by N_r and M_r, respectively, so that the sub-matrix of A ($M_r \times K_c$) and B ($K_c \times N_r$) fit into the L1 cache. The $M_r \times N_r$ elements from the matrix C fit into registers and the innermost computation of size $M_r \times N_r$ is executed as a micro-kernel. The right-bottom panel in Fig. 4 shows the various levels of tiling.

GEMM Micro-Kernel. Modern architectures are very complex and require sophisticated and highly-optimized code to fully achieve high performance. Compiler frameworks do their best to generate such code but also remain general. COMET leverages the LLVM back-end for code and binary generation which, when combined with tiling optimizations, provide good performance. However, a highly-optimized code for the specific architecture can fully leverage vector instructions, instruction-level parallelism, speculation, and other architectural features, achieving even higher performance. Also, COMET has been designed to support custom hardware accelerators that implement specific functionalities in hardware. Thus, the innermost computation in the GEMM kernel is performed using a *micro-kernel*, either a highly-specialized code for the target architecture ("soft-accelerator") or a custom hardware accelerator ("hard accelerator").

7   Modeling Custom Accelerators

Custom hardware accelerators may significantly increase performance, area, and energy efficiency of high-end compute systems. It comes as no surprise that hardware acceleration is widely employed in many domains, including mobile, automotive, high-performance computing, and machine learning. However, designing custom accelerators requires computationally-intensive simulations using software or FPGA-based tools, which may limit the scope to very small kernels.

COMET provides an opportunity to perform co-design and design space exploration (DSE) efficiently and to assess the performance of the entire application, instead of only the innermost kernel. As we explained in the previous section, the lower level dialects represent architecture-specific operations and the innermost computation in the GEMM operation is implemented as an architecture-specific, highly-optimized micro-kernel. In order to perform co-design for a target accelerator and measure the impact of realistic tensor contractions, we replace the micro-kernel with a timing model of the hardware accelerator and execute the entire contraction at native speed. To this extend, we pair COMET with Aladdin [18], a pre-register-transfer level (RTL), power-performance simulation framework that targets rapid prototyping of data parallel accelerators. Aladdin specifications are essentially C representations of the functionalities that need to be implemented in hardware. From these representations, an LLVM-based tracer extracts a dynamic data dependence graph (DDDG) that describes the accelerator. Next, Aladdin applies various optimizations and resource constraints, therefore generating a realistic design. Finally, Aladdin estimates power and performance from dynamic traces obtained from a driver program.

Performing DSE for the hardware accelerator design with Aladdin takes order of minutes (instead of hours as in traditional FPGA-based DSE) while executing tensor contraction with COMET is performed at native speed. The entire process, thus, can be completely automated and executed within minutes.

8   Evaluation

This section presents the performance code generated by the COMET compiler from the TA language. First, we show the performance impact of progressively applying the various optimizations described in Sect. 6. Next, we compare our automatically-generated code against the code that leverages hand-optimized libraries. Finally, we show a co-design case for the GEMM accelerator. We perform our experiments on a compute node featuring Intel Xeon 6126 CPU at 2.60 GHz and 192 GB of memory. We compare our results to 30 tensor contractions from the TCCG benchmark suite [20], using the reference problem sizes. The first eight contractions include tensor-matrix multiplication from machine learning domain (1st to 8th). The next three contractions are used to transform a set of two-electron integrals from an atomic orbital basis to a molecular orbital basis (9th to 11th). Finally, the following 19 contractions are from the CCSD

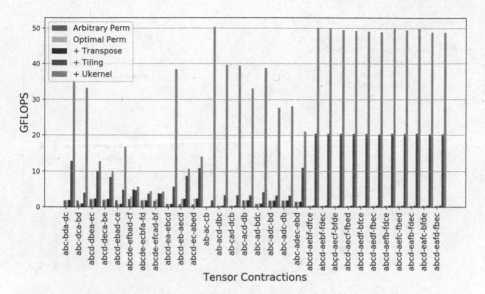

Fig. 5. Performance breakdown. The plot shows the impact of code optimizations applied incrementally to multiple tensor contractions (higher is better).

method of quantum chemistry. TCCG benchmarks are implemented in C++ and leverage highly-optimized computational libraries for tensor transpositions (HPTT) and GEMM kernels (BLIS). The results reported are the average of ten runs.

Overall Performance Evaluation. Figure 5 shows the performance impact of applying the optimizations described in Sect. 6 to the TCCG tensor contractions written with COMET DSL. The x-axis represents each tensor contraction, and the y-axis denotes the performance in terms of GFLOPS. We start from TTGT reformulations with a nested-loop GEMMs and transposes (blue bars) and progressively apply architecture-independent and architecture-specific optimizations, thus each bar in the graph shows the incremental benefits. The plot shows that each optimization brings varied performance gains on the different tensor contractions. The architecture-independent optimizations may (or may not) bring immediate benefit. This is the case of the arbitrary permutation for TTGT being already the optimal one. However, in some cases, optimizing transpose operations almost double performance (6th and 8th contractions). It is important to note that some architecture-independent optimization, such as selecting the optimal permutation, might bring performance gains after all other optimizations are applied (Fig. 6). Architecture-specific optimizations, such as GEMM tiling, bring considerable performance improvements in most of the cases, achieving 23× speedup on average and up to 56× speedup compared to the equivalent loop nest. For high-dimensional tensor contractions (e.g., the ones from CCSD), for which data movement dominates the execution time, exploiting data locality provides significant performance improvements. Finally, employing

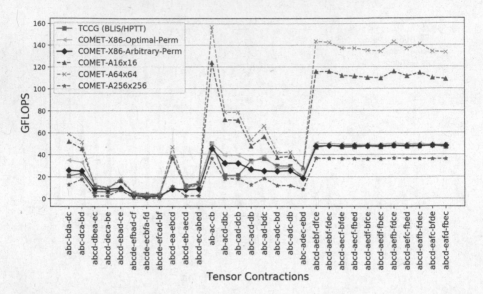

Fig. 6. COMET's performance comparison against the hand-optimized TCCG benchmarks on x86 (solid lines) and emulated platforms (dashed lines).

an architecture-specific micro-kernels that leverages AVX512 vector instructions, memory pre-fetching, and speculation, greatly improves performance, especially for the compute-bound contractions, achieving up to 51 GFLOPS. We remark that the micro-kernel is only effective once all other optimizations are performed, otherwise vector instructions cannot leverage data locality.

Figure 6 compares COMET against state-of-the-art implementation of TCCG tensor contractions. While both COMET and the C++ implementations use the TTGT method, TCCG implementations (solid blue line) leverage highly-optimized computational libraries. COMET implementations, instead, employ the optimizations described in the previous sections. In order to perform a fair comparison, we use the same micro-kernel implemented by the BLIS library, hence both hand-tuned and COMET-generated code use the same architecture-specific code. The plot shows that COMET results (solid yellow line) are comparable and, in some cases, better than the TCCG C++ implementations: COMET achieves an average of 1.22× and up to 1.98× speedup compared to the TCCG benchmarks. However, we believe that COMET has the distinct advantages of being more general (optimizations can be selectively applied), portable (different targets architectures may be chosen without re-implementing high-level optimizations), user-friendly (the TA language allows expressing equations in mathematical forms), and does not force programmers to bend algorithms to specific libraries APIs and formats. The graph also shows COMET performance when employing an arbitrary permutation instead of the best one (solid green line). Using the best permutation performs up to 4.36x better (1.38x on average) than using an arbitrary permutation. These results show that, although it

Table 1. Performance speedup of re-ordering multi-operand expressions.

Multi-operand tensor expressions	Perf.
A[c,d,m,n] * B[i,n,a,d] * C[m,c]	23.9
A[d,c,m,n] * B[i,n,a,d] * C[m,c]	21.1
A[c,d,m,n] * B[i,d] * C[n,a] * D[m,c]	4.9
A[d,c,m,n] * B[i,d] * C[n,a] * D[m,c]	4.5
A[m,n,e,j] * B[e,i] * C[a,m] * D[b,n]	1.4
A[m,n,f,e] * B[e,i] * C[f,n] * D[a,b,m,j]	1.4
A[m,n,e,f] * B[a,m] * C[f,n] * D[e,b,i,j]	2.2
A[m,n,e,f] * B[b,m] * C[f,n] * D[e,a,j,i]	1.8
A[n,m,e,f] * B[a,m] * C[f,n] * D[e,b,i,j]	2.2
A[n,m,e,f] * B[b,m] * C[f,n] * D[e,a,j,i]	1.8
A[m,n,e,f] * B[e,i] * C[f,n] * D[a,b,m,j]	1.5
A[m,n,e,f] * B[e,j] * C[f,n] * D[b,a,m,i]	1.7
A[m,n,f,e] * B[e,j] * C[f,n] * D[b,a,m,i]	1.5

Table 2. Characteristics of the emulated GEMM hardware designs.

	16×16	64×64	256×256
Perf. (cyc)	131	1026	32770
Avg. Power (mW)	5.077	13.639	73.7972
Avg. Area (uM^2)	55827	224068	4.097e+06

is not evident at first (Fig. 5), choosing an optimal permutation does increase the overall performance once architecture-specific optimizations are applied.

Overall, the results in Figs. 5 and 6 show that to achieve high performance it is imperative to employ sophisticated, architecture-specific optimizations that naturally make code much less portable. However, a compiler framework based on a multi-level IR can seamlessly apply both architecture-specific and architecture-independent optimizations, achieve optimal performance, and still maintain the high-level language specifications and semantics.

Multi-Operand Expression. Differently from a library-based approach, where programmers need to match the library-defined (binary) APIs, COMET can analyze tensor expressions and optimize the order in which each operation is executed. As stated in Sect. 6, although the final results of a multi-operand tensor contraction do not change despite of the execution order of the contractions, the number of operations does change, hence some ordering provides higher performance than others. In particular, when using a library (which normally provides an interface for contracting two tensors), programmers either have to figure out the optimal ordering manually a *priori* or may incur in performance loss if they follow the natural order of the tensor contractions. COMET, instead, automatically analyzes the entire expression and breaks it into binary operations properly ordered to achieve the highest performance by minimizing the number of overall operations. We evaluated 118 tensor contraction expressions from two NWChem methods that involve 3 and 4 operands. Table 1 shows that the multi-operand optimization reduces the total number of operations and provides performance speedup, up to 23.9×. We do not report the other expressions, as the natural order coincides with the optimal ordering. Note that in these experiments, we have employed the same optimizations introduced in Sect. 6, only difference is that the baseline executes contractions in the natural order of the expression whereas the multi-operand expression optimization identifies an ordering that reduces the overall number of operations.

Case Study: Designing Custom GEMM Accelerators. Our final experiments use COMET to perform co-design for a custom GEMM data-parallel accelerator. The main idea is to identify the best accelerator to perform GEMM operation in the TTGT method to solve tensor contractions. In this case, the GEMM accelerator is considered a "hard accelerator", as opposed to the "soft accelerator" for x86 employed in the previous section. We leverage COMET modeling capabilities and combine the code generated by our compiler framework with the timing estimates produced by Aladdin models of the GEMM designs. In particular, we replace the x86 micro-kernel with a delay that represents the execution time of the innermost GEMM computation on the hardware accelerator. We analyze three possible scenarios: small (16×16), medium (64×64), and large (256×256). Table 2 reports the hardware characteristics of the three designs in terms of performance, area, and average power. For comparison, consider that an Intel Ivy Bridge measures 160 mm^2 while an NVIDIA Volta GPU die measures 815 mm^2, which are $2,867\times$ and $14,606\times$ bigger than the 16×16 accelerator.

Figure 6 also reports the performance of a system that features custom GEMM hardware accelerators (dashed lines). The plot shows that hardware accelerators may substantially increase performance for compute-bound tensor contractions, such as the last 11 contractions, and achieve up to 156 GFLOPS, $3.1\times$ speedup over the same code employing a "soft" AVX512 accelerator. By comparing the results in Fig. 5 and 6, it is evident that the contractions that most benefit from tiling (and thus become compute-bound) also greatly benefit from hardware acceleration. The plot also shows an important point: while it seems intuitive that larger accelerators provide higher performance, this is not always the case in our experiments. There may be several reasons for this behavior, including large carry-over loops, computing GEMM for non-square matrices, caches that are not large enough to contain all the data, etc. Figure 6 does show that tensor contractions that are compute-bound with smaller hardware accelerators become memory-bound with the largest GEMM design. We infer that the lowest-level cache does not have sufficient storage to feed such large accelerators or to support data reuse. The actual point of co-design is, indeed, to figure out those trade-offs and select the best accelerator for the particular workload (64×64) instead of the best accelerator from the single operation (256×256).

9   Related Work

Among the compiler-based approaches for tensor algebra, the Tensor Contraction Engine (TCE) [8] is an early effort as a compiler framework that automatically optimizes dense tensor contractions in the quantum chemistry. TACO compiler is a C++ library that employs compiler-based techniques for dense and sparse tensors. TACO enables automatic code generation for a wide variety of linear and tensor algebra operations while supporting different storage formats. TACO provides similar notation to COMET TA language to express tensor expression, although programmers need to invoke object methods to pack/unpack data structures. Unlike TACO, COMET leverages core compiler optimizations, such as tiling or loop ordering, and supports multiple back-ends via LLVM.

There has been a lot of work on library-based approaches. The FLAME [7] focuses on formal description of linear algebra methods on matrices and the derivation of optimized implementations for distributed-memory systems. Later works [13,16,17] extend the framework for multi-dimensional tensor operations. The Cyclops Tensor Framework (CTF) [19] focuses on distributed computation of tensor operations. `libtensor` [4] focuses on describing block tensor operations using C++ templates. Recent work, such as ITensor [5] and·TensorNetwork [6], employs tensor networks to represent contractions of several tensors. Libraries-based approaches are easy to use but force scientists to re-arrange algorithms and implementations around the library APIs. This implies that, among others, library-approaches rarely support arbitrary tensor expressions. Moreover, libraries are typically implemented for specific architectures and may require heavy modifications to run on different heterogeneous systems. COMET, on the other hand, provides a programming interface close to the Einstein mathematical notation, supports arbitrary and mixed tensor expressions, and support execution on different architecture via LLVM backends.

To the best of our knowledge, none of the tools and libraries available provide an easy path to perform co-design of hardware accelerators for tensor algebra computations. COMET has been designed to support hardware accelerators and allows swapping optimizations in and out according to the target architecture.

10   Conclusions

The recent explosion of high-efficient and specialized architectures has dramatically decreased program portability and productivity. On one side, scientists prefer high-level, domain-specific languages that provide high-expressiveness and portability; on the other side, achieving high performance on modern architectures requires highly-tuned, architecture-specific implementations and support for custom hardware accelerators. This work presents COMET, a novel compiler framework that supports tensor algebra operations, specifically those related to chemistry. COMET consists of a high-level DSL, a multi-level IR, and a series of progressive lowering steps and program optimizations. COMET's multi-level IR approach allows us to change some of the dialects without the need to re-implement the entire IR stack and optimizations. We show that the code automatically generated by COMET outperforms hand-tuned tensor contractions that leverage state-of-the-art computational libraries across 30 tensor contractions from various domains. Our approach provides the distinct advantage of analyzing multi-operand expressions and identify the optimal ordering of tensor operations, achieving up to 23.9× speedup over equivalent code that follows the natural order. Finally, we show that COMET can also be used to perform co-design and identify the best GEMM accelerator for the tensor contractions under study. We plan to extend COMET in various directions, including additional support for tensor algebra operations, support for sparse operations, and support for additional architectures. We also plan to open source COMET.

Acknowledgement. This research is supported by PNNL Laboratory Directed Research and Development Program (LDRD), Data-Model Convergence Initiative, project DuoMO: A Compiler Infrastructure for Data-Model Convergence, and project Hybrid Advanced Workflows.

References

1. Abadi, M., et al.: TensorFlow: large-scale machine learning on heterogeneous systems (2015). https://www.tensorflow.org/. software available from tensorflow.org
2. Aprá, E., et al.: NWChem: past, present, and future. J. Chem. Phys. **152**(18), 184102 (2020). https://doi.org/10.1063/5.0004997
3. Einstein, A.: Die grundlage der allgemeinen relativitätstheorie. Ann. Phys. **354**(7), 769–822 (1916). https://doi.org/10.1002/andp.19163540702
4. Epifanovsky, E., et al.: New implementation of high-level correlated methods using a general block tensor library for high-performance electronic structure calculations. J. Comput. Chem. **34**(26), 2293–2309 (2013)
5. Fishman, M., White, S.R., Stoudenmire, E.M.: The itensor software library for tensor network calculations (2020)
6. Google: TensorNetwork (2020). https://github.com/google/TensorNetwork
7. Gunnels, J.A., et al.: FLAME: formal linear algebra methods environment. ACM Trans. Math. Softw. **27**(4), 422–455 (2001)
8. Hirata, S.: Tensor contraction engine: abstraction and automated parallel implementation of configuration-interaction, coupled-cluster, and many-body perturbation theories. J. Phys. Chem. A **107**(46), 9887–9897 (2003)
9. Intel: Math kernel library (2012). http://developer.intel.com/software/products/mkl/
10. Jouppi, N.P., et al.: In-datacenter performance analysis of a tensor processing unit. In: Proceedings of the 44th Annual International Symposium on Computer Architecture, pp. 1–12 (2017)
11. Lattner, C., Adve, V.: LLVM: a compilation framework for lifelong program analysis and transformation. In: CGO '04, San Jose, CA, USA, pp. 75–88 (2004)
12. Lattner, C., et al.: MLIR: a compiler infrastructure for the end of Moore's law. arXiv preprint arXiv:2002.11054 (2020)
13. Poulson, J., et al.: Elemental: a new framework for distributed memory dense matrix computations. ACM Trans. Math. Softw. **39**(2), 13:1–13:24 (2013)
14. Ragan-Kelley, J., et al.: Halide: A language and compiler for optimizing parallelism, locality, and recomputation in image processing pipelines. In: PLDI'13, pp. 519–530 (2013)
15. Raghavachari, K., et al.: A fifth-order perturbation comparison of electron correlation theories. Chem. Phys. Lett. **157**, 479–483 (1989)
16. Schatz, M., van de Geijn, R., Poulson, J.: Parallel matrix multiplication: a systematic journey. SIAM J. Sci. Comput. **38**(6), C748–C781 (2016)
17. Schatz, M.D., Low, T.M., van de Geijn, R.A., Kolda, T.G.: Exploiting symmetry in tensors for high performance: multiplication with symmetric tensors. SIAM J. Sci. Comput. **36**(5), C453–C479 (2014)

18. Shao, Y.S., et al.: Aladdin: a pre-RTL, power-performance accelerator simulator enabling large design space exploration of customized architectures. In: ISCA, pp. 97–108. IEEE Press (2014)
19. Solomonik, E., Matthews, D., Hammond, J.R., Stanton, J.F., Demmel, J.: A massively parallel tensor contraction framework for coupled-cluster computations. J. Parallel Distrib. Comput. **74**(12), 3176–3190 (2014)
20. Springer, P., Bientinesi, P.: Design of a high-performance Gemm-like tensor-tensor multiplication. ACM Trans. Math. Softw. **44**(3), 1–29 (2018)
21. Springer, P., Su, T., Bientinesi, P.: HPTT: a high-performance tensor transposition C++ library, pp. 56–62 (2017)
22. Van Zee, F.G., Van De Geijn, R.A.: BLIS: a framework for rapidly instantiating BLAS functionality. ACM Trans. Math. Softw. **41**(3), 14:1–14:33 (2015)

G-Code Re-compilation and Optimization for Faster 3D Printing

Xiaoming Li[✉]

University of Delaware, Newark, DE 19716, USA
xli@udel.edu

Abstract. The 3D printing technology has seen increasingly wider application in industrial manufacturing and the general public domain. The normal working flow of 3D printing, i.e., from Computer Aided Design (CAD), to 3D model description, and last to 3D printers, essentially uses languages such as STL (Standard Tessellation Language or STereoLithography) and G-code to pass information between the work phases from designing to manufacturing. However, the languages are produced and used literally (like using XML for only data representation), and there has not been much discussion on how these de-facto programming languages can be compiled or optimized. In this paper, we present our preliminary work that tries to improve 3D printing's efficiency at the backend of the working flow. We re-compile the G-code into a higher-level IR, design a number of physics and graphics driven optimizations, and re-generate G-code from optimized IR representation. We test our G-code compiler on several popular 3D models and show upto 10.4% speedup or save more than 16 h on printing complex models.

1 Introduction

The 3D printing is an emerging technology for product development and manufacturing. It is young, but it has passed the stage of being only a hobby activity, and has seen rapidly growing applications in industry. Some of the high-profile products that are 3D printed include Space-X's SuperDraco engine [2], Airbus aircraft parts [3] and many.

A standing-out issue for 3D printing is its speed [5]. Compared to the traditional manufacturing technologies such as casting or forging, which handle volume of material in batches, 3D printing builds up shapes with elementary forms of material such as powders or filaments. Its speed depends on both the volume of product and also the shape's complexity. It is quite common to take days to print even a seemingly simple 3D shape. For example, NASA is developing 3D printing technology for the first manned lunar base. In its latest demo, a simple chair took about 2 weeks to print [7].

This paper presents an initial and exploratory effort to improve 3D printing's speed using compiler-derived techniques. To understand the speed issue of 3D printing, we need to examine its complete workflow. 3D printing usually starts

B. Chapman and J. Moreira (Eds.): LCPC 2020, LNCS 13149, pp. 104–116, 2022.
https://doi.org/10.1007/978-3-030-95953-1_8

with a Computer Aided Design (CAD) software such as AutoCAD. The outcome of CAD is usually the 3D geometrical representation of a product. Thereafter, the 3D geometrical representation is processed by a type of software called "slicers" to be transformed into solid models and further been translated into commands that can be understood by 3D printers. 3D printers will load the commands, which are movements of servos and settings for printing such as temperatures or speeds. The embedded controller on 3D printers will execute the commands and directly control servos to move the printing nozzles and extruders.

Clearly, we can attempt to improve 3D printing's performance at any phases of the workflow. In this paper, we particularly look into the interface to the embedded 3D printer controller. The commands are usually represented in an industry standard format called G-Code. Our key observation is that while being sufficient to control the movement of servos, G-code is primitive and loses high-level information about the product being printed. The current technique that translates the 3D geometrical model to the elementary movements in G-code is direct and does have printing speed in mind. There has been a lack of proper intermediate representation for any optimization work to became possible.

The main contributions of this paper are a higher-level printing IR for G-Code, new optimization techniques that respect the physical contraints of 3D printing but reduce the total printing time, and a G-code generator that re-generates improved G-code from this IR. We evaluate our G-code compiler on a number of popular 3D printing models and achieve up to 10.4% speed improvement.

2   Background and Overview

The 3D printing technology is a new manufacturing technology to build 3D shapes. Generally speaking, traditional manufacturing methods such as forging, casting or injection molding manipulate volume of material into desired shapes. In contrast, 3D printing builds up a shape by gradually adding minuscule amount of material into place piece by piece and layer by layer. That is why 3D printing is also referred as "additive manufacturing" in many contexts.

The 3D printing workflow typical involves three phases: CAD, slicer, and 3D printer. CAD software such as AutoCAD, Fusion 360 or OpenSCAD can be used to design 3D models. CAD interfaces with slicer programs with the mesh description of 3D model. One of the industry's defacto standard format for such mesh description is STL (Standard Tessellation Language or STereoLithography).

STL files cannot be directly printed because they only describe the surface geometry of a three-dimensional object without any model attributes. Slicer programs such as *slic3r* or *Simplify3D* translate STL files into printable description of 3D model. The translation involves two main tasks: figuring out the movements of extruder to implement the 3D object, and conforming to a 3D printer's specific physical capability. Slicers also need to make sure the movements are legitimate for a specific printer, and at the same time try to maintain the print quality of the final product. Therefore, slicers will specify the physical attributes of the movements such as the extruder temperature, the building bed temperature, and the speeds of servo involved in movements.

The output of slicers is the description of all the movements, together with the specification of the printer's setup and the physical attributes of movement. All of these are written in the G-code file to be send to the printer.

2.1   System Overview

The proposed G-code compiler has three main components: (1) the geometric IR, which contains the same semantic information as the G-code, but stores it in a graph-like data-structure to facilitate the analysis and transformation; (2) front-end and backend, which convert between the G-code and the geometric IR; and (3) compiler transformations that currently include only a few essential passes including the preprocessing passes and the speed optimization passes.

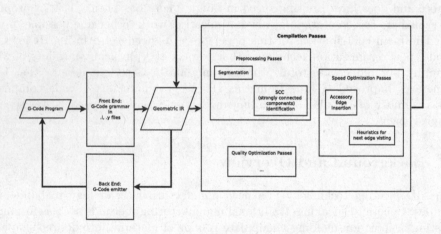

Fig. 1. Working flow of the G-code compiler.

Figure 1 shows the overall working flow of the compiler. The geometric IR and the front/back ends are described in Sect. 3 and the compiler passes in Sect. 4.

3   Intermediate Representation for G-Code

3.1   Design Consideration

What Is G-Code? G-code is a numerical control language for programming Computer Numerical Control (CNC) devices. It was born out of the MIT Servomechanisms Lab in 1950s, and has since been extended by numerous standard institutions and companies. Originally the language is designed to describe the control and movement of cutting tools, i.e., essentially telling the servos where to move and when. Since its beginning, the 3D printing technology also adopt this concept. Today G-code also becomes the de-facto programming language for 3D printers.

Just like the CNC domain, the 3D printing community has also developed numerous variants of G-code such as the Marlin, RepRap or MakerBot dialects. While the variants are largely semantically compatible, they differ in the representation of numbers and the settings of printer. Here we briefly describe the stem of the G-code that is more-or-less common among all variants.

From the programming language perspective, G-code is extremely simple. Most G-code variants don't contain any control structures such as conditional branch or loop. The language has two basic command sets—G commands that start with the letter "G", and M commands that start with the letter "M". G commands basically describe movements. For example G1 (also represented as G01) specifies a linear interpolated movement. G3 represents a counterclockwise, circular interpolated movement. M commands basically specifies settings including both movement settings and machine settings. For example, M205 sets the jerk rate (max acceleration) on the XY axis. Most M commands are modal commands, which means that the effect of the commands stays in effect until being replaced.

Geometrical Movements. The requirement for the IR to store the movements is easy to implement. The majority of a G-code file is the commands describing the servos' movements. The number of dimension in movement, or the degree of freedom in servo motion, is essentially the number of servos in a printer. The basic printers have 4 motors, and more advanced varieties have more. Usually the 3D geometrical space is consisting of the X, Y and Z dimensions and is controlled by three servos. There are two types of mapping from the three servos to the X/Y/Z dimensions. In the Cartesian style of 3D printers, each servo controls the motion along one dimension. The mapping is direct and linear. For the Delta 3D printers [4], all three servos participate in the motion control along all three dimensions. The motor movements are translated into 3D space movements through trigonometric remapping.

In addition to the three servos that control the spatial movements, 3D printers also have extruders that additively accumulate material. Normally one extruder is directly controlled by a servo. So the number of material handling servos equals, in most cases, the number of extruder equipped in a printer. An extruder servo mostly moves in one direction, that is, extruding/adding material. On the other hand, printing an object involves move the extruder motor backward, i.e., for retracting, from time to timer. For example, to avoid the leakage of material when the extruder moves from one section to another disconnected one, the corresponding extruder servo will retract and when arriving at the destination location, extruding again.

Movement Setting and System Setting. Up to this point, the IR for G-code is an abstract geometric space. Hypothetically speaking, transformations using it won't guarantee the correct printing of the transformed G-code. The reason is that a movement needs to be accomplished with proper settings such as temperatures and speeds for it to be printed correctly and with good quality. The setting is also highly contextualized, i.e., the properness depending on what happens before the movement. Therefore, a practical IR must incorporate information the printer setting, and equally importantly maintain the dependency of the settings.

The main settings relevant to movement are temperature and speed. Movements are printed with different temperatures. The reasons for doing that include to guarantee good bed adhesion, reduce material warping or improve surface quality of object. Therefore, when our compiler parses the G-code, it needs to deduce the temperatures for all the movements, and attaches the information to the edges in the Cartesian space.

A 3D printer also constantly changes printing speed in the process of printing an object. For example, when printing a small section, the speed might be reduced to give material sufficient cooling time. As another example, when the movement is across a large unsupported section, the speed might be increased to avoid sagging of the material (a.k.a "bridging" mode). Clearly the speed setting of a movement is context-sensitive, i.e., that the appropriate speed setting depends on what happens before it.

In addition to the settings related to movement, G-code also contains commands pertaining to features that are specific to slicer or printer. Those commands usually appear at the prolog or the epilog parts of G-code. The commands are usually not tied to specific movements. The compiler's frontend will recognize the start and the end of those sections, and re-emit them when transforming back into G-code.

Encoding Printer's Physical Constraints. By this point, the IR design has become capable of representing the geometrical space that a printer's motor can reach, arbitrary movements in the space, and the settings of the printer's auxiliary equipment such as heat bed or fans. One thing that needs attention is the resolution of number in the IR. The space and movements are *not* continuously reachable by the printer. The servos are mostly step-driven. That means, they can only rotate as multiples of the minimum amount of rotation, and can't go below the rotation resolution. In other words, the numbers should be discretized according to the printer's capability.

For example, a key specification parameter of 3D printer is the minimum layer height. The parameter is usually linked to the rotation resolution of the Z-axis servo. If the minimum height is 0.1 mm, any representation of the Z-axis position in the IR should be a multiple of 0.1 mm. Imaging that if a transformation introduces a new vertex in the space with $Z = 3.55$ mm, the newly created vertex, however, is meaningless because it simply won't be able to be reached precisely by the printer. Practically the printer's controller might still accept such a value in the G-code, but where it actually goes is unpredictable, and may likely create printing quality problems such as the separation of layer.

Therefore, we make the resolution of number in the IR explicitly visible in the IR. The resolution constraints are not only maintained when G-code is parsed or re-generated, but also are mandated when transformations are applied on the IR.

3.2 Definition of the Geometric IR

We have so far discussed the main points for consideration when designing the IR for G-code. Taking all these into account, we can put together a formal definition of the G-code IR. The IR has two parts, a graph representation that describes the geometric information in the G-code, and the decorating properties that store the settings for the geometric movements and the printer.

The geometric basis of the IR is a N-dimensional *graph*, N being the number of servos in the 3D printer that the IR is representing. The graph is *undirectional*, because material printing can be done on either one of the two directions of the movement. So this geometric information can be encoded as $G = (V, E)$, V is the vertex set and E is the edge set. For $v \in V$, v is a n-dimensional vector, where each element v_i represents the rotational position of the $i_t h$ servo. For $E = e_i | e_i = v_{i_0} - v_{i_1}$, each edge in the set represents the linear interpolated movements of servos between v_{i_0} and v_{i_1}. The edges are undirectional.

The graph is decorated with three categories of property: vertex property, edge property and environmental property. The vertex property in the current IR contains the position vector v^N of the vertex, and several flags that can be set by analysis or transformation passes to facilitate future processing of the graph. The flags include whether the vertex is introduced new in the segmentation pass, and the strongly connected component index that the vertex belongs to.

The edge property contains the settings for correctly printing the edge. The settings include temperature, line speed of movement, and starting/ending actions. The temperature and the speed settings are self explanatory. The starting/ending actions of an edges are those M instructions in the G-code that do not directly affect movements but still need to be done before or after the printing of the edge. Examples of such actions include $M207$—setting jerk rate, or $M212$—setting bed offset for the auto-leveling feature, etc.

The environmental property describes the printer system constraints such as the minimum resolution for servos or the sensors' precision. Even though part of such information can be reasoned from G-code, our current implementation manually provide the environmental property as an external configuration for the compiler.

3.3 Example of IR

Here we illustrate the proposed geometric IR with an example segment of G-code. The example is simplified for this illustration because in real G-code, the dimensionality is at least 4—one servo each for the X, Y, and Z dimensions and one servo for extruding. It is hard to visualize a 4 dimensional graph. So in this example, we only use the X and Y axis and one extruder dimension in the G-code program.

```
G1 X100 Y100 Z0 E1 F100
G1 X100 Y300 E2
G1 X300 Y300 E3
G1 X300 Y100 E4
G1 X100 Y300 E5
G1 X100 Y100 E5
G1 X300 Y300 E6
```
(a) G-code

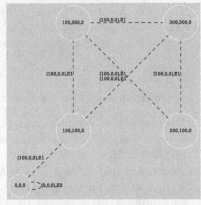

(b) IR visualization

Fig. 2. G-code example and its corresponding IR visualized.

Figure 2a shows the example G-code segment, and Fig. 2b shows the visualization of the corresponding IR. As we can see, each *G*-instruction is translated into one edge, and the *M*-instructions preceding an edge will be attached to the starting action property of the edge.

4   G-Code Optimization

The G-code IR provides a holistic representation of information contained in the G-code output of slicer. The distinctive characteristic of the IR, compared with the raw G-code format, is its high-level semantic. The IR is naturally geometrical and the raw G-code is sequential. For example, movements in a G-code file might be totally independent to each other. However, it is hard to tell that in the original form, as the G-code mandates an unnecessary order between the movements. On the other hand, the IR representation of the same movements can be easily analyzed for their dependency or even spatial locality, and further be reordered for faster printing.

The higher-level semantic of the G-code IR opens the door for 3D printing transformations. That is, transforming a G-code IR representation of an object into other equivalent IR representation, and when feeding the transformed IR to a 3D printer, still produces the same object. The concepts involved in this G-code compilation and optimization are similar to those for the typical computer programming languages. However, as we can imagine, computers compute, but 3D printers perform a very different kind of job in a very different way. We need to redefine what kind of transformation is legal, what are the optimization goals, and how to model performance (i.e., speed, quality, etc.) for the specific problem of compiling for 3D printer.

4.1   Compilation Constraints

A transformation of the G-code IR changes both the geometric description and also the order of movements or extrusion. First we need to find an operable definition of what is a valid transformation. Eventually, any valid G-code transformations should be able to print the same object that the original G-code program intends to make. The question is how this correctness requirement can be translated into a series of legality tests, like the dependency test for our computer compilers?

The correctness requirement for 3D printing basically means two things: (1) a valid transformation must extrude material exactly as the original extrusion movements do in the IR. The transformation cannot extrude more, and cannot extrude less. (2) The order of extrusion must be feasible for the 3D printer. We can use a simple example to demonstrate what is the "feasibility" here. When moving from the position $(x, y, z) = (100, 100, 2)$ to $(100, 200, 2)$, for example, there should not be any place along the moving path where the height of the printed part is higher than 2. Otherwise, the movement will damage the printed portion.

Beyond that a valid transformation must print out the same shape, like a compiler transformation should produce the same results, 3D printing has requirement on the quality of printout. Still using compiler transformations as example, in a computer program, transforming "1+1" into "1*2" will be legal but may carry different speed characteristics. The term "performance" in 3D printing not only means printing speed, but also printing quality. When the movements in a printing job are reordered, in many cases, the outcome can have drastically changed quality. It is because materials that 3D printer handle, such as PLA, ABS or Nylon, exhibit different physical properties such as layer adhesion when they are printed with different speeds, or with printing direction from the layer below, etc. Therefore, when we transform G-code, we need to respect this additional quality constraint.

4.2   Optimization for Printing Speed

Just like that our computer compiler transformations can be tuned for different goals such as speed or code size, G-code can also be transformed to improve on different 3D printing metrics such as printing speed or product quality. In this paper, we describe our exploratory study of printing speed optimization using the G-code IR.

Pre-processing with IR. Given an IR representation of a 3D printing task, the basic job is to traverse all the edges exactly once. As we will discuss later, this job sounds like an Euler Tour problem. But before we start looking into how to walk through the graph, we want to point out that the raw IR representation hides potential optimization opportunities. And these opportunities can be made available for later transformation by adding a preprocessing pass after the compiler front-end.

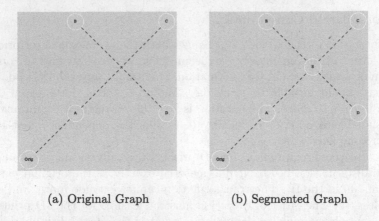

(a) Original Graph   (b) Segmented Graph

Fig. 3. IR pre-processing: graph segmentation

In this study we implement two preprocessing passes: graph segmentation and connected component identification.

The purpose of graph segmentation is to facilitate the route searching in the Euler Touring based optimization. Here is an example of how graph segmentation can help. As Fig. 3 shows, in the original G-code representation, two movements $A - C$ and $B - D$ intersect in space. However, because they are originally represented as two separate edges, the Euler Touring algorithm might not be able to take advantage of the intersection to find more efficient tours. If we segment the graph, i.e., introduce a dummy vertex for the intersection point, the touring algorithm would be able to move only parts of the original movements and find more efficient touring path. Thanks to this added flexibility of touring, after graph segmentation, the Euler Touring algorithm will find the shortest tour that uses the additional connectivity of the dummy vertex "S".

Graph segmentation itself is a conceptually very simple processing. A naive algorithm will try to intersect an edge with all other edges. If any two edges intersect, introduce the intersection point as a new vertex and break up the original two edges into four based on the intersection point. In this case, the complexity of the naive segmentation will be $O(E^2)$, where E being the number of edges. Because the newly created edges might also intersect with other edges, the iteration will continue until no further changes are made.

The naive graph segmentation algorithm won't work in practice. A typical 3D object will involve millions of edges. The complexity of $O(E^2)$ simply make the naive algorithm not viable. We use two pruning techniques to accelerate the algorithm. The first is to further preprocess the graph IR to identify connected components. So that we only need to test intercepting with a component. We use a DFS-based approach to find all connected components. Since connected components can still be huge, we further re-organize a component into layers and only try interception test with in the layer that the edge belongs to and the layer below and the layer above, where are the only place that any potential intercepting edges can reside.

4.3   Printing Speed Optimization

As previously discussed, the proposed G-code IR supports a variety of optimization goals such as speed, printing quality or physical strength. This paper describes our preliminary result of optimizing speed. Under this set up, the goal function is simply to cover all edges in the original graph exactly once, and minimize the overall *time*.

The goal sounds very much like an Euler Tour problem, i.e., finding a path in a finite graph that visits every edge exactly once. The main challenges to adapt the Euler Tour problem in the solving of the G-code printing speed problem lie in the subtle but fundamental problem setup differences. The differences are derived from how 3D printers work and perform.

The starting point of our preliminary optimization is based on the Hierholzer's algorithm [6,8] with solutions to address the specifics of the G-code optimization setup. Our main effort is spent on addressing the differences between the Euler Tour problem and our optimization problem. Next we describe the differences and our solution thereof.

- Goal: The Hierholzer algorithm finds *an* Euler tour in a graph, and that's it. There is not any optimization criteria built-in. The only guarantee is that every edge is visited exactly once. But no effort is made to find the tour that minimize the total distance or other graph metrics. Note that the total distance in an Euler tour is not fixed for a graph, as accessory edges need to be introduced in order to guarantee the existence of an Euler tour.

  Our solution is to include heuristics at several places in the algorithm to optimize the total tour time. The places include the construction of accessory edges, the choice of next edge and the choice of next vertex to visit. The final heuristics also consider the next couple of challenges, and will be detailed in Sect. 4.4.
- Complexity: The computation complexity of the Hierholzer's Algorithm is $O(V + E)$, V being the number of vertices and E being the number of edges. Real-world G-code, when transformed into the proposed IR, can contain millions of vertices and/or edges. It is impractical to blindly apply the Hierholzer's Algorithm. Our solution is motivated by a type of compiler pass, i.e., the Strongly Connected Components (SCC) passes. That is, we apply the optimization algorithm on every connected component that has been found. Also when the work on one component is finish, we use the same heuristic that finds the next vertex to identify the next component to process.
- Performance of edge visit: In the setup of the Euler Tour problem, the weights of edges are constant. In our G-code optimization problem, the weights are the distance of movement, and they are indeed constant, too. However, the time to travel through the edge is not. This is because for a 3D printing to move, the setting of the movement must be ready, which introduce overhead.

Also the change of moving direction lead to acceleration, and the involved servos need to do extra work to handle the G-force. Overall, the time to travel through an edge is contextually dependent on the previous edge. Our solution is to build a physical performance model, quite rough at this stage, for the edge traversal, and incorporate the model into the optimization heuristics.

4.4 Optimization Heuristics

Accessory Edges: In order to find an eulerian tour, accessory edges need to be introduced in a graph to connect pairs of vertices with odd degrees. We need to minimize the total distance of the introduced accessory edges to optimize the total time for traveling the eulerian tour. That is, if a graph has n odd-degree vertices, we need to find the division scheme that minimize $\sum_{\forall v} dist(v_i, v_j)$, This is another well-known algorithmic problem called the *Pairwise Optimization* problem. We use a simple heuristic to solve the problem. We build a matrix of all the pairwise distances any two of odd-degree vertices, and use Dynamic programming to iteratively remove the next shortest pair, until all odd-degree vertices are covered. We want to point out that our heuristic is *not* globally optimal.

Next Edge to Visit: In the Hierholzer's Algorithm, if a just-visited vertex has multiple un-visited outbound edges, a random choice is made. In the case of G-code IR, the choice of the next edge carries significance with regard to the edge traversal time. There are two reasons. First, if the next edge has different setting, e.g., speed or temperature, the printer need to change setting first before it can drive the servos to make the movement. That introduces overhead. Second, change of moving direction introduces G-force in servos. This is call "jerk rate" in the 3D printing terminology. Without going into too much physic details, the short conclusion is that the lower the G-force, the faster the printing. Using the example in Fig. 3b, if the current vertex is S, and the previous edge is $B - S$, the best next edge is $S - D$ but not $S - A$ or $S - C$, as $S - D$ is mostly aligned with the previous edge and will incur the least G-force.

We develop a simple heuristic here. We first check the printing setting of the edge candidates, and if possible, only choosing from the ones that have the same setting as the current edge, or if not possible, involving the least setting changes. If there are still multiple candidates, which are the majority of the cases, choose the one the involves the minimum G-force to travel.

5 Experiment and Evaluation

The G-code compiler and the printing speed optimization are evaluated with 3D models. There have been no public available compiler/optimization work on G-code, and as the result there is no "standard" benchmark for the kind of evaluation we want to do. Fortunately, due to the increasing populaty of 3D printing technology, there are multiple websites for people to share 3D printing models—sort of like github for 3D models. We use http://www.thingiverse.com (Thingiverse), one of the most widely used 3D model sharing site, and use several of the most popular models on that site as the benchmarks. The models are "Baby Groot", "Benchy", "Printer Test", and "Mid Castle". Table 1 shows the benchmark models, download links and the total number of downloads as reported by Thingiverse.

Table 1. 3D model benchmarks

Benchmarks	URL	# of Downloads
Baby Groot	https://www.thingiverse.com/thing:2014307	32402
Benchy	https://www.thingiverse.com/thing:763622	42329
3D Printer Test	https://www.thingiverse.com/thing:2656594	32235
Medieval Castle	https://www.thingiverse.com/thing:862724	18701

All the models are downloaded as STL files. We use Simplify3D [1], a widely used commercial Slicer to generate G-code for the STL. The 3D printer we use is JGAurora A8, and its controller firmware is Marlin, a Linux-based software that is widely used as the operating system in 3D printers.

The G-code output from Simplify3D is the input to our compiler and optimizer, and our output is also G-code. We measure the printing time of the before/after versions of the G-code. Actually Simplify3D also reports estimated printing time based on its own G-code output, and in almost all cases, its estimation is spot on. In this paper, we report the actual printing time.

Table 2 shows the before and the after printing time of the benchmark modes. We also collect statistics of the model before vs. after, including the number of vertices, number of edges, total distance traveled. As the result shows, our optimization achieves upto 10.4% speed or about 973 minutes for the model "Medieval Castle" that has the highest number of edges (9.08 million). On simpler models, our speed-ups are around 5%.

Table 2. Before/After comparison and speedups.

Benchmarks	Edges	Vertices	Total Distance (mm)	Time (minutes)	Speedup
Baby Groot	3.39M/3.42M	3.58M/3.65M	183.536K / 174.227K	632.945/605.71	4.7%
Benchy	2.05M/2.43M	2.43M/2.67M	5.34M/5.22M	1866.1/1766.75	5.3%
3D Printer Test	190.9K/194.2K	211.37K/213.3K	872.1K / 829.3K	380.301 362.723	4.6%
Medieval Castle	9.08M/9.76M	16.81M/17.33M	29.1M/27.51M	9358.84/8385.93	10.4%

6 Conclusion

In this paper we present the preliminary design of a G-code compiler. Particularly we introduce an appropriate IR that captures all information in G-code and in addition makes it easily to retract higher-level graphic and physical information. Furthermore, we discuss the legal test for G-code transformation on the IR and several heuristics for improving the printing performance. The evaluation using several popular 3D models shows up to 10% speedup on complex and long printing jobs.

References

1. Simplify3d. https://www.simplify3d.com/
2. SpaceX uses DMLs to 3D print Inconel SuperDraco engine chamber. https://additivemanufacturingtoday.com/spacex-uses-dmls-to-3d-print-inconel-superdraco-engine-chamber
3. Bridging the gap with 3d printing (2018). https://www.airbus.com/newsroom/news/en/2018/04/bridging-the-gap-with-3d-printing.html
4. Bell, C.: 3D Printing with Delta Printers, 1st edn. Apress, New York (2015)
5. Gibson, I., Rosen, D.W., Stucker, B.: Additive Manufacturing Technologies: Rapid Prototyping to Direct Digital Manufacturing, 1st edn. Springer, Heidelberg (2009). https://doi.org/10.1007/978-1-4419-1120-9
6. Hierholzer, C., Wiener, C.: Ueber die Möglichkeit, einen Linienzug ohne Wiederholung und ohne Unterbrechung zu umfahren (1873)
7. Staedter, T.: AI SpaceFactory wins Nasa's 3D-printed extraterrestrial habitats challenge. In: IEEE Spectrum. IEEE (2019)
8. Torrubia, G.S., Blanc, C.T., Navascués-Galante, L.: EulerPathSolver: a new application for Fleury's algorithm simulation (2009)

Machine Language and Quantum Computing

Optimized Code Generation for Deep Neural Networks

Janaan Lake$^{(\boxtimes)}$ (iD), Tharindu R. Patabandi (iD), and Mary Hall (iD)

School of Computing, University of Utah, Salt Lake City, UT, USA
u0987016@utah.edu, {tharindu,mhall}@cs.utah.edu

Abstract. As Deep Neural Networks (DNNs) become more widely used in a variety of applications, the need for performance and portability on many different architectures, including CPUs, becomes increasingly important. Compiler-based methods offer opportunities for performance gains over statically-tuned libraries by exploiting data reuse and parallelism, efficient memory access, and vectorization for specific backends with the use of abstraction. The Batch Normalization (BN) operator can accelerate the training and increase the robustness of DNNs, making it a widely-used operator in many DNNs. *LATTE* is a domain-specific language for DNNs, and *SWIRL* is a compiler that can be used with *LATTE*. We extend the applicability of *LATTE/SWIRL* by incorporating the BN operator into the *LATTE* framework and by expanding the optimizations of *SWIRL* to this operator. The optimized BN operator in *LATTE/SWIRL* is compared to existing frameworks such as TensorFlow, TensorFlow with Intel MKL-DNN, TensorFlow with XLA, PyTorch with MKL-DNN and MXNet with MKL-DNN. The results show that a compiler-based approach for the BN operator can increase performance on CPU architectures.

Keywords: Optimizing compilers · Batch normalization · Deep neural networks · Code generation

1 Introduction

Deep Neural Networks (DNNs) are currently one of the fastest growing areas in computer science, with wide-ranging applications from speech recognition to genomics. Typical DNNs require billions of operations for training and inference, making them compute intensive. Graphics Processing Units (GPUs) have been the hardware of choice for many DNNs. Due to a variety of factors, including cost and programming complexity, GPUs are not always incorporated into many computing clusters. Hence, there is a demand for performance and portability of DNNs across a variety of architectures and platforms.

Because of the large interest in DNNs, there are many frameworks that can train and run them. These high-level frameworks, such as TensorFlow [4], Torch [8], Theano [19], Caffe [11], CNTK [16] and MXNet [6], use abstraction to represent neural networks and employ one of three approaches: computation graph

© Springer Nature Switzerland AG 2022
B. Chapman and J. Moreira (Eds.): LCPC 2020, LNCS 13149, pp. 119–133, 2022.
https://doi.org/10.1007/978-3-030-95953-1_9

engines, layer-specific libraries, and domain-specific languages. Most of these implementations use statically-tuned libraries such as cuDNN [3] for GPUs and Eigen [1] or Intel MKL-DNN [2] for CPUs to achieve performance. These libraries lack optimization across operators, and the execution of each operation varies dramatically for different data sizes, data layouts, configurations for operators, memory hierarchies and specific hardware features. When a new operator is developed for use in DNNs that does not fit into these preoptimized library functions, the computation efficiency decreases dramatically [22]. Because of these challenges, compiler-based approaches have recently garnered more interest for achieving performance in neural networks. Compiler-based methods can separate algorithms from schedules, which allows users to experiment with different options for parallelism and data locality on a wide range of platforms. This approach was demonstrated by Halide [13].

LATTE is a domain-specific language for DNNs with a graph-like implementation that uses a compiler-based approach for optimization. *SWIRL* is a domain-specific compiler for neural networks that can be used with *LATTE*. *SWIRL* takes *LATTE* as input and uses high-level transformation recipes to generate efficient C++ code. These transformation commands span both data and computation planes. *SWIRL* has demonstrated comparable performance with TensorFlow integrated with MKL-DNN on both training and inference for a variety of neural networks, including AlexNet, Overfeat and VGG [21].

Batch Normalization is a novel operator used in many DNNs that standardizes the inputs to other layers. Currently *LATTE* does not have a Batch Normalization operator. Extending *LATTE* to include this operator and *SWIRL* to generate optimizations for the BN operator will broaden the efficacy and applicability of the *LATTE* language and the *SWIRL* compiler for DNNs.

The key contributions of this paper are:

- An extension of *LATTE* and *SWIRL* to include the BN operator and compiler optimizations that can be applied to this operator.
- An application of scalar replacement for reduced memory access and loop interchange and fusion for increased parallelism in the BN *LATTE* code implementation.
- A transformation recipe for *SWIRL* to create a SIMD vectorization and parallelization strategy for optimizing BN in *LATTE*.
- A performance evaluation of the BN operator and of the combined Convolution-BN-ReLU layer on the Intel SkyLake platform, comparing *LATTE* and *SWIRL* to TensorFlow, PyTorch and MXNet all integrated with the MKL-DNN library, TensowFlow XLA and native TensorFlow.

2 Background

This section provides a brief description of Batch Normalization and its benefits for training DNNs. The compilation workflow of *LATTE* and *SWIRL* is described along with details of how the Batch Normalization layer is expressed in *LATTE*.

2.1 Batch Normalization

Batch Normalization is a technique introduced in [10] that decreases the training time and increases the robustness of neural networks. Deep neural networks are challenging to train, in part because the input from prior layers can change after weight updates during each training pass. The inputs to each layer are affected by the parameters of all preceding layers, which creates an amplifying effect as the network depth increases. This variance in the input distribution, referred to as internal covariate shift, slows down the training by requiring lower learning rates and careful parameter initialization. Because Batch Normalization reduces the variance in the inputs and activations in a network, it can allow for higher learning rates during training. The BN transform has been shown to decrease training time and to match performance for inference on many popular DNN models [15], and its use has become rather ubiquitous in many neural networks.

Batch Normalization is achieved through a normalization step that fixes the means and variances of the inputs. Each dimension of the input data is normalized to a mean of zero and a standard deviation of one. The BN transform is performed on mini-batches ($\mathcal{B}$) since these are used during stochastic gradient training. Therefore, the mean (μ) and variance (σ^2) of each input dimension are calculated over a mini batch. Because normalizing each input of a layer may change what the layer can represent, the BN transform includes a pair of parameters, γ and β, which scale and shift the normalized values. These parameters are learned during training. The Batch Normalization transform algorithm is shown in Fig. 1.

An important piece of the Batch Normalization technique is allowing the gradient of the loss with respect to the model parameters to account for the normalization. The BN transform is differentiable, and the gradient of the loss with respect to the different parameters can be computed directly with the chain rule. See [10] or [12] for the back propagation equation of the BN operator.

2.2 LATTE and SWIRL

LATTE is a DNN domain-specific language that provides abstraction for the user to create a neural network, and *SWIRL* uses high-level transformation recipes to generate efficient CPU code. The transformation recipe abstraction allows an expert programmer to explicitly enumerate the transformations that can be applied to each individual layer within *LATTE*. The main *SWIRL* transformations used for the BN operator include tiling, loop unrolling, vectorization and parallelization. Tiling can improve cache locality. Unrolling certain loop iterations by a factor reduces branch penalties and improves register reuse. Vectorization creates intrinsics to be used on SIMD architectures, and parallelization uses OpenMP to parallelize one or more loops for increased performance. These optimizations can be tailored for performance on a variety of CPU backends [21].

122   J. Lake et al.

Input: Values of x over a mini-batch: $\mathcal{B} = \{x_1...x_m\}$;
Parameters to be learned: γ, β
Output: $\{y_i = BN_{\gamma,\beta}(x_i)\}$

$$\mu_{\mathcal{B}} \leftarrow \frac{1}{m}\sum_{i=1}^{m} x_i \qquad\qquad mini\text{-}batch\ mean \qquad (1)$$

$$\sigma_{\mathcal{B}}^2 \leftarrow \frac{1}{m}\sum_{i=1}^{m}(x_i - \mu_{\mathcal{B}})^2 \qquad\qquad mini\text{-}batch\ variance \qquad (2)$$

$$\widehat{x_i} \leftarrow \frac{x_i - \mu_{\mathcal{B}}}{\sqrt{\sigma_{\mathcal{B}}^2 + \epsilon}} \qquad\qquad normalize \qquad (3)$$

$$y_i \leftarrow \gamma\widehat{x_i} + \beta \equiv BN_{\gamma,\beta}(x_i) \qquad scale\ and\ shift \qquad (4)$$

Fig. 1. Algorithm for Batch Normalization Transform. Ioffe, S., Szegedy, C.: Batch Normalization: Accelerating deep network training by reducing internal covariate shift. CoRR abs/1502.03167 (2015).

A DNN is created in *LATTE* by stacking layers on top of each other, starting with an input layer, adding various hidden layers and ending with a fully-connected layer that applies an activation function. These layers are represented as ensembles of neurons that are connected using mapping functions [20]. *LATTE* uses an implicit data-flow graph model of the DNN. The nodes represent computations in layers, and the edges are data dependencies between layer inputs and outputs. This data-flow graph is represented by a dictionary of mapping functions, which connects the inputs and outputs of layers. This allows *LATTE* to store complex graphs without incurring extra memory costs. For training and inference, *SWIRL* generates kernels for computations as a set of nested for-loops for each forward, backward and weight update pass of each layer.

Figure 2 shows a Python code sequence for expressing Batch Normalization in *LATTE*. The `BatchNormLayer` function takes three arguments: the network object (`net`), the input ensemble (`input_ensemble`) and `epsilon`. The neurons are created in Line 8 and added to the BN ensemble in Line 10. A mapping function is defined on Lines 13–14, which connects the `input_ensemble` to the `bn_ensemble`.

Once the user has defined a neural network in *LATTE*, the description is then lowered to a standard Python AST. Next, the *SWIRL* compiler uses transformation recipes on the Python AST. Lastly, the transformed Python AST is translated to C++ code using the *ctree* package, which is then lowered to optimized x86 machine code using the Intel C++ Compiler. High-quality vector code is also generated via intrinsics rather than relying on compiler directives. See Fig. 3 for a visual representation of this workflow.

```
1   def BatchNormLayer(net, input_ensemble, epsilon=0.001):
2       input_channels, input_height, input_width = input_ensemble.shape
3       shape = (input_channels, input_height, input_width)
4       neurons = np.empty(shape, dtype='object')
5       batch_num = net.batch_size
6
7       #Create an ensemble and initialize it
8       neurons[:,:,:] = BNNeuron(input_ensemble, batch_num, epsilon)
9       bn_ensemble = BNEnsemble(neurons)
10      net.add_ensemble(bn_ensemble)
11
12      #Mapping function for add_connections
13      def mapping(c,x,y):
14          return (range(c), range(x), range(y))
15       net.add_connections(input_ensemble, bn_ensemble, mapping)
```

Fig. 2. Python code for batch normalization layer in *LATTE*

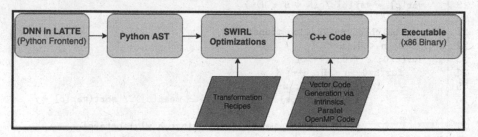

Fig. 3. *LATTE/SWIRL* workflow

3   Methods

The code for the Batch Normalization transform, backpropagation and parameter updates can be optimized in a number of ways. Some general optimization techniques, such as scalar replacement combined with loop interchange and loop fusion, were performed on the loop nests directly within *LATTE*. *SWIRL* transformation recipes were used for the rest of the optimizations.

3.1   Batch Normalization Pseudo Code

The Batch Normalization transform, represented by the equations in Fig. 1, is expressed by the loop nests in Fig. 4. Since the transform is applied to mini-batches, the batch dimension N is used. The mean and variance are calculated per feature map or channel dimension C, as shown in Lines 6 and 16 of Fig. 4. The heights and widths of the inputs are H and W respectively. The normalized inputs are referenced as x_hat on Line 26 and are scaled by gamma and shifted by beta on Line 27. The inputs and outputs are x and y respectively.

```
1    //Calculate the mean per channel dimension
2    for (n=0; n < N; n++) { // mini-batch size
3        for(c=0; c < C; c++) { //channel dimension
4            for(h=0; h < H; h++) { //height
5                for(w=0; w < W; w++) { //width
6                    mean[c] += x[n,c,h,w]
7    } } } }
8    for(c=0; c < C; c++) {
9        mean[c] = mean[c] / (N * H * W) }
10
11   //Calculate the variance per channel dimension
12   for (n=0; n < N; n++) {
13       for(c=0; c < C; c++) {
14           for(h=0; h < H; h++) {
15               for(w=0; w < W; w++) {
16                   var[c] += (x[n,c,h,w]-mean[c])*(x[n,c,h,w]-mean[c])
17   } } } }
18   for(c=0; c < C; c++) {
19       var[c] = var[c] / (N * H * W) }
20
21   //Apply batch normalization transform
22   for (n=0; n < N; n++) {
23       for(c=0; c < C; c++) {
24           for(h=0; h < H; h++) {
25               for(w=0; w < W; w++) {
26                   x_hat[n,c,h,w] = (x[n,c,h,w] - mean[c]) / sqrt(var[c] +
                         epsilon)
27                   y[n,c,h,w] = gamma[c] * x_hat[n,c,h,w] + beta[c]
28   } } } }
```

Fig. 4. Batch normalization forward pass

3.2   Scalar Replacement, Loop Interchange and Loop Fusion

The goal of scalar replacement is to identify repeated accesses made to the same memory address, either within an iteration or across iterations, and to remove the redundant accesses by keeping the data in registers. Compilers are effective in allocating scalar variables to registers but often fail to do so with array references. Data dependences provide opportunities for reuse of array variables in registers through scalar replacement [5, Chapter 8].

The loop nests that represent the forward, backward and parameter update passes of the BN operator during training exhibit data dependences that can be exploited through scalar replacement. For example, in Fig. 4 the array reference on Line 6 for mean has both an output and a true dependence carried by all but the C loop. Line 16 has similar dependences for the array reference to var and also an input dependence for the array reference to mean carried by all of the loops except C. In the last loop nest structure, there are input dependences for mean and var on line 26 and gamma and beta on line 27 carried by all of the loops except C. Lastly, there is a loop-independent true dependence for x_hat on line 27.

Figure 5 reflects the changes made for scalar replacement in the Batch Normalization forward pass. To fully exploit the benefits of the scalar replacement, loop interchange of the C and N loops is performed. Because the C loop does not carry any dependences, moving the N loop inside of the C loop allows for more reuse of the values by keeping them in registers during the iterations of the N, H and W loops. Since the C loop is now the outermost loop and does not carry any dependences, all of the C loops can be fused. This fusion can increase the level of parallelism and data locality that can be exploited in the compiler transformations applied to this code by *SWIRL*. It also decreases the loop control overhead. Lastly, a final optimization technique is used for the expensive square root and division operations shown on Line 26 of Fig. 4. This operation is an input dependence carried in the C loop, which means that this time-consuming calculation needs only to be performed once per C loop iteration rather than for each iteration of every loop. A multiplication operator replaces the more expensive division operator. On Line 21 of Fig. 4 these calculations are stored in a register and reused on Line 26.

The backward pass exhibits even more opportunities for register reuse. As was done in the forward pass, the two outer loops are interchanged, after which loop fusion is performed on the outermost C loop. Expensive operations involving division operators are performed once per outer loop and replaced with scalars. The parameter update loop nest is optimized in a similar manner. For more details on these optimizations, the reader is directed to [12].

3.3 Transformation Recipes

SWIRL uses the concept of transformation recipes to generate high-quality code and to customize optimizations to the target hardware. A recipe consists of a set of commands that include both data and code transformations. A more detailed explanation of these commands can be found at [21]. The transformation recipe used for the BatchNormLayer forward pass implementation is shown in Fig. 6. The feature map dimensions of the input and output are tiled by the SIMD vector length for the given platform to aid vectorization (Lines 4–5). The loops corresponding to the batch dimension are specified for concurrent execution via the parallelize command in Lines 6 and 8. During code generation these loops are annotated with OpenMP pragmas. The inner-most loop of the 4-D loop nest is vectorized and unrolled by a factor that allows for the data locality to be fully exploited by the SIMD instructions and to reduce loop overhead (Lines 10–11).

A sample transformation recipe for the backward and weight update passes used in the BatchNormLayer is illustrated in [12]. The transformations are similar to those used in the forward pass. Applying the transformation recipe in Fig. 6 to the Batch Normalization layer in *LATTE* generates optimized code for the Intel SkyLake platform. The final C++ code generated by the *SWIRL* compiler for the forward pass is shown in Fig. 7.

```
1    for(c=0; c < C; c++) {
2        mean_temp = 0.0
3        var_temp = 0.0
4        gamma_temp = gamma[c]
5        beta_temp = beta[c]
6        for (n=0; n < N; n++) {
7            for(h=0; h < H; h++) {
8                for(w=0; w < W; w++) {
9                    mean_temp += x[n,c,h,w]
10       } } }
11       mean_temp = mean_temp / (N * C * W)
12       mean[c] = mean_temp
13
14       for (n=0; n < N; n++) {
15           for(h=0; h < H; h++) {
16               for(w=0; w < W; w++) {
17                   var_temp += x[n,c,h,w] - mean_temp
18       } } }
19       var_temp = var_temp / (N * C * W)
20       var[c] = var_temp
21       divisor = 1 / sqrt(var_temp + epsilon)
22
23       for (n=0; n < N; n++) {
24           for(h=0; h < H; h++) {
25               for(w=0; w < W; w++) {
26                   x_hat_temp = (x[n,c,h,w] - mean_temp) * divisor
27                   y[n,c,h,w] = gamma_temp * x_hat_temp + beta_temp
28                   x_hat[n,c,h,w] = x_hat_temp
29   } } } }
```

Fig. 5. Batch normalization forward pass with scalar replacement, loop interchange and loop fusion optimizations

4   Results

The performance results of using *LATTE* and *SWIRL* for the Batch Normalization operator compared to other state-of-the-art frameworks were generated on an Intel Skylake platform with AVX-512 support. The frameworks used for comparison include TensorFlow release version 1.11.0, TensorFlow release version 2.0.0 configured with Intel Math Kernel Library for Deep Neural Networks (MKL-DNN), TensorFlow release version 2.0.0 using XLA, MXNet version 1.5.1 with MKL-DNN, and Pytorch version 1.4.0+cpu with MKL-DNN.

```
1   if "value" in input_ensemble.tiling_info:
2       tiled_dims = input_ensemble.tiling_info["value"]
3       for dim, factor in tiled_dims:
4           bn_ens.tile('inputs', dim=dim, factor=factor)
5           bn_ens.tile('value', dim=dim, factor=factor)
6           bn_ens.parallelize(phase="forward",loop_var="_neuron_index_1_outer
                ")
7   else:
8       bn_ens.parallelize(phase="forward",loop_var="_neuron_index_1")
9
10  bn_ens.vectorize(phase="forward", loop_var="_neuron_index_3", factor=
        latte.config.SIMDWIDTH)
11  bn_ens.unroll(phase="forward",loop_var="_neuron_index_3", factor=4,
        unroll_type=0)
```

Fig. 6. An example transformation recipe for the forward pass of the batch normalization layer created in Fig. 2.

4.1 Hardware Platform and Environment

The hardware platform used is a high-performance server class dual socket Intel Xeon Gold 6130 SkyLake processor with 2×16 2.1 Ghz (max 3.7 Ghz) turbo-enabled cores. This is an AVX-512 platform with 512-bit vector support. The processor has 98 GB of DDR4-2666 memory, with 32KB of L1 cache, 1MB of L2 cache and 22 MB of L3 Cache. The code is generated via the Intel C++ Compiler (ICC) v18.0.1.163 with "-O3 -qopenmp -xCORE-AVX512" flags and NUM_OMP_THREADS=32.

4.2 Performance Comparison of Batch Normalization

The performance of the *LATTE/SWIRL* implementation of the BN operator used for training is compared with the five frameworks described above. The training step involves a forward, backward and weight update pass. The testing was carried out on ten different input sizes. The dimensions of these input layers are representative of the sizes found in GoogleNet [18], VGGNet [17] and ResNet [9] architectures. The results of six of these tests are displayed in Fig. 8. The graphs show the number of images per second each implementation can process with a batch size of 64 and the image size listed as C, H/W where C represents the number of channels and H/W represent the height and width dimensions respectively. *LATTE/SWIRL* outperforms all of the other frameworks. On average, *LATTE/SWIRL* has 2x greater throughput than MXNet with MKL-DNN, 4x more throughput than PyTorch with MKL-DNN, 5x greater throughput than TensorFlow using XLA, 6x more throughput than TensorFlow with MKL-DNN and 100x greater throughput than TensowFlow.

All of the implementations used SIMD vectorization and parallelization for compute performance. All of them except TensorFlow used cache blocking to decrease memory latency. The dimensions of the cache blocking were varied.

```cpp
1   #pragma omp parallel for
2   for (int _neuron_index_1 = 0; _neuron_index_1 < 2; _neuron_index_1 += 1) {
3       __m512 mean_temp_0 = _mm512_set1_ps(0.0);
4       __m512 mean_temp_1 = _mm512_set1_ps(0.0);
5       __m512 mean_temp_2 = _mm512_set1_ps(0.0);
6       __m512 mean_temp_3 = _mm512_set1_ps(0.0);
7       double mean_t1 = 0.0;
8       for (int _neuron_index_0 = 0; _neuron_index_0 < 2; _neuron_index_0 += 1) {
9           for (int _neuron_index_2 = 0; _neuron_index_2 < 64; _neuron_index_2 += 1) {
10              for (int _neuron_index_3 = 0; _neuron_index_3 < 64; _neuron_index_3 += 64) {
11                  mean_temp_0 = _mm512_add_ps(mean_temp_0, _mm512_load_ps(& inputs[_neuron_index_0][
                        _neuron_index_1][_neuron_index_2][(_neuron_index_3 + 0)]));
12                  mean_temp_1 = _mm512_add_ps(mean_temp_1, _mm512_load_ps(& inputs[_neuron_index_0][
                        _neuron_index_1][_neuron_index_2][(_neuron_index_3 + 16)]));
13                  mean_temp_2 = _mm512_add_ps(mean_temp_2, _mm512_load_ps(& inputs[_neuron_index_0][
                        _neuron_index_1][_neuron_index_2][(_neuron_index_3 + 32)]));
14                  mean_temp_3 = _mm512_add_ps(mean_temp_3, _mm512_load_ps(& ensemb le2inputs[
                        _neuron_index_0][_neuron_index_1][_neuron_index_2][(_neuron_index_3 + 48)] ));
15  } } }
16      mean_t1 += _mm512_reduce_add_ps(_mm512_div_ps(mean_temp_0, _mm512_set1_ps(8192)));
17      mean_t1 += _mm512_reduce_add_ps(_mm512_div_ps(mean_temp_1, _mm512_set1_ps(8192)));
18      mean_t1 += _mm512_reduce_add_ps(_mm512_div_ps(mean_temp_2, _mm512_set1_ps(8192)));
19      mean_t1 += _mm512_reduce_add_ps(_mm512_div_ps(mean_temp_3, _mm512_set1_ps(8192)));
20      mean[_neuron_index_1] = mean_t1;
21      __m512 mean_t2 = _mm512_set1_ps(mean[_neuron_index_1]);
22      __m512 var_temp_0 = _mm512_set1_ps(0.0);
23      __m512 var_temp_1 = _mm512_set1_ps(0.0);
24      __m512 var_temp_2 = _mm512_set1_ps(0.0);
25      __m512 var_temp_3 = _mm512_set1_ps(0.0);
26      double var_t = 0.0;
27      for (int _neuron_index_0 = 0; _neuron_index_0 < 2; _neuron_index_0 += 1) {
28          for (int _neuron_index_2 = 0; _neuron_index_2 < 64; _neuron_index_2 += 1) {
29              for (int _neuron_index_3 = 0; _neuron_index_3 < 64; _neuron_index_3 += 64) {
30                  __m512 diff_0 = _mm512_sub_ps(_mm512_load_ps(& inputs[_neuron_index_0][_neuron_index_1][
                        _neuron_index_2][(_neuron_index_3 + 0)]), mean_t2);
31                  __m512 diff_1 = _mm512_sub_ps(_mm512_load_ps(& 2inputs[_neuron_index_0][_neuron_index_1][
                        _neuron_index_2][(_neuron_index_3 + 16)]), mean_t2);
32                  __m512 diff_2 = _mm512_sub_ps(_mm512_load_ps(& 2inputs[_neuron_index_0][_neuron_index_1][
                        _neuron_index_2][(_neuron_index_3 + 32)]), mean_t2);
33                  __m512 diff_3 = _mm512_sub_ps(_mm512_load_ps(& inputs[_neuron_index_0][_neuron_index_1][
                        _neuron_index_2][(_neuron_index_3 + 48)]), mean_t2);
34                  var_temp_0 = _mm512_fmadd_ps(diff_0, diff_0, var_temp_0);
35                  var_temp_1 = _mm512_fmadd_ps(diff_1, diff_1, var_temp_1);
36                  var_temp_2 = _mm512_fmadd_ps(diff_2, diff_2, var_temp_2);
37                  var_temp_3 = _mm512_fmadd_ps(diff_3, diff_3, var_temp_3);
38  } } }
39
40      var_t += _mm512_reduce_add_ps(_mm512_div_ps(var_temp_0, _mm512_set1_ps(8192)));
41      var_t += _mm512_reduce_add_ps(_mm512_div_ps(var_temp_1, _mm512_set1_ps(8192)));
42      var_t += _mm512_reduce_add_ps(_mm512_div_ps(var_temp_2, _mm512_set1_ps(8192)));
43      var_t += _mm512_reduce_add_ps(_mm512_div_ps(var_temp_3, _mm512_set1_ps(8192)));
44      var[_neuron_index_1] = var_t;
45      __m512 gamma_temp = _mm512_set1_ps(gamma[_neuron_index_1]);
46      __m512 beta_temp = _mm512_set1_ps(beta[_neuron_index_1]);
47      __m512 divisor = _mm512_set1_ps(1.0 / sqrt(var_t + 0.001));
48      for (int _neuron_index_0 = 0; _neuron_index_0 < 2; _neuron_index_0 += 1) {
49          for (int _neuron_index_2 = 0; _neuron_index_2 < 64; _neuron_index_2 += 1) {
50              for (int _neuron_index_3 = 0; _neuron_index_3 < 64; _neuron_index_3 += 64) {
51                  __m512 x_hat_0 = _mm512_mul_ps(_mm512_sub_ps(_mm512_load_ps(& inputs[_neuron_index_0][
                        _neuron_index_1][_neuron_index_2][(_neuron_index_3 + 0)]), mean_t2), divisor);
52                  __m512 x_hat_1 = _mm512_mul_ps(_mm512_sub_ps(_mm512_load_ps(& inputs[_neuron_index_0][
                        _neuron_index_1][_neuron_index_2][(_neuron_index_3 + 16)]), mean_t2), divisor);
53                  __m512 x_hat_2 = _mm512_mul_ps(_mm512_sub_ps(_mm512_load_ps(& inputs[_neuron_index_0][
                        _neuron_index_1][_neuron_index_2][(_neuron_index_3 + 32)]), mean_t2), divisor);
54                  __m512 x_hat_3 = _mm512_mul_ps(_mm512_sub_ps(_mm512_load_ps(& inputs[_neuron_index_0][
                        _neuron_index_1][_neuron_index_2][(_neuron_index_3 + 48)]), mean_t2), divisor);
55                  _mm512_store_ps(& x_hat[_neuron_index_0][_neuron_index_1][_neuron_index_2][(_neuron_index_3 + 0)
                        ], x_hat_0);
56                  _mm512_store_ps(& x_hat[_neuron_index_0][_neuron_index_1][_neuron_index_2][(_neuron_index_3 +
                        16)], x_hat_1);
57                  _mm512_store_ps(& x_hat[_neuron_index_0][_neuron_index_1][_neuron_index_2][(_neuron_index_3 +
                        32)], x_hat_2);
58                  _mm512_store_ps(& x_hat[_neuron_index_0][_neuron_index_1][_neuron_index_2][(_neuron_index_3 +
                        48)], x_hat_3);
59                  _mm512_store_ps(& value[_neuron_index_0][_neuron_index_1][_neuron_index_2][(_neuron_index_3 + 0)
                        ], _mm512_fmadd_ps(gamma_temp, x_hat_0, beta_temp));
60                  _mm512_store_ps(& value[_neuron_index_0][_neuron_index_1][_neuron_index_2][(_neuron_index_3 +
                        16)], _mm512_fmadd_ps(gamma_temp, x_hat_1, beta_temp));
61                  _mm512_store_ps(& value[_neuron_index_0][_neuron_index_1][_neuron_index_2][(_neuron_index_3 +
                        32)], _mm512_fmadd_ps(gamma_temp, x_hat_2, beta_temp));
62                  _mm512_store_ps(& value[_neuron_index_0][_neuron_index_1][_neuron_index_2][(_neuron_index_3 +
                        48)], _mm512_fmadd_ps(gamma_temp, x_hat_3, beta_temp));
63  } } } };
```

Fig. 7. Generated C++ code from the *SWIRL* transformation recipe shown in Fig. 6

For example the frameworks using MKL-DNN blocked the inner dimension by a factor of 16 while *SWIRL* used a factor of 64. Because the batch normalization operation is limited by memory bandwidth, scalar replacement, loop interchange and fusion allowed the vectorization and parallelization to exploit even more performance gains in the *LATTE/SWIRL* implementation.

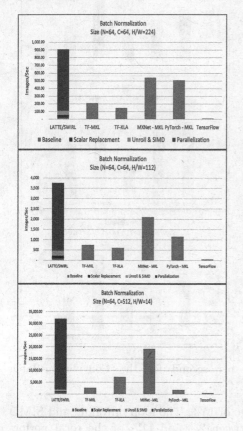
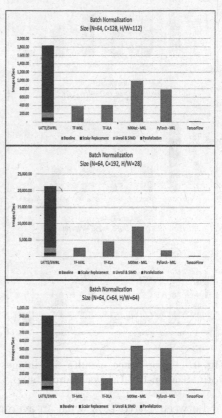

Fig. 8. Performance results and breakdown for the batch normalization training step. Demonstrates the effects of different optimizations towards overall performance for the *LATTE/SWIRL* implementation.

The code optimizations and the transformation recipes discussed earlier incorporate several compiler optimizations, including scalar replacement, loop unrolling, SIMD vectorization and parallelization. The individual effects of each optimization on the *LATTE/SWIRL* implementation are included in the performance results of the Batch Normalization operator in Fig. 8. The breakdown is shown only for *LATTE/SWIRL* results, with the blue area representing the baseline performance, the orange area displaying the performance with scalar replacement included, the grey area showing the performance with the loop unrolling and SIMD vectorization in addition to scalar replacement, and the gold area exhibiting the performance with all of the optimizations, including parallelization. Of the total performance improvement, scalar replacement accounts

130   J. Lake et al.

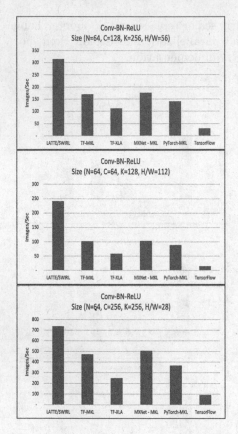 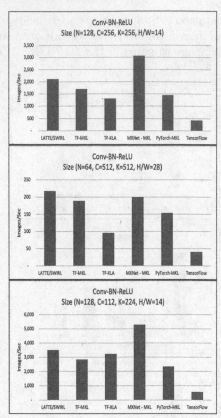

Fig. 9. Performance results in images per second for the Convolution-Batch Normalization-ReLU layer training step.

for between 4% to 18%, with an average of 15%. The loop unrolling and SIMD vectorization performance boost is between 2% and 11% of the total performance gains, with an average of 9%. Parallelization provides the greatest benefit. Between 69% to 93% of the total performance gain, with an average of 77%, is attributable to parallelization.

4.3 Performance Comparison for Conv-BN-ReLU Layer

A comparison is presented for a training layer composed of Convolution, Batch Normalization and ReLU activation operators. This layer configuration is commonly found in many deep learning architectures and is suggested in [10]. The layer dimensions are representative of layers found in the GoogleNet [18], VGGNet [17] and ResNet [9] architectures. Some of the results can be seen in Figs. 9 and 10. Figure 9 shows the images per second that each implementation can process with batch sizes of either 64 or 128 with varying image sizes. C represents the number of in-channels for the convolution layer, K represents the out-channels for the Convolution operator and hence the number of channels for

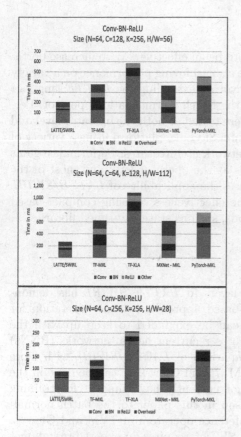
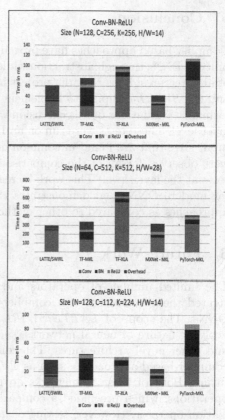

Fig. 10. Performance results in time (ms) for the Convolution-Batch Normalization-ReLU layer training step. Displays the time spent on each operator.

the BN and ReLU operators, and H/W are the height and width respectively of the image for all of the operators. Figure 10 displays a time comparison for computing the Conv-BN-ReLU layer. This comparison is presented so a breakout of the performance of each operator can be observed. Note that the results from the native TensorFlow implementation are not included so the graph would not be distorted and the information from the other frameworks could be seen more easily. A larger sample of results can be found in [12].

LATTE/SWIRL outperforms the other implementations on most of the tests. For those dimensions where H/W is small (i.e. ≤ 14), the Convolution operator in *LATTE/SWIRL* is not as efficient as the Convolution operator in TensorFlow with MKL-DNN and MXNet with MKL-DNN. The largest performance gains by *LATTE/SWIRL* are observed for the test dimensions where H/W is large (i.e. 112). This demonstrates that the loop unrolling and SIMD vectorization in *LATTE/SWIRL* on the inner dimensions can be more fully exploited when the inner dimensions are large. For all of the test sizes, *LATTE/SWIRL* was more efficient than the other frameworks for the memory-bound operations of BN and ReLU.

5   Conclusion

Compiler-based approaches have proven to be an effective way to increase portability of DNNs through abstraction while also achieving performance on a variety of architectures. This research project involved extending the *LATTE* language and the *SWIRL* compiler to implement the Batch Normalization operator. Performance evaluations of this extension were tested at both the operator level and layer level. These tests were run on an Intel SkyLake platform using a variety of input sizes that are found in common network architectures. Performance gains were observed for all of the comparisons at the operator level and most of the tests at the layer level. This work increases the applicability of *LATTE/SWIRL* for modern DNNs and demonstrates the effectiveness of using compiler-based approaches as compared to other methods, such as statically-tuned libraries.

6   Future Work

The limited number of operators and layers in *LATTE/SWIRL* has demonstrated the effectiveness of a compiler-based approach to code generation for DNNs. The scope of *LATTE/SWIRL* can be expanded to keep up with the evolving nature of neural networks, such as recurrent neural networks (RNNs) and other novel architectures. The comparison of *LATTE/SWIRL* with more compiler-based approaches, such as TVM [7] and Glow [14], can be done in the future. Both of these frameworks do not currently have support for training operations, which precluded a comparison in this paper to the batch normalization operator. However, testing of inference operators in TVM and Glow to *LATTE/SWIRL* would be appropriate. *SWIRL* requires an expert programmer to create the optimized transformation recipes. Therefore, the use of autotuning and machine learning tools to prune the optimization search space and to reduce the time involved in creating transformation recipes can provide future research opportunities as well.

References

1. Eigen (2019). http://eigen.tuxfamily.org/
2. Intel math Kernal library for deep learning networks (2019). https://software.intel.com/en-us/articles/intel-mkl-dnn-part-1-library-overview-and-installation
3. NVIDIA cuDNN (2019). https://developer.nvidia.com/cudnn
4. Abadi, M., et al.: Tensorflow: large-scale machine learning on heterogeneous distributed systems. arXiv e-prints 1603.04467 (March 2016)
5. Allen, R., Kennedy, K.: Optimizing Compilers for Modern Architectures. Academic Press, London (2002)
6. Chen, T., et al.: MXNet: a flexible and efficient machine learning library for heterogeneous distributed systems. arXiv e-prints arXiv:1512.01274 (2015)
7. Chen, T., et al.: TVM: an automated end-to-end optimizing compiler for deep learning. arXiv e-prints arXiv:1802.04799 (2018)

8. Collobert, R., Kavukcuoglu, K., Farabet, C.: Torch7: a Matlab-like environment for machine learning. In: BigLearn, NIPS Workshop (2011)
9. He, K., Zhang, X., Ren, S., Sun, J.: Deep residual learning for image recognition. In: 2016 IEEE Conference on Computer Vision and Pattern Recognition (CVPR), pp. 770–778 (2016)
10. Ioffe, S., Szegedy, C.: Batch normalization: accelerating deep network training by reducing internal covariate shift. CoRR abs/1502.03167 (2015)
11. Jia, Y., et al.: Caffe: convolutional architecture for fast feature embedding. In: Proceedings of the 22nd ACM International Conference on Multimedia, MM '14, pp. 675–678. Association for Computing Machinery, New York (2014). https://doi.org/10.1145/2647868.2654889
12. Lake, J.: Optimized code generation for deep learning networks using LATTE and SWIRL (2020). Unpublished bachelor's thesis
13. Ragan-Kelley, J., Barnes, C., Adams, A., Paris, S., Durand, F., Amarasinghe, S.: Halide: a language and compiler for optimizing parallelism, locality, and recomputation in image processing pipelines. In: Proceedings of the 34th ACM SIGPLAN Conference on Programming Language Design and Implementation, PLDI '13, pp. 519–530. Association for Computing Machinery, New York (2013). https://doi.org/10.1145/2491956.2462176
14. Rotem, N., et al.: Glow: graph lowering compiler techniques for neural networks. arXiv e-prints arXiv:1805.00907 (2018)
15. Schilling, F.: The effect of Batch Normalization on deep convolutional neural networks (Dissertation) (2016). http://urn.kb.se/resolve?urn=urn:nbn:se:kth:diva-191222
16. Seide, F., Agarwal, A.: CNTK: Microsoft's open-source deep-learning toolkit. In: Proceedings of the 22nd ACM SIGKDD International Conference on Knowledge Discovery and Data Mining, KDD '16, p. 2135. Association for Computing Machinery, New York (2016). https://doi.org/10.1145/2939672.2945397
17. Simonyan, K., Zisserman, A.: Very deep convolutional networks for large-scale image recognition. CoRR abs/1409.1556 (2015)
18. Szegedy, C., et al.: Going deeper with convolutions. In: 2015 IEEE Conference on Computer Vision and Pattern Recognition (CVPR), pp. 1–9 (2015)
19. Theano Development Team: Theano: A Python framework for fast computation of mathematical expressions. arXiv e-prints abs/1605.02688 (2016)
20. Truong, L., et al.: Latte: a language, compiler, and runtime for elegant and efficient deep neural networks. SIGPLAN Not. 51(6), 209–223 (2016)
21. Venkat, A., Rusira, T., Barik, R., Hall, M.W., Truong, L.: SWIRL: high-performance many-core CPU code generation for deep neural networks. Int. J. High Perform. Comput. Appl. 33, 1275–1289 (2019)
22. Xing, Y., Weng, J., Wang, Y., Sui, L., Shan, Y., Wang, Y.: An in-depth comparison of compilers for deep neural networks on hardware. In: 2019 IEEE International Conference on Embedded Software and Systems (ICESS), pp. 1–8 (2019). https://doi.org/10.1109/ICESS.2019.8782480

Thermal-Aware Compilation of Spiking Neural Networks to Neuromorphic Hardware

Twisha Titirsha[ID] and Anup Das[✉][ID]

Drexel University, Philadelphia, PA 19104, USA
{tt624,anup.das}@drexel.edu

Abstract. Hardware implementation of neuromorphic computing can significantly improve performance and energy efficiency of machine learning tasks implemented with spiking neural networks (SNNs), making these hardware platforms particularly suitable for embedded systems and other energy-constrained environments. We observe that the long bitlines and wordlines in a crossbar of the hardware create significant current variations when propagating spikes through its synaptic elements, which are typically designed with non-volatile memory (NVM). Such current variations create a thermal gradient within each crossbar of the hardware, depending on the machine learning workload and the mapping of neurons and synapses of the workload to these crossbars. This thermal gradient becomes significant at scaled technology nodes and it increases the leakage power in the hardware leading to an increase in the energy consumption. We propose a novel technique to map neurons and synapses of SNN-based machine learning workloads to neuromorphic hardware. We make two novel contributions. First, we formulate a detailed thermal model for a crossbar in a neuromorphic hardware incorporating workload dependency, where the temperature of each NVM-based synaptic cell is computed considering the thermal contributions from its neighboring cells. Second, we incorporate this thermal model in the mapping of neurons and synapses of SNN-based workloads using a hill-climbing heuristic. The objective is to reduce the thermal gradient in crossbars. We evaluate our neuron and synapse mapping technique using 10 machine learning workloads for a state-of-the-art neuromorphic hardware. We demonstrate an average 11.4K reduction in the average temperature of each crossbar in the hardware, leading to a 52% reduction in the leakage power consumption (11% lower total energy consumption) compared to a performance-oriented SNN mapping technique.

Keywords: Neuromorphic computing · Spiking Neural Network · Non-Volatile Memory (NVM) · Phase-Change Memory (PCM) · Temperature · Leakage power consumption · Crossbar

1 Introduction

Spiking Neural Networks (SNNs) are machine learning models designed with spike-based computations and bio-inspired learning algorithms [36]. Neurons

B. Chapman and J. Moreira (Eds.): LCPC 2020, LNCS 13149, pp. 134–150, 2022.
https://doi.org/10.1007/978-3-030-95953-1_10

communicate information using spikes via synapses. SNNs are used to implement both supervised and unsupervised machine learning approaches. Our focus is on supervised approaches, where a machine learning model is first trained using training data, and then deployed for inference with in-field data.

Neuromorphic hardware such as TrueNorth [23], Loihi [22], and DYNAP-SE [38] can significantly improve the energy efficiency of SNNs, thanks to their event-driven computations, efficient implementations of biological neurons using CMOS and FinFET technologies, and the use of Non-Volatile Memory (NVM) such as Phase-Change Memory (PCM) [9,45,47–49], Oxide-base Resistive RAM (OxRRAM) [37], and Spin-Transfer Torque Magnetic or Spin-Orbit-Torque RAM (STT- and SoT-MRAM) [40] for high density synaptic storage. Therefore, neuromorphic hardware can be used to implement machine learning tasks on power-constrained environments such as embedded systems, and sensor and edge devices of the Internet-of-Things (IoT) [26].

A neuromorphic hardware is implemented as a tile-based architecture [10] with a shared interconnect in the form of Networks-on-Chip (NoC) or Segmented Bus [8] (see Fig. 1a). A tile in a neuromorphic hardware is designed as a crossbar, which is an organization of top electrodes (wordlines) and bottom electrodes (bitlines), with NVM-based synaptic elements at their intersections (Fig. 1b). A synaptic element is connected to a bitline and a wordline using an access transistor (Fig. 1c). Within a crossbar, the pre-synaptic neurons are mapped on the wordlines, while the post-synpatic neurons are mapped along the bitlines. An $n \times n$ crossbar has n pre-synaptic neurons, n post-synaptic neurons, and n^2 NVM cells. A pre-synaptic neuron's spike voltage from a wordline is multiplied with the conductance of the NVM to generate a current. Currents from multiple wordlines are integrated on a bitline, implementing forward propagation of neuron excitation. This is illustrated in Fig. 1b.

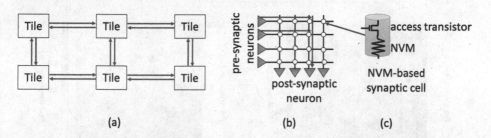

Fig. 1. (a) Tile-based neuromorphic hardware. (b) A crossbar of a neuromorphic tile. (c) An NVM-based synaptic cell consisting of an access transistor and an NVM.

We investigate the internal architecture of a crossbar and observe that the bitlines and wordlines of a crossbar consist of parasitic elements, which consist of capacitance and resistance of the metal interconnect as shown in Fig. 2. These parasitic elements create variation in current propagating along different paths in the crossbar. The figure illustrates the shortest and the longest current paths

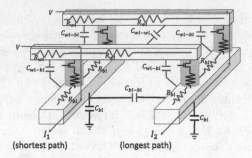

Fig. 2. Parasitc components on the bitlines and wordlines in a crossbar.

in a crossbar, where the length of a path is measured in terms of the number of parasitic components that are present on the path. Current differences create variation in access speed of the different synaptic elements in the crossbar [25, 50,54]. A conservative design practice is to use a common spike voltage to obtain the required access speed of the synaptic element on the longest current path.

We argue that this conservative approach creates current differences in a crossbar, leading to a wide thermal gradient. Figure 3 illustrates the current and thermal variations in a 128×128 PCM crossbar at 65nm technology node. Accessing the synaptic cells on shorter current paths (bottom left corner of Fig. 3b) generate higher temperatures than those on longer current paths (top right corner). Due to the exponential dependency of leakage current on temperature [35], the leakage current through cells with higher temperature is much higher than the current through cells with lower temperature. So, frequently accessing the cells on shorter current paths when executing a workload can lead to higher leakage power consumption in the crossbar.

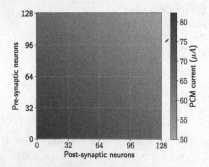

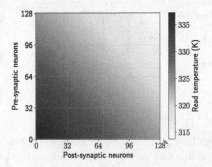

(a) Current variation for PCM access operations in a 128x128 crossbar.

(b) Temperature gradient in a 128x128 crossbar.

Fig. 3. Current variation and temperature gradient in a 128×128 crossbar at 65 nm process node with $T_{amb} = 298K$. The PCM crystallization point is 360K.

Existing techniques to map neurons and synapses of SNNs to neuromorphic hardware have mostly focused on improving performance and circuit aging [1, 4–7, 16, 21, 43, 44, 46]. These techniques do not consider the thermal gradient in a crossbar and therefore, they can increase the leakage power significantly. We build the case for one such mapping technique – SpiNeMap [5]. The leakage energy using this technique constitute between 20% to 30% of the total energy consumption for the typical machine learning workloads (see Sect. 4), where the total energy of a neuromorphic hardware includes the energy to generate spikes, the energy to communicate spikes, and the leakage energy. Therefore, reducing the leakage power (which we demonstrate in this work) will lead to a significant reduction of the total energy consumption.

Our **goal** is to minimize the leakage power consumption. We achieve this goal by lowering the average temperature of each crossbar using the proposed mapping technique. To this end, we make the following two key contributions.

– **Contribution 1:** We propose a new comprehensive thermal model of a crossbar designed with phase-change memory (PCM). Our model incorporates 1) workload dependency, i.e., the temperature obtained in processing spike trains from a given SNN-based machine learning workload, and 2) spatial thermal dependencies, i.e., the temperature contributions from the neighboring cells based on their synaptic excitation in the workload.
– **Contribution 2:** We propose a novel neuron and synapse mapping approach incorporating the thermal model using a hill climbing heuristic. The objective of the heuristic is to allocate the neurons and synapses of an SNN to the crossbars of the hardware such that the maximum average temperature of all crossbars is minimized, which lowers its leakage power consumption.

We evaluate the proposed technique with 10 machine learning applications from three most commonly-used neural network topology – convolution neural network (CNN), multilayer perceptron (MLP), and recurrent neural network (RNN). Evaluation for DYNAP-SE [38], a state-of-the-art neuromorphic hardware demonstrates the reduction of temperature, leading to a significant reduction in the leakage current.

2   Workload-Dependant Thermal Model of Crossbars

In this section, we develop a workload-dependent thermal model of crossbars in a neuromorphic hardware, considering PCM-based synaptic elements. We start by reviewing the internals of a PCM device. The proposed thermal model can be generalized to other NVMs such as OxRRAM and SOT-/STT-MRAM exploiting their specific structures.

Figure 4(a) illustrates how a chalcogenide semiconductor alloy is used to build a PCM cell. The amorphous phase (logic '0') in this alloy has higher resistance than the crystalline phase (logic '1'). $Ge_2Sb_2Te_5$ (GST) is the most commonly used alloy for PCM [53] due to its high amorphous-to-crystalline resistance ratio, fast switching between phases, and high endurance. However, other

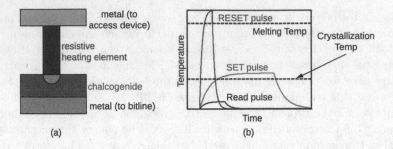

Fig. 4. (a) A PCM cell and (b) Current needed to operate a PCM cell.

chalcogenide alloys are also explored due to their better data retention properties [39]. Phase changes in a PCM cell are induced by injecting current into the resistor-chalcogenide junction and heating the chalcogenide alloy.

Figure 4(b) shows the different current profiles needed to program and read in a PCM device. To RESET a PCM cell, a high power pulse of short duration is applied and quickly terminated. This first raises the temperature of the chalcogenide alloy to 650°C, above its melting point. The melted alloy subsequently cools extremely quickly, locking into an amorphous phase. To SET a PCM cell, the chalcogenide alloy is heated above its crystallization temperature, but below its melting point for a sufficient amount of time. Finally, to read the content (i.e., know the phase) of a PCM cell, a small electrical pulse is applied that is sufficiently low so as not to induce phase change in the PCM cell. We focus on PCM read for the inference of supervised machine learning approaches.

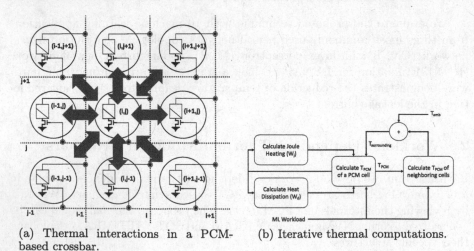

(a) Thermal interactions in a PCM-based crossbar.

(b) Iterative thermal computations.

Fig. 5. Building thermal model of a PCM-based crossbar.

Many prior works have developed thermal models for PCM devices [11,31, 51]. However, these models are developed for individual PCM cell considering the effect of crystallization and amorphization (synaptic weight updates in the context of machine learning). In other words, these models have the following two key limitations for their use in the context of neuromorphic computing. First, they do not consider spatial dependencies, i.e., the thermal contributions from neighboring PCM cells considering their utilization in a machine learning workload. Second, the thermal impact due to PCM reads (as required for machine learning inference) is not modeled. Figure 5a shows the thermal interactions in a crossbar. When a cell is accessed repeatedly within a short time window, there remains very little scope for heat inside the cell to be dissipated. As a result temperature keeps rising on every access, building on the undissipated components, and dissipating the heat to its neighboring cells, raising their temperature.

Figure 5b shows the proposed iterative approach of computing the temperature of a crossbar. The model computes the temperature of a single PCM cell incorporating 1) thermal contributions from its neighbors and 2) its activation within a workload.

The temperature of a single PCM cell is computed using Joule heating, W_j and heat dissipation, W_d which is given by the following equation [34],

$$T_{PCM} = \int \frac{W_j - W_d}{C \times V} dt \tag{1}$$

where C and V are heat capacity of GST and volume of the active region of the cell respectively. The heat generation in the PCM cell is given by,

$$W_j - I_{PCM}^2 \times R_{PCM} \tag{2}$$

where I_{PCM} is the current through the PCM cell and R_{PCM} is the effective resistance of the cell. We use $R_{PCM} = 10\,K\Omega$ in the low resistance (SET) state and $200\,K\Omega$ in the high resistance (RESET) state. A part of this generated heat is dissipated to the surrounding and this heat dissipation is given by the Equation [33],

$$W_d = -k \sum \Delta T \tag{3}$$

where ΔT represents the temperature dispersion around the active region and expressed as,

$$\Delta T = \frac{\partial T_{PCM}}{\partial x} + \frac{\partial T_{PCM}}{\partial y} + \frac{\partial T_{PCM}}{\partial z} \tag{4}$$

For simplicity we assume that the heat is mainly dispersed along the thickness of the cell and the temperature outside the dispersion region is close to the temperature surrounding the cell. Therefore, Eq. 3 can be written as [30,52],

$$W_d = \frac{kV}{l^2} (T_{PCM} - T_{surrounding}) \tag{5}$$

where l is the thickness of the GST material and k is the thermal conductivity. Substitution of Eqs. 2 and 5 in Eq. 1 yields,

$$\frac{dT_{PCM}}{dt} = \frac{W_j - W_d}{C \times V} \tag{6}$$

Solving this ODE gives,

$$T_{PCM} = \frac{I_{PCM}^2 R_{PCM} l^2}{kV} - C_1 exp\left(-\frac{kt}{l^2 C}\right) + T_{surrounding} \qquad (7)$$

Initially the PCM cell's temperature is assumed to be the same as its surrounding temperature. This boundary condition is used to determine the constant C_1. Finally the cell temperature is modeled as,

$$T_{PCM} = \frac{I_{PCM}^2 R_{PCM} l^2}{kV} - \left[1 - exp\left(-\frac{kt}{l^2 C}\right)\right] + T_{surrounding} \qquad (8)$$

The surrounding temperature $T_{surrounding}$ is computed as

$$T_{surrounding} = T_{amb} + \sum_j k \cdot T_{PCM_j}/D_j \qquad (9)$$

where D_j is the thermal distance of the PCM cell from its neighboring cell j, T_{PCM_j} is the temperature of the neighboring cell, and T_{amb} is the ambient temperature of the neuromorphic hardware.

Equations 8 and 9 combine the following effects—1) temporal thermal effect of accessing a PCM cell in a machine learning workload, 2) the spatial thermal contributions from the neighboring cell based on their activation.

Finally, we use the PCM temperature T_{PCM} to compute the leakage current through the access transistor of the PCM cell using Eq. 10, where the fitting parameters A and η, and the nominal parameters $I_{nominal}$ and $T_{nominal}$ are obtained using [3,14,17,18,20,35,41].

$$I_{leakage} \approx A \cdot I_{nominal} \left(T_{PCM} - T_{nominal}\right)^\eta \qquad (10)$$

3 Proposed Neuron and Synapse Mapping Technique

Figure 6 shows an overview of the proposed neuron and synapse mapping approach. A machine learning application is first simulated using PyCARL [2], a framework for simulating SNN-based applications. PyCARL internally uses the CARLsim [12] simulator to extract the precise spike times on every synaptic element in the SNN for representative training data. These spike times, together

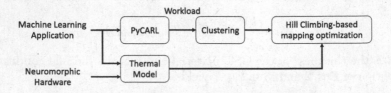

Fig. 6. Overview of the proposed technique.

with the neuron and synapse information constitute the SNN workload for the machine learning application.

Next, the SNN workload is clustered using a greedy clustering approach, roughly based on the Kernighan-Lin Graph Partitioning algorithm of SpiNe-Map [28]. Each cluster is a collection of pre- and post-synaptic neurons, synapses connecting these neurons, and the spike times on these synapses. From the mapping perspective, each cluster maps to a crossbar in the hardware, while the inter-cluster communication channels are mapped on the shared interconnect of the hardware. Therefore, the clustering technique ensures that the neurons and synapses of a cluster can fit onto the resources of the crossbar. PyCARL clusters an SNN to minimize the inter-cluster communication. This reduces the spike congestion on the shared interconnect which improves application latency.

The final step in our approach is the cluster mapping to the hardware. To describe this step, let $G(C,S)$ be the machine learning workload with set C of clusters and a set S of connections between the clusters. The workload is to be executed on the hardware $H(\mathcal{T},L)$ with a set $\mathcal{T}$ of tiles (each tile has one crossbar) and a set L of links between the tiles. The mapping of the application G to the hardware H, $\mathcal{M} = \{m_{x,y}\}$ is defined as

$$m_{x,y} = \begin{cases} 1 & \text{if cluster } c_x \in C \text{ is mapped to tile } t_y \in T \\ 0 & \text{otherwise} \end{cases} \tag{11}$$

Algorithm 1: Generate neuron and synapse mapping $\mathcal{M}$ to minimize the average temperature of crossbars.

Input: G, H
Output: $\mathcal{M}$

1   **for** i *in MaxIter* **do**
2     $\mathcal{M}_{\text{init}}$ = allocate clusters to crossbars randomly;
3   T_{init} = CalculateAvgTemperature($\mathcal{M}_{\text{init}}$);
4   **do**
5   **for** $c_x \in C$ **do**
6   **for** $t_y \in \mathcal{T}$ **do**
7             $\mathcal{M}_y = \mathcal{M}_{\text{init}} \big| m_{x,z} = \begin{cases} 1 & \text{if } z = y \\ 0 & \text{otherwise} \end{cases}$ /* Move c_x to tile t_y and generate the new mapping $\mathcal{M}_y$.   */
8   T_y = CalculateAvgTemperature($\mathcal{M}_y$);
9   **end**
10   x_{idx} = argmin $\{T_y | y \in 1, 2, \cdots, |\mathcal{T}|\}$/* Find the index of the mapping with the minimum temperature.   */
11   **if** $T_y < T_{min}$ **then**
12           $T_{\text{min}} = T_y$ and $\mathcal{M}_{\text{min}} = \mathcal{M}_y$/* Update the mapping if the average temperature reduces.   */
13   **end**
14   **end**
15   **while** $T_{min} < T_{init}$;
16   **end**
17 Return $\mathcal{M}_{\text{init}}$

Algorithm 1 provides the pseudo-code of the hill-climbing based average temperature minimization algorithm. The algorithm takes the clustered application G and the neuromorphic hardware H as input. The algorithm returns the mapping of G to H, which minimizes the average temperature of the crossbars. The algorithm is iterated for $MaxIter$ iterations (outer loop lines 1–16). For each iteration of the outer loop, the algorithm generates a random allocation of the clusters to the tiles (line 2) and calculate the average temperature (line 3). The routine `CalculateAvgTemperature` calculates the temperature of each crossbar for a mapping $\mathcal{M}$ using the iterative approach of Fig. 5b, specifically utilizing Eqs. 8 & 9, and return the maximum average temperature of all crossbars in the neuromorphic hardware.

At each iteration of the Algorithm 1, a cluster is moved to one of the tiles (line 7), computing the average temperature of this new mapping (line 8). The one mapping that leads to reduction of the average temperature is retained as the new mapping (lines 10–13) and the process is repeated for the next cluster (5–14). Once every cluster is analyzed, the iteration is repeated (lines 4–15) to check if the clusters can be remapped again to reduce the average temperature. The user-defined parameter $MaxIter$ governs the convergence of the algorithm.

Algorithm Complexity: The complexity of Algorithm 1 is calculated as follows. Let the inner loop (lines 4–15) be executed ζ times on average. At each of these iterations, the algorithm performs $|C| \times |T|$ operations. Therefore, the complexity of Algorithm 1 is $O(MaxIter \times \zeta \times |C| \times |T|)$.

4 Evaluation

4.1 Evaluated Applications

We evaluated 10 machine learning applications that are representative of three most commonly used neural network classes—convolutional neural network (CNN), multi-layer perceptron (MLP), and recurrent neural network (RNN). Table 1 summarizes the topology, the number of neurons and synapses of these applications, and their baseline accuracy.

Table 1. Applications used to evaluate the proposed technique.

Class	Applications	Synapses	Neurons	Topology	Accuracy
CNN	LeNet [32]	282,936	20,602	CNN	85.1%
	AlexNet [29]	38,730,222	230,443	CNN	90.7%
	VGG16 [42]	99,080,704	554,059	CNN	69.8 %
	HeartClass [3, 15]	1,049,249	153,730	CNN	63.7%
MLP	DigitRecogMLP	79,400	884	FeedForward (784, 100, 10)	91.6%
	EdgeDet [12]	114,057	6,120	FeedForward (4096, 1024, 1024, 1024)	100%
	ImgSmooth [12]	9,025	4,096	FeedForward (4096, 1024)	100%
RNN	HeartEstm [13]	66,406	166	Recurrent reservoir	100%
	VisualPursuit [27]	163,880	205	Recurrent reservoir	47.3%
	R-DigitRecog [24]	11,442	567	Recurrent reservoir	83.6%

4.2 Hardware Models

We model the DYNAP-SE neuromorphic hardware [38] with the following configurations.

- A tiled array of 4 tiles, each with a 128×128 crossbar. There are 65,536 memristors per crossbar.
- Spikes are digitized and communicated between cores through a mesh routing network using the Address Event Representation (AER) protocol.
- Each synaptic element is a PCM-based memristor.

Table 2 reports the hardware parameters of DYNAP-SE.

Table 2. Major simulation parameters extracted from [38].

Neuron technology	32 nm FD-SOI
Synapse technology	PCM
Supply voltage	1.0 V
Energy per spike	50 pJ at 30 Hz spike frequency
Energy per routing	147 pJ
Switch bandwidth	1.8 G. Events/s

4.3 Evaluated Techniques

We evaluate the following two approaches.

- **SpiNeMap** [5]: This is a performance-oriented approach to map SNN-based applications to neuromorphic hardware. This approach first generates clusters of neurons and synapses, where each cluster can fit on to the resources of a tile in the hardware. Then, it uses an optimization algorithm to place these clusters to the hardware, maximizing performance of the machine learning application on the hardware. Temperature gradients are not incorporated in the mapping process.
- **Proposed:** In this technique the neurons and synapses of an SNN are mapped to the hardware considering the thermal gradient. It uses the clustering technique of SpiNeMap to generate clusters of neurons and synapses, where each cluster can fit on to the resources of a tile. The clusters are mapped to the crossbar using a hill-climbing approach to minimize the average temperature. This reduces the leakage power consumption.

4.4   Evaluated Metrics

We evaluate the following metrics.

- **Average Temperature:** This is the average temperature of each crossbar in the hardware. We report the highest average temperatures of all crossbars.
- **Leakage Power:** This is the total leakage power consumed in the hardware.
- **Performance:** This is the latency, i.e., the time it takes to execute each model on hardware.
- **Compilation Time:** This is the time it takes to generate the minimum temperature mapping of an application for the hardware.

5   Results and Discussion

5.1   Average Temperature

Figure 7 compares the maximum average temperature of the crossbars for each evaluated application on DYNAP-SE using SpiNeMap and the proposed technique. We make the following *two* key observations.

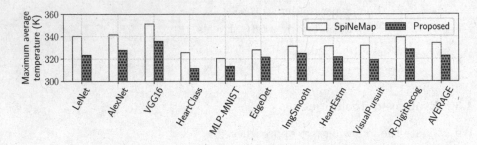

Fig. 7. Maximum average temperature of the crossbars on DYNAP-SE.

First, the maximum average temperature increases with model size. VGG16, which has more neurons and synapses than AlexNet (see Table 1), results in higher average temperature than AlexNet for both SpiNeMap and the proposed technique. MLP-MNIST, on the other hand, have lower temperature than both these models due to its lower model complexity. Although R-DigitRecog has comparatively fewer neurons and synapses, the average temperature is much higher. This is because R-DigitRecog has higher activation, i.e., spikes in its workload, which increases the temperature. These results clearly demonstrate the *workload-dependent* nature of the temperature obtained on the hardware. Second, the temperature obtained using the proposed mapping technique is lower than SpiNeMap by an average 11.4 K (between 6.4 K and 17 K) for these 10 applications. This reduction is because of the proposed hill climbing algorithm (Algorithm 1), which incorporates the thermal gradient in optimizing the mapping of neurons and synapses to the crossbars of the hardware.

5.2   Leakage Power

Figure 8 compares the leakage power on DYNAP-SE for each evaluated application using SpiNeMap and the proposed technique. The leakage power constitute between 20%–30% (average 22.8%) of the total energy consumption in the hardware. Results are normalized with respect to the leakage power obtained on the hardware using SpiNeMap. We observe that the leakage power obtained using the proposed technique is lower than SpiNeMap by an average 52%. This significant improvement in the leakage power is due to the reduction of the average temperature of the crossbars, which we analyzed in Sect. 5.1. This reduction in leakage power results in a reduction of the total energy consumption by 11%.

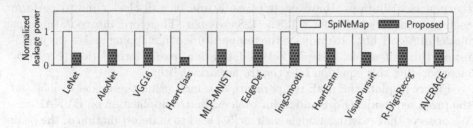

Fig. 8. Normalized leakage power on DYNAP-SE.

5.3   Performance

Figure 9 compares the latency of SpiNeMap and the proposed technique on DYNAP-SE for the evaluated applications. We observe that the latency of the proposed technique is only 5% higher (average) than SpiNeMap. Although the optimization objective of SpiNeMap (which is performance) is different from the optimization objective of the proposed technique (which is temperature), the proposed technique uses the clustering technique of SpiNeMap to first generate clusters, minimizing the spike communication on the shared interconnect of the hardware. This results in lower spike latency. Therefore, in the next step when the proposed technique optimizes for temperature during placement of the clusters to crossbars of the hardware, the latency is not significantly higher than SpiNeMap.

5.4   Thermal Model Validation

We validate our thermal model against 1) the thermal model of [55], which models the temperature of a single PCM cell and 2) the detailed model of [19], which performs a detailed layout-based thermal simulations. The individual PCM cell model is fast. However, it does not incorporate the thermal contributions from neighboring PCM cells in a crossbar. Therefore, this model is not accurate. On

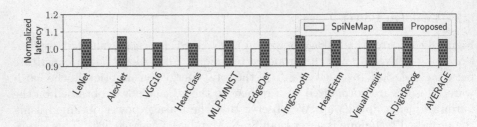

Fig. 9. Normalized latency on DYNAP-SE.

the other hand, the model in [19] is accurate because it incorporates the spatial thermal contributions. However, it takes 30 min of wall clock time to perform each thermal simulation for a 128 × 128 crossbar. Therefore, incorporating this model in Algorithm 1 to evaluate the temperature of a mapping makes the exploration time infeasible. Instead, we validated our spatial formulation (Eq. 9) by incorporating this equation into the framework of [19].

Figure 10 plots the peak temperature obtained using the model of [55] and the proposed model (Eq. 8 and 9) for each evaluated application on DYNAP-SE. We observe that existing models such as [55] lead to underestimation of the peak temperature by an average 1.6K for these applications. This is because they do not incorporate the spatial dependency. Underestimation of temperature leads to an underestimation of the leakage power consumption of the hardware.

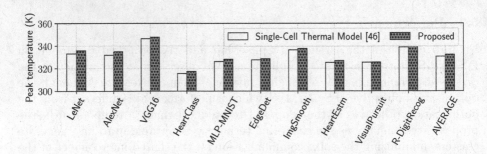

Fig. 10. Comparison of Peak temperature.

Figure 11 plots the spatial contribution obtained using the model of [19] and the proposed model (Eq. 9) for 10 synthetic applications. We observe that the accuracy of the proposed spatial model is close to that of the detailed model [19]. The spatial contribution obtained using Eq. 9 is on average 8.2% lower than [19] (0.3K in absolute terms).

These results validate the thermal model proposed in this work.

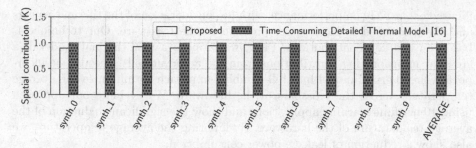

Fig. 11. Comparison of spatial contribution.

5.5   Compilation Time and Solution Tradeoff

Table 3 reports the compilation time and the average temperature obtained for three different settings of the variable *MaxIter*. We observe that as *MaxIter* is increased, the average temperature reduces for all applications. This is because with increase in the number of iterations, Algorithm 1 is able to find a better solution. However, the compilation time also increases. Finally, we observe that increasing *MaxIter* from 100 to 1000 results in a significant increase in compilation time with a minimal improvement of the average temperature. We conclude that setting *MaxIter* = 100 gives the best trade-off in terms of compilation time and the solution quality. User can use this *MaxIter* parameter to set a limit on the compilation time of their algorithm by analyzing the complexity of their model against the ones we evaluate (see Table 1).

Table 3. Compilation time and solution tradeoff.

Application	MaxIter = 10		MaxIter = 100		MaxIter = 1000	
	Compilation time (sec)	Avg. temperature (K)	Compilation time (sec)	Avg. temperature (K)	Compilation time (sec)	Avg. temperature (K)
LeNet	26	326.3	259	323.2	2641	322.2
AlexNet	114	330.1	1144	327.6	11480	326.0
VGG16	241	344.6	2413	335.8	24180	335.3
HeartClass	96	315.1	965	311.3	9699	309.9
MLP-MNIST	14	319.7	149	313.2	1520	311.6
EdgeDet	12	323.5	132	321.5	1337	320.8
ImgSmooth	26	327.11	268	324.7	2740	322.8
HeartEstm	12	328.2	125	321.8	1255	320.4
VisualPursuit	27	329.1	284	319.2	2883	318.7
R-DigitRecog	15	336.3	159	328.5	1615	327.9

6   Conclusions

We propose a technique to map the neurons and synapses of SNN-based machine learning applications to neuromorphic hardware. Prior work in this space have focused extensively on performance, with no consideration of the thermal aspects and the associated leakage power problem in the hardware. Our technique is based on two key contributions. First, we propose a new thermal model of a crossbar incorporating contributions from the adjacent cells. Second, we incorporate this thermal model in a hill-climbing approach to minimize the average temperature across the crossbars of the hardware. We evaluate our approach using 10 machine learning applications and show the significant reduction of the average temperature of the hardware. By lowering the average temperature, we also show a reduction of leakage power consumption.

Acknowledgment. This work is supported by the National Science Foundation Faculty Early Career Development Award CCF-1942697 (CAREER: Facilitating Dependable Neuromorphic Computing: Vision, Architecture, and Impact on Programmability).

References

1. Balaji, A., et al.: A framework to explore workload-specific performance and lifetime trade-offs in neuromorphic computing. CAL **18**, 149–152 (2019)
2. Balaji, A., Adiraju, P., Kashyap, H.J., Das, A., Krichmar, J.L., Dutt, N.D., Catthoor, F.: PyCARL: a PyNN interface for hardware-software co-simulation of spiking neural network. In: IJCNN (2020)
3. Balaji, A., Corradi, F., Das, A., Pande, S., Schaafsma, S., Catthoor, F.: Power-accuracy trade-offs for heartbeat classification on neural networks hardware. JOLPE **14**, 508–519 (2018)
4. Balaji, A., Das, A.: A framework for the analysis of throughput-constraints of snns on neuromorphic hardware. In: ISVLSI (2019)
5. Balaji, A., et al.: Mapping spiking neural networks to neuromorphic hardware. TVLSI **28**, 76–86 (2020)
6. Balaji, A., Marty, T., Das, A., Catthoor, F.: Run-time mapping of spiking neural networks to neuromorphic hardware. JSPS **92**, 1293–1302 (2020)
7. Balaji, A., et al.: Enabling resource-aware mapping of spiking neural networks via spatial decomposition. ESL **13**, 142–145 (2021)
8. Balaji, A., Wu, Y., Das, A., Catthoor, F., et al.: Exploration of segmented bus as scalable global interconnect for neuromorphic computing. In: GLSVLSI (2019)
9. Burr, G.W., Shelby, R.M., et al.: Neuromorphic computing using non-volatile memory. Adv. Phys.: X **2**, 89–124 (2017)
10. Catthoor, F., Mitra, S., Das, A., Schaafsma, S.: Very large-scale neuromorphic systems for biological signal processing. In: Mitra, S., Cumming, D.R.S. (eds.) CMOS Circuits for Biological Sensing and Processing, pp. 315–340. Springer, Cham (2018). https://doi.org/10.1007/978-3-319-67723-1_13
11. Chen, I.R., Pop, E.: Compact thermal model for vertical nanowire phase-change memory cells. TED **56**, 1523–1528 (2009)
12. Chou, T.S., et al.: CARLsim 4: an open source library for large scale, biologically detailed spiking neural network simulation using heterogeneous clusters. In: IJCNN (2018)
13. Das, A., et al.: Unsupervised heart-rate estimation in wearables with Liquid states and a probabilistic readout. Neural Netw. **99**, 134–147 (2018)
14. Das, A., Catthoor, F., Bourdoux, A., Gyselinckx, B.: Energy-efficient mapping of LTE-A PHY signal processing tasks on microservers. TGCN **2**, 397–407 (2018)

15. Das, A., Catthoor, F., et al.: Heartbeat classification in wearables using multi-layer perceptron and time-frequency joint distribution of ECG. In: CHASE (2018)
16. Das, A., Kumar, A.: Dataflow-based mapping of spiking neural networks on neuromorphic hardware. In: GLSVLSI (2018)
17. Das, A., Kumar, A., Veeravalli, B.: Communication and migration energy aware design space exploration for multicore systems with intermittent faults. In: DATE (2013)
18. Das, A., Kumar, A., Veeravalli, B.: Communication and migration energy aware task mapping for reliable multiprocessor systems. FGCS **30**, 216–228 (2014)
19. Das, A., Kumar, A., Veeravalli, B.: Reliability and energy-aware mapping and scheduling of multimedia applications on multiprocessor systems. TPDS **27**, 869–884 (2015)
20. Das, A., Walker, M.J., Hansson, A., Al-Hashimi, B.M., Merrett, G.V.: Hardware-software interaction for run-time power optimization: a case study of embedded Linux on multicore smartphones. In: ISLPED (2015)
21. Das, A., Wu, Y., Huynh, K., Dell'Anna, F., Catthoor, F., Schaafsma, S.: Mapping of local and global synapses on spiking neuromorphic hardware. In: DATE (2018)
22. Davies, M., Srinivasa, N., et al.: Loihi: a neuromorphic manycore processor with on-chip learning. IEEE Micro **38**, 82–99 (2018)
23. Debole, M.V., Taba, B., et al.: TrueNorth: accelerating from zero to 64 million neurons in 10 years. Computer **52**, 20–29 (2019)
24. Diehl, P.U., Cook, M.: Unsupervised learning of digit recognition using spike-timing-dependent plasticity. Front. Comput. Neurosci. **9**, 99 (2015)
25. Fouda, M.E., Eltawil, A.M., Kurdahi, F.: Modeling and analysis of passive switching crossbar arrays. TCAS I: Regular Pap. **65**, 270–282 (2017)
26. Gubbi, J., Buyya, R., Marusic, S., Palaniswami, M.: Internet of Things (IoT): a vision, architectural elements, and future directions. FGCS **29**, 1645–1660 (2013)
27. Kashyap, H.J., et al.: A recurrent neural network based model of predictive smooth pursuit eye movement in primates. In: IJCNN (2018)
28. Kernighan, B.W., Lin, S.: An efficient heuristic procedure for partitioning graphs. Bell Syst. Techn. J. **49**, 291–307 (1970)
29. Krizhevsky, A., Sutskever, I., Hinton, G.E.: ImageNet classification with deep convolutional neural networks. In: NeurIPS (2012)
30. Kwong, K.C., Li, L., He, J., Chan, M.: Verilog-a model for phase change memory simulation. In: ICSICT (2008)
31. Le Gallo, M., Athmanathan, A., Krebs, D., Sebastian, A.: Evidence for thermally assisted threshold switching behavior in nanoscale phase-change memory cells. J. Appl. Phys. **119**, 025704 (2016)
32. LeCun, Y., et al.: LeNet-5, convolutional neural networks (2015)
33. Liao, Y.B., Chen, Y.K., Chiang, M.H.: An analytical compact PCM model accounting for partial crystallization. In: EDSSC (2007)
34. Liao, Y.B., Lin, J.T., Chiang, M.H.: Temperature-based phase change memory model for pulsing scheme assessment. In: ICICDT (2008)
35. Liu, Y., Dick, R.P., Shang, L., Yang, H.: Accurate temperature-dependent integrated circuit leakage power estimation is easy. In: DATE (2007)
36. Maass, W.: Networks of spiking neurons: the third generation of neural network models. Neural Netw. **10**, 1659–1671 (1997)
37. Mallik, A., Garbin, D., Fantini, A., Rodopoulos, et al.: Design-technology co-optimization for OxRRAM-based synaptic processing unit. In: VLSIT (2017)

38. Moradi, S., Qiao, N., Stefanini, F., Indiveri, G.: A scalable multicore architecture with heterogeneous memory structures for dynamic neuromorphic asynchronous processors (DYNAPs). TBCAS **12**, 106–122 (2017)
39. Morikawa, T., Kurotsuchi, K., Kinoshita, M., et al.: Doped in-Ge-Te phase change memory featuring stable operation and good data retention. In: IEDM (2007)
40. Ramasubramanian, S.G., Venkatesan, R., Sharad, M., et al.: SPINDLE: spintronic deep learning engine for large-scale neuromorphic computing. In: ISLPED (2014)
41. Shafik, R.A., Das, A., Yang, S., Merrett, G., Al-Hashimi, B.M.: Adaptive energy minimization of OpenMP parallel applications on many-core systems. In: PARMA-DITAM (2015)
42. Simonyan, K., Zisserman, A.: Very deep convolutional networks for large-scale image recognition. arXiv (2014)
43. Song, S., Balaji, A., Das, A., Kandasamy, N., Shackleford, J.: Compiling spiking neural networks to neuromorphic hardware. In: LCTES (2020)
44. Song, S., Das, A.: A case for lifetime reliability-aware neuromorphic computing. In: MWSCAS (2020)
45. Song, S., Das, A., Kandasamy, N.: Exploiting inter- and intra-memory asymmetries for data mapping in hybrid tiered-memories. In: ISMM (2020)
46. Song, S., Das, A., Kandasamy, N.: Improving dependability of neuromorphic computing with non-volatile memory. In: EDCC (2020)
47. Song, S., Das, A., Mutlu, O., Kandasamy, N.: Enabling and exploiting partition-level parallelism (PALP) in phase change memories. TECS **18**, 1–25 (2019)
48. Song, S., Das, A., Mutlu, O., Kandasamy, N.: Improving phase change memory performance with data content aware access. In: ISMM (2020)
49. Song, S., Das, A., Mutlu, O., Kandasamy, N.: Aging aware request scheduling for non-volatile main memory. In: ASP-DAC (2021)
50. Titirsha, T., Das, A.: Reliability-performance trade-offs in neuromorphic computing. In: CUT (2020)
51. Warren, R., Reifenberg, J., Goodson, K.: Compact thermal model for phase change memory nanodevices. In: ICTTPES (2008)
52. Wei, Y., Lin, X., Jia, Y., Cui, X., He, J., Zhang, X.: A SPICE model for a phase-change memory cell based on the analytical conductivity model. JOS **33**, 114004 (2012)
53. Wong, H.S.P., et al.: Phase change memory. In: Proceedings of the IEEE (2010)
54. Woo, J., Yu, S.: Resistive memory-based analog synapse: the pursuit for linear and symmetric weight update. IEEE Nanotechnol. Mag. **12**, 36–44 (2018)
55. Xi, L., Zhitang, S., Daolin, C., Xiaogang, C., Houpeng, C.: An spice model for phase-change memory simulations. JOS **32**, 094011 (2011)

A Quantum-Inspired Model for Bit-Serial SIMD-Parallel Computation

Henry Dietz[✉], Aury Shafran, and Gregory Austin Murphy

University of Kentucky, Lexington, KY 40506, USA
hankd@engr.uky.edu
http://aggregate.org/hankd

Abstract. Bit-serial SIMD-parallel execution was once commonly used in supercomputers, but fell out of favor as it became practical to implement word-level operations directly in MIMD hardware. Word-level primitive operations simplify programming and significantly speed-up sequential code. However, aggressive gate-level compiler optimization can dramatically reduce power consumed in massively-parallel bit-serial execution without a performance penalty. The model described here, Parallel Bit Pattern Computing, not only leverages gate-level just-in-time optimization of bit-serial code, but also uses a quantum-inspired type of symbolic execution based on regular expressions to obtain a potentially exponential reduction in computational complexity while using entirely conventional computer hardware.

Keywords: Bit-serial SIMD · Quantum computing · Qubit · Logic optimization · Regular expressions · Just in time compilation · C++

1 Introduction

Bit-serial SIMD supercomputing is not a new topic for the Languages and Compilers for Parallel Computing (LCPC) community; much of the work presented in the first two decades of this workshop series targeted such machines. However, the current work is largely focused on applying compiler technology at the level of individual gate operations, and such techniques are far less well studied. The 2017 "How Low Can You Go?" paper [1] was an attempt to inspire more work in that direction, and much of what it suggested is implemented in the system described in this paper.

The *parallel bit pattern* model of computation [2] shares two important properties with quantum computing:

– Both quantum computing and parallel bit pattern computing provide execution mechanisms that have the potential for a single unit of computational work to produce results for exponentially many data values using the concepts of *superposition* and *entanglement*. Quantum computers seek these benefits

© Springer Nature Switzerland AG 2022
B. Chapman and J. Moreira (Eds.): LCPC 2020, LNCS 13149, pp. 151–159, 2022.
https://doi.org/10.1007/978-3-030-95953-1_11

by implementing *qubits* using quantum phenomena. In contrast, *pattern bits*, or *pbits*, use **symbolic computation on a compressed bit vector representation − a bit pattern**, which can be manipulated efficiently using conventional computer hardware.
- Both focus on optimizing computations at the gate level. Quantum computers are directly programmed at that low level, expecting programmers to manually optimize the gate-level code. In contrast, parallel bit pattern computing leverages **gate-level compiler optimization technology at runtime** to allow not only programming at the gate level, but also at a higher level, using relatively conventional operators and data types including variable-precision integers: *pints*.

Parallel bit pattern computing is neither a simulation of quantum computing nor a compatible replacement for quantum hardware. It offers a new high-level programming model, and bit-serial parallel execution model, that together enable conventionally-constructed computers to efficiently use superposition and entanglement to implement a large class of quantum-inspired algorithms. The model is fundamentally stronger than quantum models because it allows non-destructive measurement and values may be maintained for arbitrarily long without decoherence. Of course, all this is accomplished while aggressively using compiler optimization to dramatically reduce the total number of gate-level operations that must be executed to perform each computation, thus potentially reducing the power consumed.

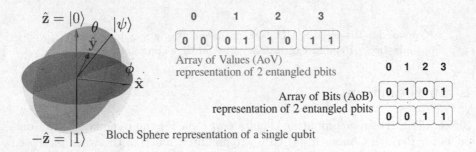

Fig. 1. Representations: Bloch Sphere *qubit*; AoV and AoB 2-way entangled *pbit*

1.1   Representation of Entangled Superposition

Figure 1 shows three different ways in which superposed values can be represented. The value of a *qubit* is commonly modeled as a real-valued, two-dimensional, probability density function: the Bloch Sphere [3]. Instead of using that model, an e-way entangled *pbit* value can be represented as an array of 2^e values (AoV), in which each possible multi-bit value is an element: an entangled pair of *pbit* initialized to equiprobable $\{0, 1, 2, 3\}$ is shown. However, the AoV

layout does not provide the benefits sought by bit-serial execution. Thus, consider *turning* that representation – a trick used to integrate word-based floating point units with massively-parallel bit-serial execution in the Thinking Machines CM2 [4]. Thus, the value of each *pbit* is an array of 2^e bits (*AoB*), entangled values are bits with the same array index (i.e., using the same *entanglement channels*), and value probabilities are not real numbers, but always integer parts per 2^e.

The *AoB* representation offers one more huge benefit: low entropy. The bit values often have relatively simple repeating patterns, which we can compress by representation as a *regular expression* (*RE*). In the *AoB* example above, {0,1,0,1} can reduce to $(01)^2$ and {0,0,1,1} is $0^2 1^2$ by simple *run-length encoding*. By storing and operating directly on REs, parallel bit pattern computing reduces both storage requirements and computational complexity by as much as an exponential factor... essentially the same goal sought by quantum computing, but achieved using partially symbolic parallel execution on conventional hardware.

1.2   A pbit-Level Example

Even at the *pbit* level, storage space for values is automatically managed. Also unlike quantum computers, programs are not restricted to using reversible gates like NOT (Pauli X), CNOT, SWAP, CCNOT (Toffoli), and CSWAP (Fredkin). They can be used, but so can conventional gates and fanout. For example, a 1-bit full adder computing a+b+cin to produce sum and cout could be:

```
pbit sum = pbit_xor(pbit_xor(a,b),cin);
pbit cout = pbit_or(pbit_and(a,b),pbit_and(pbit_xor(a,b),cin));
```

Of course, pbit_xor(a,b) will be evaluated only once, but the really interesting thing is that values for a, b, and cin can be 3-way entangled superpositions of all 8 possible input values. To do this, each input must be given a Hadamard value on it's own *entanglement channel* (a concept unique to parallel bit patterns):

```
pbit a = PBIT_H(0);    // a is (01)+
pbit b = PBIT_H(1);    // b is (0011)+
pbit cin = PBIT_H(2);  // cin is (00001111)+
```

The result of performing the add is thus that sum gets the value (01101001)+ and cout gets (00010111)+. Unlike quantum computers, this entangled superposition does not collapse into a single value when measured; any or all of the values can be read. In fact, the entire probability distribution can be read without need to repeat the computation: in this case, the 2-bit {cout,sum} results would be 1/8 {0,0}, 3/8 {0,1}, 3/8 {1,0}, and 1/8 {1,1}.

These REs can be simplified using run-length encoding: cout is $(0^3 1^1 0^1 1^3)$+. Execution walks these RE patterns without expanding them to AoB form. Overhead of this symbolic manipulation is reduced by using larger symbols in the

RE; rather than patterns of individual bits, the current prototype treats each 4096-bit *chunk* as a symbol. This also allows massively-parallel execution of gate operations over the bits within each chunk, and *applicative caching* can avoid recomputation when a chunk result is available from a prior computation.

1.3   Two pint-Level Examples

Moving up to the pint level, consider the problem of computing the square root of the 16-bit value 29929, which is 173. Rather than using a conventional algorithm, this can be computed by squaring all 8-bit values and selecting only the values that produced 29929. The complete code is simply:

```
int main(int argc, char **argv) {
  pint_init();
  pint a = pint_mk(16, 29929);   // 16-pbit value 29929
  pint b = pint_h(8, 0xff);      // H(0) .. H(7)
  pint c = pint_mul(b, b);       // square them
  pint d = pint_eq(c, a);        // where square equals 29929
  pint e = pint_mul(d, b);       // make non-sqrts all 0
  pint_measure(e);               // prints 0, 173
}
```

Notice that multiplying two 8-bit values naturally produces a 16-bit result (which here is 8-way entangled). This *pint* computation is implemented by just 310 gate-level *pbit* operations. The obvious algorithm to find all factors of 221 is similar, but creates a 16-way entangled space from two 8-way entangled values:

```
int main(int argc, char **argv) {
  pint_init();
  pint a = pint_mk(8, 221);      // 8-pbit value 221=13*17
  pint b = pint_h(8, 0x00ff);    // H(0) .. H(7)
  pint c = pint_h(8, 0xff00);    // H(8) .. H(15)
  pint d = pint_mul(b, c);       // multiply them
  pint e = pint_eq(d, a);        // where product equals 221
  pint f = pint_mul(e, b);       // make non-factors all 0
  pint_measure(f);               // prints 0, 1, 13, 17, 221
}
```

The number of values found in this measurement trivially determines primality. Any value thus factored will list at least 0, 1, and itself; if that is all, the number is prime. If there are four listed, then the number is the square of a prime. If there are five, the number is the product of two primes – the prime factors. Of course, much more efficient algorithms are possible, but the elegance of this example is a compelling argument for investigating this model further.

The remainder of this paper discusses some of the more interesting aspects of the current implementation of the parallel bit pattern computing model.

2   The Prototype Implementation

The latest prototype implementation consists of 2,713 lines (59KB) of C source code, originally written by Dietz and significantly improved by Shafran in Spring 2020. There are expected to be five major layers in the implementation of this model, four of which are operational at this writing. The lowest level is the chunk management. Above that layer is the factored bit parallel (FBP) or pattern layer, which manages regular expression values of *pbits*. The `pbit` layer is next, constructing optimized DAGs (directed acyclic graphs) for *pbit*-level computations. The `pint` layer handles arithmetic and other operations on variable-precision multi-*pbit* signed and unsigned integer values. The top layer, which is not yet complete, essentially wraps the `pint` layer in C++ constructs that allow `pints` to be directly manipulated in a C++ program as though they were a built-in data type. These layers are described in the following subsections.

2.1   The Chunk Management Layer

As mentioned in Sect. 1.2, the REs are currently expressed as patterns of 4096-bit chunk values within a potential 4294967296-bit AoB representation for 32-way entanglement. The chunk management layer implements a pool for allocation of chunk data blocks in an aligned, contiguous, region of memory. The data is kept separate from the management structures to ensure optimal alignment with cache lines, page table entries, and parallel execution structures. In Spring 2020, Murphy began work on parallel evaluation within a CUDA GPU, but parallel execution is currently within the host processor.

Chunks are indexed by a hash table containing many buckets (to keep loading light), each of which heads a dual-linked list of hash entries. Each hash entry not only points at the corresponding chunk data, but also contains a reference count tracking how many higher-level structures still have live pointers to this chunk entry. Duplicate chunks are recognized and only unique live chunks are stored. Reusing chunk memory as soon as possible is intended to improve cache and translation lookaside buffer performance.

2.2   The Factored Bit Parallel (FBP) Pattern Layer

The representation of a *pbit* value as a regular expression in which chunks are the basic symbols is managed by the factored bit parallel (FBP) layer.

As Table 1 shows, many FBP operations still have worst-case complexity that is exponential. Note that, using a more conventional (e.g., AoV) model of computation, all of the *pbit* operations would have at least 2^{32} work complexity, and there would be more total work to perform because bit-serial optimizations [1] would not have been applied. In contrast, RE-based FBP makes 2^{32} an unlikely worst case. The 2^{20} limits come from operations acting only on the symbols within a regular expression, rather than operating (in parallel) on the 4096 bits in each chunk. Lower-entropy regular expressions and applicative caching of chunk operations make the expected complexities far lower; any operation with no more than 12-way entanglement takes unit time, and a symbol repeated N times in an FBP regular expression typically would be evaluated only once.

Contrast these complexities with a true quantum computer supporting 32-way entanglement (which none yet support). Complexity would be constants for SWAP, CSWAP, CCNOT, and NOT. However, the other operations are not directly implementable. In fact, the *no cloning theorem* implies implementing operations like POP or even non-destructive measurement is impossible. Many complex quantum algorithms, such as Shor's algorithm [5], owe their complexity to statistically approximating such operations (typically using phase interference).

Table 1. Complexities of 32-way entangled FBP operations with 4096-bit chunks

Time	Work	Operations
1	1	SWAP gate; ALL, ANY reduction; non-destructive measurement
$1..2^{20}$	$1..2^{20}$	DUP; POPulation count; simplify regular expression
$1..2^{20}$	$1..2^{32}$	CSWAP, CCNOT, NOT, AND, OR, XOR gates

2.3 The pbit Layer

Quantum computing compilation and/or simulation environments generally define, and expose to users, some simple syntax for expressing operations on *qubit*s: a "quantum assembly language." For example, Quil [6], OpenQASM [7], and cQASM [8] all implement similar syntax for specifying operations on *qubit*s. However, that approach is not well suited to specification of FBP operations. One problem is the mismatch between basic operations provided: the various quantum assembly languages all provide direct operations on quantum wave functions and only adiabatic logic gates, whereas FBP does not model wave functions at all and provides a variety of both adiabatic and conventional types of logic gates. However, there is a larger incompatibility: pbit layer operations are normally not textually represented in a program, nor are they static; aggressive optimization and pbit (register) allocation are done at runtime.

As is discussed in Sect. 2.4, the pbit layer is really intended to serve as an internal framework for just-in-time compilation and optimization of work specified at the pint level. When specifying a computation using sequences of operations on multi-bit integers, as was observed by Dietz [1], it is common that a very large fraction of the intermediate bit-level operations will end-up being unnecessary. Logic optimization can symbolically recognize and remove many of these operations at compile time without ever incurring the overhead of constructing and evaluating FBP data structures. Thus, the pbit layer is literally an optimizing compiler used to cheaply remove as many unnecessary operations as possible before causing any FBP-layer evaluation.

Although pbit operations should look a lot like the FBP operations that are used to implement whatever computation remains, there is no need to use every type of instruction that the underlying machine supports. The current `pbit` layer simplifies optimizations by decomposing all operations into `ANY`, `NOT`, `OR`, `AND`, and `XOR`. The only constants available are 0, 1, and Hadamard superpositions for up to 32-way entangled *pbits* (i.e., `H(0)` .. `H(31)`).

Various algebraic simplifications are performed on-the-fly as `pbit` expression DAGs are created. For example, `AND` of anything with the constant 1 does not create an AND gate, but returns the other operand. A few multi-level simplifications also are performed, such as removal of `NOT NOT` and recursive searches to see if an item being ORed or ANDed into a sequence of that operation has already been included – e.g., (a `AND` (b `AND` (a `AND` c))) becomes just (b `AND` (a `AND` c)). Every potential operation also has its operand order normalized and a new operation will only be generated if that normalized computation is not already an available expression.

Originally, to maximize the probability of finding available expressions, no `pbit` DAG operation created during the expression compilation process was ever deleted. However, the latest version greedily reclaims no-longer-referenced `pbit` data structures to reduce memory usage. When the `pbit` layer is initialized, only 0, 1, and the Hadamard superpositions are available, but the set of available expressions grows as calls are made to compile additional operations. When the value of a `pbit` is demanded, the DAG producing that value is evaluated by executing a simple bottom-up tree walk that decorates the DAG with the results from executing each operation using the FBP layer. Values shared between DAGs are evaluated only once because the first walk to visit a node decorates it with a pointer to the FBP result, thus making it the bottom node in that walk. The nodes that correspond to dead code are not reachable via any walk, hence they are never evaluated using FBPs.

2.4   The `pint` Layer

In most quantum computer programming systems, the next level up from the quantum assembly languages described in the previous section is one in which quantum computations are still specified at the level of individual operations on *qubits*, but the quantum manipulations are embedded in a full-featured conventional programming language. For example, both IBM's Qiskit [9] and Microsoft's Q# [10] essentially add a variety of functions to existing languages to allow *qubit*-level specification of computations. Higher-level (e.g., integer) operations must be built using the primitive operations. The system described in the current work also augments a conventional language (C/C++), but the `pint` layer directly understands integer operations.

A `pint` is represented as a data structure which contains an array of `pbit` references, a current precision, and a flag specifying if the value is signed (as opposed to unsigned). All the usual integer operations are supported for `pint` containing from 1 to 32 `pbits`.

Lowering operations on `pint` to operate on `pbits` is a lot like lowering operations on integers to gate-level code operating on individual bits. Some multi-bit integer operations are trivially lowered to operations on individual bits. For example, bitwise AND of two `pint` values trivially produces a result using ANDs of corresponding component `pbit` values from the two operands. Other operations are significantly less straightforward. For example, addition of two `pint` values performs a sequence of `pbit` operations that is equivalent to implementing a ripple carry adder circuit. Multiply builds upon that to implement a purely combinatorial shift-and-add circuit.

The primary complication in implementing these `pint` operations at the `pbit` level lies in the fact that precision and signedness can dynamically vary. It does not make sense to bitwise OR values of different precision; the less precise one should be promoted to have the same number of `pbits` as the more precise one. If two k-`pbit` `pint` values are added, the result generally has $k + 1$ `pbits`. On the other hand, if the two unsigned integers being added are 0 and 1, only a single bit is needed to express that the result is 1. Implementation of `pint` operations involves a variety of automatic promotion and precision-minimization operations.

When the `pint` layer is initialized, all the layers below also are initialized. Operations on `pint` simply compile DAGs for the component `pbit` operations. At the end of a sequence of `pint` operations, a call to evaluate each `pint` will cause the component `pbit` DAGs to be evaluated and decorated with references to their FBP results. Arbitrarily complex intermediate steps combining `pint` values do not cause any computation until it is demanded by calling for evaluation of a particular `pint`, e.g., by measuring the value. Measurement results can be printed, but normally would be storing a single value into an ordinary `int` or all superposed values into an `int` array.

3   Conclusion

The current work begins by describing, and giving a few motivating examples for, the quantum-inspired parallel bit pattern model for energy-efficient execution using conventional computer hardware. The efficiency comes partly from extensive gate-level optimization implemented using just-in-time compilation, but also from use of symbolic computation on regular grammars to obtain the quantum-like property of a single operation on an entangled, superposed, value producing up to exponentially many results. The structure of a prototype implementation is also detailed.

Although the prototype system is operational, it is not yet complete: we are improving/debugging the system and implementing a C++ wrapper, and plan an open source release. We are working on offloading the massively-parallel evaluation of chunks to a GPU. Dietz also has created a greatly simplified parallel bit pattern computer architecture called *Tangled*, which provides coprocessor support for parallel AoB chunk operations and is being implemented in Verilog by the students taking his undergraduate CPE480 Computer Architecture course at the University of Kentucky in Fall 2020. In the more distant future, we envision compiler technology for automatic parallelization targeting this new model.

References

1. Dietz, H.G.: How low can you go? In: 30th International Workshop on Languages and Compilers for Parallel Computing (LCPC 2017), College Station, Texas, p. 8, 11 October 2017
2. Dietz, H.: Parallel bit pattern computing. In: IEEE 2019 Tenth International Green and Sustainable Computing Conference (IGSC) (2019). https://doi.org/10.1109/IGSC48788.2019.8957188
3. Rieffel, E., Polak, W.: An introduction to quantum computing for non-physicists. ACM Comput. Surv. (CSUR) **32**(3), 300–335 (2000). https://doi.org/10.1145/367701.367709
4. Tucker, L.W., Robertson, G.G.: Architecture and applications of the connection machine. IEEE Comput. **21**(8), 26–38 (1988)
5. Shor, P.W.: Algorithms for quantum computation: discrete logarithms and factoring. In: Proceedings 35th Annual Symposium on Foundations of Computer Science, pp. 124–134. IEEE Comput. Soc. Press (1994). https://doi.org/10.1109/sfcs.1994.365700
6. Smith, R.S., Curtis, M.J., Zeng, W.J.: A practical quantum instruction set architecture. arXiv preprint arXiv:1608.03355 (2016)
7. Cross, A.W., Bishop, L.S., Smolin, J.A., Gambetta, J.M.: Open quantum assembly language. arXiv preprint arXiv:1707.03429 (13 July 2017)
8. Khammassi, N., Guerreschi, G.G., Ashraf, I., Hogaboam, J.W., Almudever, C.G., Bertels, K.: cqasm v1. 0: Towards a common quantum assembly language. arXiv preprint arXiv:1805.09607 (2018)
9. Wille, R., Van Meter, R., Naveh, Y.: IBM's Qiskit tool chain: working with and developing for real quantum computers. In: Design, Automation & Test in Europe Conference & Exhibition (DATE), pp. 1234–1240. Florence, Italy (2019)
10. Svore, K.M., et al.: Q#: Enabling scalable quantum computing and development with a high-level domain-specific language. arXiv preprint arXiv:1803.00652 (2018)

Performance Analysis

Enhancing the Top-Down Microarchitectural Analysis Method Using Purchasing Power Parity Theory

Yectli A. Huerta[1,2]([⊠]), Brent Swartz[3], and David J. Lilja[2]

[1] Scientific Computation, Minnesota Supercomputing Institute, Minneapolis, USA
[2] Department of Electrical and Computer Engineering, University of Minnesota, Minneapolis, USA
yhuerta@umn.edu
[3] Minneapolis, USA

Abstract. The Top-Down method makes it possible to identify bottlenecks as instructions traverse the CPU's pipeline. Once bottlenecks are identified, incremental changes to the code can be made to mitigate the negative effects bottlenecks might have in performance. This is an iterative process that could potentially result in a more optimal use of CPU resources. It can be difficult to compare bottleneck metrics of the same program generated by different compilers running on the same system. Different compilers could potentially generate different instructions, arrange the instructions in different order, and require different number of cycles to execute the program. Ratios with relatively similar values could hide valuable information that could be used to identify differences in magnitude and influence of bottlenecks. To amplify magnitude differences of bottleneck metrics, we use the cycles required to complete the program as a reference point. We can then quantify the relative difference the effect a bottleneck has when compared with the bottleneck of the reference compiler. This study's proposed approach is based on the Purchasing Power Parity theory, which is used by economists to compare the purchasing power of different currencies by comparing similar products. We show that this approach can give us more information on how effective each compiler is in using the CPU's architectural features by comparing their respective bottlenecks. For example, using conventional methods, our measurements show that for the *363.swim* benchmark, BackEnd Bound rates for GCC4 was 0.949, and 0.956 for GCC6 and GCC7 respectively. However, using the PPP normalization approach, we showed that there were differences of 55.3% for GCC6 and 54.9% for GCC7 over GCC4.

1 Introduction

Parallel programming frameworks, such as OpenMP, have made it possible to use highly complex computational resources efficiently. But compilers and programming frameworks have a wide variety of features and options that can make

---

B. Swartz—Independent Researcher.

B. Chapman and J. Moreira (Eds.): LCPC 2020, LNCS 13149, pp. 163–177, 2022.
https://doi.org/10.1007/978-3-030-95953-1_12

it challenging to obtain optimal performance without some significant effort. It
is essential to have analysis tools and techniques that can provide users with precise and detailed information on the compiler's performance to assess whether
or not the generated code uses all of the architectural features of the CPU efficiently, as measured in overall runtime. The user could select different compiler
flags, modify the code, or select a different compiler version that might further
enhance performance. When designing compilers, developers are interested in
in-depth profiling to quantify the impact of new features on performance.

Performance analysis can be a challenging and time-consuming endeavor.
Modern CPUs have complex microarchitectures that improve overall code performance. The use of deep pipelines, buffers and prefetchers makes it possible
to hide and mitigate stalls – delays in the processing of an operation. Stalls can
occur when an operation has to wait for needed resources to become available
before it can be completed. This microarchitectural complexity makes it difficult to analyze bottlenecks – portions of the code where stalls occur, and that
should be examined for a possible change to improve performance, once they are
properly identified, and their effects quantified. Features that minimize stalls
and improve overall performance will tend to make it difficult to pinpoint such
bottlenecks by hiding latencies. For example, a CPU will reduce its data retrieval
time by guessing which data value an instruction will need next, or by storing
frequently used instructions or memory contents in its caches.

To better understand the behavior of the CPU, computer chip manufacturers
include performance counter units in their CPUs to track hardware and software
events. Performance counters will keep track of the number of times a particular
event occurs for a user-defined sampling interval. These events include cache-
misses, cycles, page-faults, and branches. Kernel tools like *perf* [7] will interact
with the performance counters and report the results. These reports can provide
useful information on how the program behave on the CPU as it was executed,
e.g., how a component is being efficiently utilized.

Performance analysis is an iterative process. Users will profile the code to
get baseline bottleneck metric values. Based on those values, the user will then
make appropriate changes to the code, environment, or compiler flag to reduce
the effect of the bottleneck. Then the code will be recompiled, executed, and
profiled again. The goal is to understand the effects the change had on performance and how it is reflected in CPU bottlenecks. Further, the goal is to
identify and mitigate bottlenecks to improve performance. Bottleneck identification and quantification of their effects are crucial in this optimization process. In
this paper, we extend current analysis techniques to compare and quantify how
different compilers use CPU features. Our goal is to improve the performance
analysis process by making it easier to compare different compilers.

This study shows the following:

– For many programs, newer versions of GNU compilers [2] will not always
  entail better performance.
– Current analysis techniques show and quantify the difference in reported bottlenecks between programs generated by the same compiler. Our study shows

that these bottleneck comparisons, across programs generated by different compilers, can differ greatly, and this variation is not captured using the regular technique.

- The PPP normalization technique can be used to better compare bottlenecks across multiple compiler versions using a specific compiler as a reference. In our study, we use GCC4 compiled programs to compare the magnitude of bottleneck changes across different compiler versions.
- PPP normalized rates make it easy to make bottleneck comparisons show trends and highlight differences.

2   Background

2.1   The Top-Down Method

When optimizing a program, a developer will make changes to the program or compiler options until the desired performance gains are made, or there are no longer resources to continue the process. This technique, called differential analysis [16], can be combined with a systematic approach to bottleneck iden-tification, called the Top-Down method [19]. The Top-Down method focuses on accounting for the use of pipeline resources, making it possible to highlight micro-architectural components that generate stalls, and narrow down the list of possible components, accounting for the most stalls. This iterative Top-Down method is used by the Intel VTune profiler suite [4] and has been used to analyze different systems [11, 20, 21].

The Top-Down method divides the instruction pipeline into two parts: the Front End and the Back End. The Front End is the portion of the pipeline where instructions are fetched, decoded into *uops* – low-level instructions – and then queued to wait their turn to be executed by the Back End. The Back End will schedule *uops* for execution, for example, integer store/load or floating-point operations. The results will then be committed or retired.

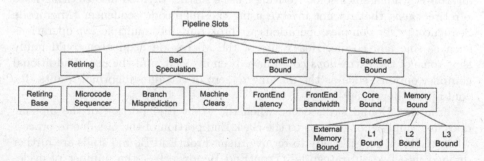

Fig. 1. Top-Down hierarchy breakdown used in this study. Retiring, Bad Speculation, FrontEnd Bound and BackEnd Bound are the main categories used to classify pipeline slots. Subsequent subcategories give more granular information on specific architectural components.

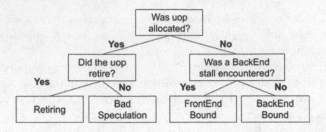

Fig. 2. Top-Down *uop* classification tree.

The Top-Down method has four categories to track the progress of *uops* as they traverse the pipeline. The categories are FrontEnd Bound, BackEnd Bound, Bad Speculation, and Retiring. Figure 1 shows the Top-Down classification hierarchy used in this study. The category assignment occurs as follows – if a *uop* is allocated, then it will be either retired or not retired. If it is retired, it will be assigned to the Retiring classification. If it is not retired, it will be classified as Bad Speculation. Retiring and Bad Speculation account for non-stalled slots. If the *uop* is not allocated, then there are two choices, if there is a Back End stall, then it will be classified as BackEnd Bound. If it is not a Back End stall, then it will be classified as FrontEnd Bound. Figure 2 shows the decision tree used in *uop* classifications.

The BackEnd Bound stalls occur when *uops* are not delivered to the execution pipeline due to lack of resources at the Back End. This could be due to a data-cache miss or a stall due to lack of execution resources. BackEnd Bound stalls are divided into Memory Bound stalls – stalls related to the memory subsystem and Core Bound stalls – all other BackEnd Bound stalls. L1 Bound, L2 Bound, L3 Bound, and External Memory are stalls when accessing data already present in the specific memory subsystem.

The Retiring category focuses on the last stage of the pipeline in which the *uops* are completed and retired. Ideally, this should be the largest category of all Top-Down classifications. Retiring can be further divided into Retiring Base – retired *uops* that do not involve using the microcode sequencer (Microcode Sequencer) when complex operations are broken up into multiple *uop* operations such as sine and cosine. Heavy use of the Microcode Sequencer could imply that some of the extra *uops* could have been avoided, and the use of additional compiler options, such as the flushing to zero of certain subnormal results -*ftz*, could prove beneficial [5].

FrontEnd Bound stalls occur when the Front End portion of the pipeline does not supply enough *uops* to the Back End portion of the pipeline to process when the Back End is ready to receive them. FrontEnd Bound stalls are further divided into two subcategories, FrontEnd Bandwidth – the number of cycles when the number of *uops* is less than the maximum allowable of 4 and FrontEnd Latency – the number of cycles when no *uops* were issued to the available Back End.

The Bad Speculation category involves wasted pipeline resources with operations that are not useful. There might be *uops* that were issued speculatively and will never be retired, thus wasting pipeline slots, or stalls that occur when the pipeline recovers from an earlier misspeculation. The subcategories that make up Bad Speculation are Branch Mispredicts and Machine Clears. The Branch Mispredictions category is used when a bad speculated branch takes place, while *uops* are classified as Machine Clears when the pipeline is flushed to recover from a misspeculation.

Table 1. Results of tuning matrix-multiply case [19].

Metric	multiply1	multiply2	multiply3
Speedup	1.0x	11.8x	16.5x
IPC	0.17	1.19	0.80
Frontend Bound	0.00	0.07	0.02
Retiring	0.05	0.41	0.28
Bad Speculation	0.00	0.00	0.00
Backend Bound	0.95	0.52	0.70
Memory Bound	0.84	0.12	0.31
L1 Bound	0.05	0.07	0.03
L2 Bound	0.03	–	0.05
L3 Bound	0.05	–	0.01
Stores Bound	–	–	–
Core Bound	0.15	0.64	0.55
Divider	–	–	–
Ports Utiliz	0.15	0.64	0.55

Table 1 shows the analysis of a matrix multiplication example. The formulas needed to compute the different Top-Down metrics are given in [8,19]. The first step, *multiply1*, is a simple matrix multiplication that is Memory Bound. The use of loop interchange optimization in the second step, *multiply2*, achieves a significant performance gain by shifting the bottleneck from Memory Bound to Compute Bound. Loop interchange takes advantage of locality through better use of memory access patterns. In the last step, *multiply3* uses vectorization to further improve performance by reducing the use of port utilization [19]. These optimization examples show that different bottlenecks can be identified, and their effects mitigated in order to obtain performance enhancements. The incremental changes between versions of the program generated by the same compiler is manageable. Code changes will potentially affect the specific bottleneck in question and their effects potentially mitigated with each change.

Comparisons between programs generated by different compilers or compiler versions are more difficult. Each compiler could generate different instructions, and the number of cycles required to complete those instructions could vary widely for the same program, resulting in widely different bottlenecks. To make it easier to compare and analyze programs generated by different compilers, we propose the use of the Purchasing Power Parity (PPP) economic theory. PPP will be used to normalize Top-Down metrics with respect to a single compiler, GCC4, to be able to better compare metrics generated by different compilers. We describe this approach in the next subsection.

2.2 Purchasing Power Parity

PPP states that *the exchange rate is proportional to the ratio of price levels in two countries.* [13]. Essentially, it allows for the comparison of the same good in different countries to see if a country's currency is overvalued (when the good is more expensive), or undervalued (when the good is cheaper) relative to another currency [6]. The Big Mac Index [1] is the most famous application of the PPP theory, and it compares the value of Big Mac burgers across many countries. Equations 1 and 2 show an example of how to compute the Big Mac Index. Assume that the cost of a Big Mac in the US is \$3.57. The same burger costs 7.50 reales in Brazil. The PPP exchange rate is shown in Eq. 1, which is 2.10. The currency exchange rate at that time was of 1.58 reales for \$1. In Eq. 2, we compute the Big Mac Index by subtracting 1.58 from the PPP exchange rate and then dividing by 1.58. According to the index, the real is overvalued almost 33% as compared to the US dollar [13].

$$7.50/3.57 = 2.10 \tag{1}$$

$$(2.10 - 1.58) * 100/1.58 = 32.91\% \tag{2}$$

In our study, the products we compare are benchmarks, and the currency that we are comparing are the cycles that it took to complete those benchmarks. PPP theory allows us to compare different compiler generated Top-Down metrics to determine if the metrics are undervalued or overvalued relative to the same metrics generated by the GCC4 compiler. An undervalued metric signifies that a bottleneck has a relatively lesser effect when compared with the baseline GCC4 metric. Overvalued metrics translate into bottlenecks that have a relatively greater effect than the baseline. We compute the PPP exchange rate, Eq. 3, by dividing the *cpu_clk_unhalted.thread* event value of a given compiler by the same performance event value that was collected when the same benchmark ran with a binary generated with the GCC4 compiler. We use *cpu_clk_unhalted.thread* for all computed metrics, except for the FrontEnd Bandwidth metric. This metric uses the *cpu_clk_unhalted.thread_any* performance event, which is also used to calculate its corresponding metric PPP exchange rate. Our choice of *cpu_clk_unhalted.thread* and *cpu_clk_unhalted.thread_any* as normalization metrics is because they account for cycles when the thread is not in a halt state [3], as oppose to using execution time, which is a less granular metric.

$$PPP\_Exchange\_Rate = CPU\_clk/CPU\_clk_{gcc4} \tag{3}$$

The Metric variable represents all of the Top-Down Method categories described earlier. As Eq. 2 shows, we divide a Metric by its GCC4 generated counterpart before using the PPP_Exchange_Rate variable to compute the PPP normalized percentage.

$$PPP = 100 * ((Metric/Metric_{gcc4}) - PPP\_Exchange\_Rate)/PPP\_Exchange\_Rate \tag{4}$$

For a metric to be overvalued, the metric rate, $Metric/Metric_{gcc4}$, needs to be positive and bigger than $PPP\_Exchange\_Rate$. This occurs when the GCC4 baseline metric is smaller than the number of events of the other compiler. Undervalued metrics occur when the metric rate has a smaller magnitude than the $PPP\_Exchange\_Rate$. We have parity when the PPP normalized rate is zero or very close to zero.

Equations 5 and 6 show an example of the PPP normalization index for the 350.md benchmark for GCC6 using GCC4 as the baseline. The PPP exchange rate is 0.92. The Bad Speculation metric values are 0.0204 for GCC6, and 0.0206 for GCC4. In this, case we see that there is a 7.64% relative increase of Bad Speculation for GCC6 over GCC4. The metric is overvalued.

$$270956056194992/294654034404202 = 0.92 \tag{5}$$

$$((0.0204/0.0206) - 0.92) * 100/0.92 = 7.64\% \tag{6}$$

3 Experimental Setup

In this study, we use the Top-Down method in combination with the SPEC OMP2012 benchmarks [9,17] to evaluate versions 4.8.5, 6.3.1, and 7.3.1 of the C, C++, and Fortran GCC compiler suite. It is a freely available and widely used suite of compilers that can run in multiple platforms and operating systems. All benchmarks were compiled using the following flags: *-fopenmp -O3 -march=native*. The only exception was *371.applu331*, which used these flags: *-fopenmp -O2 -march=native*. Additionally, *-ffree-form -fno-range-check* were used for *350.md* and *-std=c99* for *367.imagick*. The SPEC OMP2012 benchmarks include a wide variety of commonly used computational kernels written in Fortran, C, and C++. These kernels make it possible to stress different system components, including CPU, memory, and parallel support libraries, making possible to highlight how each compiler handles bottlenecks. The OMP2012 benchmark suite is widely used to compare HPC systems using OpenMP applications. Benchmarks results that meet the SPEC group reporting guidelines are published for comparison in a public repository where different systems with a variety of designs and compilers can be compared [10].

A two socket Intel(R) Xeon(R) Silver 4110 CPU @ 2.10GHz with 8 cores per socket, 2 threads per core was used running the CentOS 7.6.1810 Linux operating system installed. Figure 3 was generated using the walltime reported by the

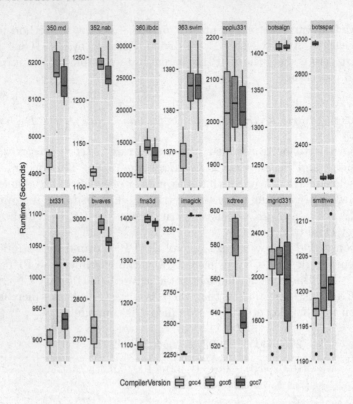

Fig. 3. Runtimes for SPEC OMP2012 benchmarks using 32 threads with SMT enabled. Lower is better.

SPEC framework and includes the results for the 14 SPEC OMP2012 benchmarks. Figures 4, 5, and 6 were generated using *perf* and include 6 additional programs to the original total of 14. These programs were included because the *367.imagick* benchmark is made up of a process that involves 6 different steps, *convert11, convert2, convert9, vall11, val2,* and *val9. 372.smithwa* has a two step process, *refset1* and *refset2*.

4   Results and Analysis

Table 2 gives the description of the 14 benchmarks that make up the SPEC OMP2012 suite. Figure 3 shows that for many of the benchmarks, runtimes can vary significantly depending on the choice of compiler. On average, eight of the benchmarks, 350.md, 352.nab, botsalgn, 360.ilbdc, bt331, bwaves, fma3d, and imagick, perform better when using the GCC4 compiler. While benchmark runtimes might differ, their respective Top-Down metrics might be relatively similar for 360.ilbdc, 350.md, and bt331, Figs. 4(a), 5(a) and 6(a). Our goal is to show that Top-Down metrics, even when they have similar values, can diverge

Table 2. SPEC OMP2012 benchmark description [9]

Benchmark Name	Programming Language	Description
350.md	Fortran	Physics: Molecular Dynamics
351.bwaves	Fortran	Physics: Computational Fluid Dynamics (CFD)
352.nab	C	Molecular Modeling
357.bt331	Fortran	Physics: Computational Fluid Dynamics (CFD)
358.botsalgn	C	Protein Alignment
359.botsspar	C	Sparse LU
360.ilbdc	Fortran	Lattic Boltzmann
362.fma3d	Fortran	Mechanical Response Simulation
363.swim	Fortran	Weather Prediction
367.imagick	C	Image Processing
370.mgrid331	Fortran	Physics: Computational Fluid Dynamics (CFD)
371.applu331	Fortran	Physics: Computational Fluid Dynamics (CFD)
372.smithwa	C	Optimal Pattern Matching
376.kdtree	C++	Sorting and Searching

in magnitude when normalized with a reference compiler. Using Eqs. 3 and 4, we computed the PPP normalized metrics using the benchmark results from the three different compilers using the performance metrics results collected via *perf*. The results are shown in Figs. 4(b), 5(b) and 6(b). These plots can give us better information of how stalls, BackEnd and FrontEnd Bound categories, and non-stalls, Retiring and Bad Speculation categories, are overvalued, undervalued or have bottleneck parity for each compiler. In the following subsections, we show how these results allow us to extract important insights about the relative magnitude difference of bottlenecks between compilers.

– **Overvalued bottlenecks:** The refset1 and refset2 programs are an example of how PPP normalized values can give us a better picture of the magnitude of bottleneck differences when different versions of compilers are used. refset1 has a Bad Speculation rate of 0.000474 for GCC4, 0.000624 for GCC6 and 0.0307 for GCC7. If we take the ratio of GCC7 and GCC4, we get 64.77 and the ratio of GCC6 and GCC4 is 1.316. To compute the PPP normalized rate, we need to use the PPP exchange rates of 0.994 for GCC6 and 0.884 for GCC7, which yield a PPP normalized rate of 32.5% for GCC6 and 7222% for GCC7. The normalization value, by taking into account the cycles it took to complete the program, shows the effectiveness of the cycles used by the

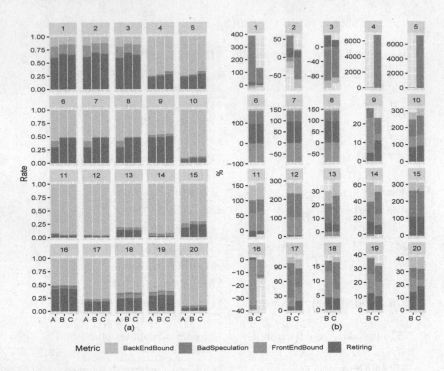

Fig. 4. Top-Down method categories for SPEC OMP2012 benchmarks: 1. val9, 2. val2, 3. val11, 4. refset2, 5. refset1, 6. convert9, 7. convert2, 8. convert11, 9. 376.kdtree, 10. 371.applu331, 11. 370.mgrid331, 12. 363.swim, 13. 362.fma3d, 14. 360.ilbdc, 15. 359.botsspar, 16. 358.botsalgn, 17. 357.bt331, 18. 352.nab, 19. 351.bwaves, 20. 350.md using compilers: A. GCC4, B. GCC6, C. GCC7. (a) is the regular metric. (b) is the PPP normalized metric.

GCC6 and GCC7 generated binaries. In the context of Bad Speculation, GCC7 is massively overvalued – the bottleneck cost in terms of cycles is higher relative to the cycle cost when using GCC4 binaries, and GCC6 is relatively overvalued when compared to the GCC4.

- **Undervalued bottlenecks:** Undervalued rates occur when the reference compiler underperforms the other compilers in a given bottleneck metric. As a result, a bottleneck will take more GCC4 cycles than the number of cycles it takes when using a different compiler. In the case of the 358.botsalgn benchmark, we have FrontEnd Bound rates of 0.0206 for GCC4, 0.0133 for GCC6 and 0.0183 for GCC7, Fig. 4(a). The PPP exchange rates are 1.01 for both GCC6 and GCC7. The resulting PPP normalized FrontEnd Bound rates are −35.5% for GCC6 and −11.7% for GCC7, Fig. 4(b). For the given number of cycles, the GCC6 FrontEnd Bound bottlenecks are not as significant as compared to GCC4 and GCC7.
- **Similar bottleneck rates:** There are instances when compilers have similar Top-Down rates and their PPP normalized rates will be similar due to the PPP exchange rate. The 371.applu331 benchmark has GCC4 FrontEnd

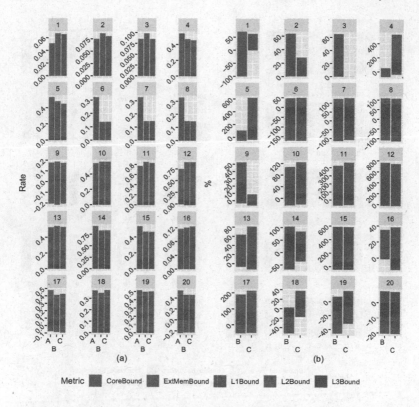

Metric ■ CoreBound ■ ExtMemBound ■ L1Bound ■ L2Bound ■ L3Bound

Fig. 5. BackEnd Bound subcategories, Core Bound and Memory Bound (ExtMem-Bound, L1Bound, L2Bound and L3Bound) for SPEC OMP2012 benchmarks: 1. val9, 2. val2, 3. val11, 4. refset2, 5. refset1, 6. convert9, 7. convert2, 8. convert11, 9. 376.kdtree, 10. 371.applu331, 11. 370.mgrid331, 12. 363.swim, 13. 362.fma3d, 14. 360.ilbdc, 15. 359.botsspar, 16. 358.botsalgn, 17. 357.bt331, 18. 352.nab, 19. 351.bwaves, 20. 350.md using compilers: A. GCC4, B. GCC6, C. GCC7. (a) is the regular metric. (b) is the PPP normalized metric.

Bound rate of 0.0188, a GCC6 FrontEnd Bound rate of 0.0211 and a GCC7 FrontEnd Rate of 0.0210, Fig. 4(a). The PPP exchange rate for GCC6 is 0.697 and 0.685 for GCC7. The resulting normalized PPP FrontEnd Bound rates for GCC6 and GCC7 are 61.5 and 63.6, Fig. 4(b). GCC6 and GCC7 are overvalued for the FrontEnd Bound category as compared to GCC4 for the 371.applu331 benchmark.

– **Similar PPP rates:** Figure 5(a) shows that for 359.botsspar, GCC6 and GCC7 have similar BackEnd Bound rates. Figure 5(b) shows that the PPP rates are nearly identical. The CoreBound subcategory is over 400% greater than GCC4, while the External Memory and L3 Bound subcategories add up close to an additional 200% difference. We can conclude that for 359.botsspar, GCC6 and GCC7 are both significantly more BackEnd Bound than GCC4 at a relatively identical rate.

174   Y. A. Huerta et al.

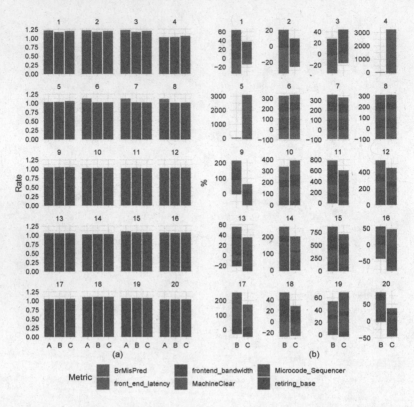

(a)   (b)

Metric
BrMisPred   frontend_bandwidth   Microcode_Sequencer
front_end_latency   MachineClear   retiring_base

Fig. 6. FrontEnd Bound (front_end_latency, frontend_bandwidth), Retiring (retiring_base, Microcode_Sequencer) and Bad Speculation (BrMisPred, MachineClear) subcategories for SPEC OMP2012 benchmarks: 1. val9, 2. val2, 3. val11, 4. refset2, 5. refset1, 6. convert9, 7. convert2, 8. convert11, 9. 376.kdtree, 10. 371.applu331, 11. 370.mgrid331, 12. 363.swim, 13. 362.fma3d, 14. 360.ilbdc, 15. 359.botsspar, 16. 358.botsalgn, 17. 357.bt331, 18. 352.nab, 19. 351.bwaves, 20. 350.md using compilers: A. GCC4, B. GCC6, C. GCC7. (a) is the regular metric. (b) is the PPP normalized metric.

- **PPP parity (PPP rates that equal zero):** We have seen that there have been instances where the non-normalized Top-Down rates are equal, but the PPP normalized metrics showed that there was a relative difference between bottlenecks. There are cases when the metrics are equal and the PPP normalized values are zero, or close to it. In those cases, we can conclude that there is relatively little to no difference between the GCC4 baseline metric and the other compiler generated metric. The magnitude of the bottleneck effect is similar for both compilers. For example, in Fig. 5(a), there is little difference between GCC4 and GCC7 for val11. Figure 5(b) shows that the resulting PPP column for GCC7 is empty. We can conclude that the BackEnd Bound subcategories are relatively equal for GCC4 and GCC7 while there is a difference between GCC4 and GCC6 in the Core and L1 Bound subcategories of over 60%.

5   Related Works

The Top-Down method introduced a hierarchical classification that uses a number of performance counters to identify bottlenecks as instructions traverse the instructional pipeline. VTune is a tool that uses the Top-Down to identify portions of the code that generate bottlenecks with the biggest negative effect. Table 1 shows an example of the iterative process to identify and mitigate bottlenecks.

The Metric-Guided Method (MGM) [15] extends the Top-Down method. In addition to the regular Top-Down bottleneck metrics, it employs additional performance metrics such as IPC and IPFLOPs to identify, via multiple iterations, changes in metrics. Once a set of metrics is identified, a specially designed microbenchmark kernel is created to further examine the drift in the metrics with the goal of identifying the causes for the changes. The process ends when enough data is collected that explains the performance drifts captured by the metrics.

Top-Down based analysis techniques can identify bottlenecks and provide information on the magnitude of the bottleneck. In combination with differential analysis, bottlenecks could potentially be mitigated with each iteration. The limitation is, Top-Down methodology does not give information on the magnitude of the change with each iteration. Knowing the relative differences between iterations can shed important information. For instance, whether or not a change made the program more core bound or more memory bound and by how much. As Figs. 4, 5 and 6 showed, there are instances in which bottleneck metrics had similar magnitudes but PPP normalized rates showed high relative differences in rate magnitude. This translates in bottlenecks having larger or smaller effects in the system.

There are other approaches to bottleneck identification. An analysis of a 64-bit ARMv8 system [15] involved the use of Partial Least Squares (PLS) Path Modeling [14] to identify and compare bottlenecks with other x86 and x86_64 based systems. Computational resources and subsystems were identified. All available performance counters were collected and a subset was selected based on their correlation with others, in order to minimize the number of counters to be analyzed. The selected counters were associated with corresponding architectural resources of interest. PLS Path Model analysis, in combination with Bootstrapping, assigned coefficients to each of the architectural features, making it possible to identify the significance of these features. The approach taken in this study will make it difficult to quantify relative differences among bottlenecks. This approach creates a statistical model with regression coefficients. The path coefficient is not a value of the magnitude of the bottleneck effect on the system, as it is the case in Top-Down metrics.

The roofline model [18] is used to visually identify performance bottlenecks. The model was extended to include non-throughput resource related bottlenecks such as cache capacity [12]. The extended model uses Directed Acyclic Graphs (DAG) to abstract microarchitectural features. Nodes represent operations and edges represent data dependencies. Work is defined by the number of nodes in the DAG. LLVM intermediate representation (IR), a representation of computation or memory operations, will generate instructions that will become DAG nodes. The LLVM interpreter will use the IR to generate the schedule of the DAG nodes. The resulting scheduled DAG is used to compute bottleneck and performance estimates. The issue with high level abstractions is that they reduce the accuracy. They are focused on high level code simulations that are common to many computer platforms. Bottleneck analysis based on Top-Down methods is accurate because bottleneck metrics are computed using CPU specific performance counters. This makes it possible to compute relative magnitude changes in bottleneck metrics when changes are made to the code or a different compiler is used.

6   Conclusion

In this study, we proposed the use of normalized Top-Down bottleneck metrics using the *purchasing power parity* theory to quantify the relative difference in bottleneck metrics for different compilers, GCC4, GCC6 and GCC7. PPP based indexes have been used to track the purchasing power of many currencies by comparing specific goods. The widely known Big Mac Index is an example of a PPP metric where local prices of Big Macs from different countries are compared against US priced Big Macs. The aim is to use the US dollar as the baseline for currency comparisons. The Big Mac Index makes it possible to determine if currencies are undervalued or overvalued when compared to the purchasing power of the US dollar.

We take a similar approach by determining if bottlenecks have a relatively greater or lesser effect on performance when comparing different compilers versions using cycles as the common currency. Our method uses Top-Down bottleneck metrics of benchmark programs as the *good* that is to be compared across different versions of compilers. We use cycles as the currency for the comparison. Each compiler version has the potential of generating bottlenecks of varying magnitude for the same program. Each of these versions could potentially require a different number of cycles to run the program to completion. Our goal is to use bottleneck metrics obtained from GCC4 compiler binaries as a baseline to normalize other bottleneck metrics generated by other compilers. This normalization makes it possible to quantify relative increases or decreases in magnitude of bottlenecks when compared to the baseline compiler.

Our goal was to provide a simple technique to compare complex systems, and we found PPP normalization is a suitable technique that can accomplish this task. Our approach makes it possible for computer architects and compiler developers to track the drift of bottlenecks by easily identifying trends, and magnify differences that otherwise would go unnoticed. Quantification of the bottleneck drift makes it possible to assess the effects changes to programs or compilers have in the effective use of CPU architectural features.

References

1. The big mac index. https://www.economist.com/news/2020/01/15/the-big-mac-index
2. The gnu compiler collection website. http://gcc.gnu.org
3. Intel microarchitecture code named skylake events. https://download.01.org/perfmon/index/skylake.html
4. Intel vtune profiler. https://software.intel.com/content/www/us/en/develop/tools/vtune-profiler.html
5. Intel vtune profiler performance analysis cookbook. https://software.intel.com/content/www/us/en/develop/documentation/vtune-cookbook/top.html
6. The latte index: Using the impartial bean to value currencies. https://www.visualcapitalist.com/latte-index-currencies/
7. perf: Linux profiling with performance counters. http://perf.wiki.kernel.org
8. pmu-tools: Intel pmu profiling tools. https://github.com/andikleen/pmu-tools
9. Spec omp2012 documentation. https://spec.org/omp2012/Docs/index.html
10. Spec omp2012 results. https://www.spec.org/omp2012/results/
11. Ayers, G., Ahn, J.H., Kozyrakis, C., Ranganathan, P.: Memory hierarchy for web search. In: 2018 IEEE International Symposium on High Performance Computer Architecture (HPCA), pp. 643–656 (2018)
12. Cabezas, V.C., Püschel, M.: Extending the roofline model: bottleneck analysis with microarchitectural constraints. In: 2014 IEEE International Symposium on Workload Characterization (IISWC). pp. 222–231 (2014)
13. Clements, K.: Currencies, Commodities and Consumption. Cambridge University Press, Cambridge (2013)
14. Jöreskog, K., Wold, H.: Systems under indirect observation: causality, structure, prediction. No. no. 139, pt. 2 in Contributions to Economic Analysis, North-Holland (1982)
15. Laurenzano, M.A., Tiwari, A., Cauble-Chantrenne, A., Jundt, A., Ward, W.A., Campbell, R., Carrington, L.: Characterization and bottleneck analysis of a 64-bit armv8 platform. In: 2016 IEEE International Symposium on Performance Analysis of Systems and Software (ISPASS), pp. 36–45 (2016)
16. McKenney, P.E.: Differential profiling. In: MASCOTS 1995. Proceedings of the Third International Workshop on Modeling, Analysis, and Simulation of Computer and Telecommunication Systems, pp. 237–241 (1995)
17. Müller, M.S., et al.: SPEC OMP2012 — an application benchmark suite for parallel systems using OpenMP. In: Chapman, B.M., Massaioli, F., Müller, M.S., Rorro, M. (eds.) IWOMP 2012. LNCS, vol. 7312, pp. 223–236. Springer, Heidelberg (2012). https://doi.org/10.1007/978-3-642-30961-8_17
18. Williams, S., Waterman, A., Patterson, D.: Roofline: an insightful visual performance model for multicore architectures. Commun. ACM 52(4), 65–76 (2009)
19. Yasin, A.: A top-down method for performance analysis and counters architecture. In: 2014 IEEE International Symposium on Performance Analysis of Systems and Software (ISPASS), pp. 35–44 (2014)
20. Yasin, A., Ben-Asher, Y., Mendelson, A.: Deep-dive analysis of the data analytics workload in cloudsuite. In: 2014 IEEE International Symposium on Workload Characterization (IISWC), pp. 202–211 (2014)
21. Yasin, A., Haj-Yahya, J., Ben-Asher, Y., Mendelson, A.: A metric-guided method for discovering impactful features and architectural insights for skylake-based processors. ACM Trans. Archit. Code Optim. 16(4) (2019). https://doi.org/10.1145/3369383

Code Generation

Cain: Automatic Code Generation for Simultaneous Convolutional Kernels on Focal-plane Sensor-processors

Edward Stow[1]([✉]), Riku Murai[1], Sajad Saeedi[2], and Paul H. J. Kelly[1]

[1] Department of Computing, Imperial College London, 180 Queens Gate,
London SW7 2AZ, UK
{edward.stow16,riku.murai15,p.kelly}@imperial.ac.uk
[2] Department of Mechanical and Industrial Engineering, Ryerson University,
350 Victoria Street, Toronto, ON M5B 2K3, Canada
s.saeedi@ryerson.ca

Abstract. Focal-plane Sensor-processors (FPSPs) are a camera technology that enable low power, high frame rate computation, making them suitable for edge computation. Unfortunately, these devices' limited instruction sets and registers make developing complex algorithms difficult. In this work, we present Cain, an open-source compiler that targets SCAMP-5, a general-purpose FPSP – which generates code from multiple convolutional kernels. As an example, given the convolutional kernels for an MNIST digit recognition neural network, Cain produces code that is half as long, when compared to the other available compilers for SCAMP-5.

Keywords: Convolution · SIMD · Image sensor · Analogue computing · Edge inference

1 Introduction

Real-time computer vision applications are currently bound to traditional camera sensors that transfer each pixel at each frame to a host where it is processed. This requires high-performance buses between the sensors and hosts, especially where high frame-rates are required. A self-driving car may need to receive new information for every 1 cm travelled to be vigilant of unexpected scenarios, so at 80 km/hr a frame rate 2222 Hz would be required. A 2 mega-pixel camera, with 10-bit pixel depth, running at such a frame rate, requires a bus capable of 45.6 Gbit/s—which is currently only possible with devices such as a PCI-e x8 Gen3 interface [21]. For many applications, however, streaming data at such volumes is too demanding – both in power and computation time – hence requiring an alternative solution.

Codesign of hardware and software for computer vision applications is an emerging research field to address the limitations of conventional systems [17].

© Springer Nature Switzerland AG 2022
B. Chapman and J. Moreira (Eds.): LCPC 2020, LNCS 13149, pp. 181–197, 2022.
https://doi.org/10.1007/978-3-030-95953-1_13

Focal-plane Sensor-processors (FPSPs) are a promising avenue for reducing the data transfer between the camera and the processing unit. FPSPs, often synonymous with Cellular Processor Arrays (CPAs) and Pixel Processor Arrays (PPAs), perform processing on the sensor chip itself and are often designed for tasks which require high frame rates or low latency [22]. The principle behind them is that a small processor is embedded directly with each pixel of the sensor. While FPSPs come in various forms for specific applications, we in this paper we explore a general-purpose fine-grain architecture SCAMP-5 [5], but one can imagine alternatives that could be designed for various use cases.

One of the most widely used methods for image analysis is convolution kernels. From edge detection using Sobel filters to document recognition using Convolutional Neural Networks [13], convolutional kernels are the foundation for many complex computer vision applications. Traditionally, application of the convolutional kernels to the image data occurs on a CPU, but more recently GPUs and FPGAs are used to accelerate the computations in parallel [1,9]. Several systems have been designed to optimise the processing of convolutional kernels on GPUs and FPGAs, leading to a vast array of techniques to reduce the number of operational cycles needed to apply kernels to input data. While this significantly increased throughput, these methods are still bounded in latency as the image must make its way from the camera through to the host system. As for FPSPs, the ability to process the data on the focal plane enables the kernels to be applied to the image data at very low latency. Furthermore, the unique ability to select the data which is transferred from the device to the host reduces the data volume, which allows for high frame rates. However, the technology is comparatively new. By design, they offer novel ways to interact with the data, and while work has been done to provide a Domain-Specific-Language and associated tools to program such hardware [14], there has been less work done so far to produce code generation systems to make efficient use of their architectural features when applying convolutional kernels in particular.

One such system that does exist, however, is AUKE [11]. Given an $N \times N$ convolutional kernel, AUKE's reverse-split algorithm generates code for SCAMP-5 which applies the kernel efficiently to the captured image on the focal-plane using analogue computation. AUKE is, however, limited to compiling just a single convolutional kernel at a time using a reduced instruction set that omits the more powerful instructions available in SCAMP-5.

In this work, we present an improved alternative to AUKE, with the ability to produce code for applying multiple convolutional kernels at a time. The problem is presented as a dynamic graph search problem in which we must efficiently generate and traverse possible processor states to find a path that describes the relevant convolutional computation. By incorporating instruction selection and instruction scheduling into the core of search process, we enable the use of more novel features of CPA architectures than AUKE is able to use. By optimising the code for multiple kernels simultaneously, common sub-expressions between kernels can be exploited and produced only once rather than for each kernel. This reduces the computational expense of applying the kernels, enabling applications to run at a faster frame rate.

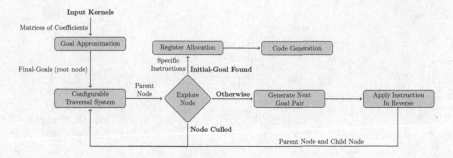

Fig. 1. Cain system overview.

The primary objective of this work is to push the boundary of code generation for FPSP devices through simultaneous kernel optimisation. We offer the following contributions:

- Cain: A code generation algorithm which effectively makes use of common sub-expressions across filters consisting of multiple convolutional kernels. Our graph search strategy – which enables Cain to efficiently search large graphs – combines instruction scheduling, instruction selection and register-allocation constraints into the core of the search to make better use of specific hardware capabilities in SIMD processors.
- We show how this search can be tractable for problems of interest through a problem formulation based on AUKE's multi-set-of-Atoms problem representation, combined with a ranking heuristic and a hybrid graph-generator–graph-search exploration strategy.
- We show how this approach allows flexible exploitation of hardware capabilities (such as three-operand adds and multi-step shifts), and generates very efficient use of additions to avoid multiplies.
- Evaluation of the effectiveness of Cain on the SCAMP-5 Focal-plane Sensor-processor. We compare against AUKE and test the effectiveness of simultaneous kernel optimisation. We conclude by exploring how our simultaneous kernel optimisation extends to future devices with more registers per pixel.

The remainder of the paper is organised as follows. Section 2 describes the SCAMP-5 and its instruction sets, Sect. 3 explains our proposed code generation algorithm Cain, and in Sect. 4 detailed comparison is made between Cain and AUKE, together with an evaluation of the effectiveness of simultaneous kernel optimisation. Section 5 reviews the related work AUKE in detail. Finally, Sect. 6 concludes our work, with a discussion about potential future research.

2   Background: SCAMP-5 Focal-Plane Sensor-Processor

In this section, we discuss the capabilities of the next generation camera technology SCAMP-5, and give an overview of the functionality used by Cain.

SCAMP-5 has been demonstrated in many different computer vision applications, ranging from Visual Odometry systems [3, 10, 16], an end-to-end neural

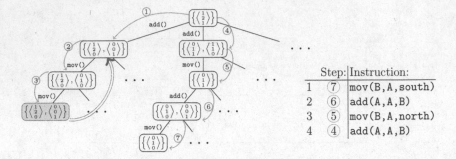

Fig. 2. Graph showing how Cain might search a simplified 1-dimensional problem using CGDS. Numbered steps show the order that the paths are explored with child nodes generated the first time a search step starts at a parent node. Nodes are checked for being the Initial-Goal when pointed too. The red node, and edge, correspond to a dead-end where a duplicate node has been found at a higher cost than previously seen and so the node is not traversed further. We see a path to the Initial-Goal is found after 7 steps, and the code produced by this path is presented on the right. The `mov()` instruction in step 5 exploits a common sub-expression such that the two Goals in its output Goal-Bag are produced together, thus shortening the code.

sensor which performs learnt pixel exposures [15], to Convolutional Neural Networks [4,20]. Its distinctive ability to perform computation on the focal-plane reduces power consumption and data transfers, making the device promising for edge computation.

The SCAMP-5 architecture is a general-purpose fine-grain SIMD FPSP [6]. It has a 256×256 pixel array, and along with each pixel is a small Processing Element (PE). All 65,536 processors execute the same instruction at one time. In addition to 14 binary registers, each PE has analogue registers A through to F as well as a *NEWS* register. Each PE can also address an *XN*, *XE*, *XS*, and *XW* register that is actually that PE's respective neighbours' *NEWS* registers. Each PE uses an analogue bus to link its available analogue registers, and because values are stored as charge; analogue arithmetic is done directly on the bus that connects the registers rather than on a separate arithmetic unit.

Instructions in the architecture control how register values are let into and out of the bus with the caveat that values are inverted due to the nature of the analogue electronics. Each macro instruction like `add`, `sub`, and `mov` are made of multiple bus instructions that create the desired behaviour, where the $busn(w_1, ..w_n, r_0..r_k)$ instruction has the general rule that the values of registers $r_0..r_k$ are summed up, negated, and divided equally between the n receiving-registers $w_1..w_n$. Since a bus operation directly controls which registers are opened to the PE's common analogue bus, a register may only appear once in each `bus` instruction. Each bus instruction also incurs significant noise and error factors, especially for `bus2` and `bus3` [8].

Macro instruction arguments are written as if they are assignment statements. For example; the macro instruction `add(A, B, C)` means $A := B + C$

and is made up of two bus instructions: bus(NEWS, B, C) meaning the $NEWS$ register now contains the value of $-(B+C)$; and then bus(A, NEWS) so that register A contains $B+C$. We can see here that the add instruction has additional constraints, such that the two operands cannot be the same register, and that the $NEWS$ register is overwritten, and left containing $-(B+C)$ as a side effect. When using macro instructions, we restrict the registers to A to F, and allow the macros themselves to make use of the $NEWS$ and neighbouring $NEWS$ registers for us by means of a direction value. We use subscripts to denote the registers of neighbouring PEs. For example: mov2x(A, B, north, east) computes $A :=$ $B_{\text{north,east}}$ in two bus instructions: bus(XS, B); bus(A,XE). The first means that $XS_{\text{north,east}} := B_{\text{north,east}}$ which is equivalent to $NEWS_{\text{east}} := B_{\text{north,east}}$ and then the second instruction means $A := XE = NEWS_{\text{east}} \implies A = B_{\text{north,east}}$.

While interesting uses of the bus instructions exist, allowing adding and subtracting from neighbouring PEs, individual macro instructions are still highly restricted in comparison to most modern instruction sets. Only primitive analogue operations are available to each PE such as: Move, Add, Subtract, Divide by two, and to acquire the value from the sensor [8]. The lack of a multiplication instruction means the problem of generating convolutional filter code for SCAMP-5 builds on the theory of multiplier-free FIR filters [7].

The chip has been shown to be capable of operating at 100,000 FPS, largely because it is not limited by the speed of an output bus to transfer all the pixel data [5]. Instead of only offering an analogue or digitally encoded output of all pixels at a time, like traditional camera sensors, the SCAMP-5 architecture allows binary outputs per pixel, and even event driven outputs. This allows each PE to come to a judgement on its input pixel data and fire its own event that sends the coordinates of the PE to the host; allowing information transfer without divulging the actual image.

The architecture uses an off-chip controller to manage the fetch-decode-execute cycle, with every pixel's processor receiving the same instruction, making it a single-instruction-multiple-data (SIMD) design. This has benefits in terms of simplicity and efficiency as none of the Processing Elements need to be able to fetch instructions for themselves. There is also provision for masking pixels such that only selected PEs execute instructions.

One important consideration to be made when using and designing algorithms related to the SCAMP-5 chip is noise introduced by the nature of the analogue computation. Every use of the 7 analogue registers introduces noise to the values stored. This makes finding optimal code to perform the convolutions ever more vital for accurate results.

3   Cain

Cain is a framework for compiling convolutional filters, designed to search through a configurable Cellular Processor Array (CPA) instruction set to find efficient code. A fundamental concept Cain uses is to only consider a single arbitrary PE in the CPA, and perform everything relative to it. This works for SIMD architecture like SCAMP-5 because every PE will be executing the same steps synchronously in parallel. The assumption we make when producing code is that the neighbours of our arbitrary PE will exist and so will have done the same work but at a relative offset in the input image. The aim is to search through the graph of possible Processing Element states in such a way that common sub-expressions in the given kernels are exploited and used to reduce the cost of any path from initial to final PE states. To do this Cain searches backwards, starting with a set of final kernels, these are the convolutional filter, and applying instructions in reverse to simplify the kernels until only the identity kernel[1] is left. Figure 1 shows a high level overview of this process. Searching backwards is a design choice that makes the search more effective because it means the aim at each step is to make what needs to be solved simpler than before. This means heuristics can be produced to always direct the search towards the identity kernel rather than a system of heuristics trying to accurately predict the path towards an arbitrary set of final Goals. We present this as a dynamic graph search problem because the size of the graph is intractable. Given the AnalogNet2 filter in Eq. 1, Cain identifies 37163 potential children nodes in the first step alone. This can be reduced to 239 if we are willing to accept a less than exhaustive search of the solution space. This restriction is applied when the computational cost of computing the full set of children nodes is too high.

3.1 Definitions

This section provides an overview of notation and definition used in this paper. Cain is designed such that different definitions could be used without changing the fundamental search algorithm but the definitions we use here for SCAMP-5 are based largely on AUKE's, which provides an elegant way to conceptualise the convolutional kernels without multiplication.

Example 1. We will look at a simple example of how a convolutional kernel is represented in Cain. Here we use AnalogNet2 [12,20] which is a CNN designed for SCAMP-5.

$$AnalogNet2 = \left\{ \frac{1}{4}\begin{bmatrix} 0 & 0 & 0 \\ -3 & 1 & 0 \\ -3 & 0 & 2 \end{bmatrix}, \frac{1}{4}\begin{bmatrix} -4 & -1 & -1 \\ -1 & 2 & 0 \\ 1 & 1 & 0 \end{bmatrix}, \frac{1}{4}\begin{bmatrix} -1 & 2 & 0 \\ -1 & 1 & -3 \\ 0 & -3 & 0 \end{bmatrix} \right\} \tag{1}$$

Since SCAMP-5 does not have multiplication we must approximate the kernel and because it does have division-by-two instructions the natural approximation to make is to find the nearest integer multiple of $\frac{1}{2^d}$ for each coefficient in the kernel, given some number of divisions d. In our example we have already extracted the common denominator such that $d = 2$ and this perfectly represents the kernel. The larger d is, the larger the search space and complexity of the problem, so d can be limited to allow an acceptable amount of approximation error such that the resulting program is shorter and computational expense of compiling it is reduced.

---

[1] Single-entry matrix. Not to be confused with identity matrix.

Definition 1. *Let an Atom, denoted as $(x, y, z, sign)$, be a representation of $\frac{1}{2^d}$ of a pixel value at coordinate x, y, on the zth channel. x, y are coordinates relative to the arbitrary PE and so also the centre of the kernel, and z refers to an image input channel. The sign is used to negate the value if necessary.*

Definition 2. *Let a Goal, denoted as $\{atom_1, atom_2, ...\}$, be a multi-set of Atoms. The Goal represents an arbitrary kernel, however, scaled by 2^d. The aggregate of the values represented by each of the Atoms yields the same result as applying the scaled kernel.*

Representing a convolutional kernel as a Goal is a convenient way to support multiply-free instruction set, such as SCAMP-5. One can simply view this as unrolling the multiply instruction into additions. Using Goals simply re-frames the problem by scaling everything by 2^d, and approximating coefficients to the nearest number of Atoms.

Definition 3. *Let a Goal-Bag, denoted as $\{goal1, goal2, ...\}$, be a multi-set of Goals. The Goal-Bag is used to capture the state of our arbitrary PE. This includes defining the Final-Goals, the set of convolution kernels we wish to compute; and the Initial-Goals, the set of Goals which the computation will start from.*

Using these definitions of Goals and Atoms we see that the first kernel from Example 1 can be represented by G

$$K = \frac{1}{4}\begin{bmatrix} 0 & 0 & 0 \\ -3 & 1 & 0 \\ -3 & 0 & 2 \end{bmatrix}, \quad G = \left\{ \begin{array}{lll} (1,0,0,-), & (-1,0,0,-), & (-1,0,0,-), \\ (0,0,0,+), & (-1,-1,0,-), & (-1,-1,0,-), \\ (-1,-1,0,-), & (1,-1,0,+), & (1,-1,0,+) \end{array} \right\}$$

As our Goal notation is verbose, we provide a compact version that disambiguates Goals from kernels

$$G = \left\langle \begin{array}{ccc} 0 & 0 & 0 \\ -3 & 1 & 0 \\ -3 & 0 & 2 \end{array} \right\rangle \implies \frac{1}{2^2}\begin{bmatrix} 0 & 0 & 0 \\ -3 & 1 & 0 \\ -3 & 0 & 2 \end{bmatrix} \star \text{Image Input} \tag{2}$$

where the $\star$ operator applies the left-hand convolutional kernel to the right-hand array

By repeating this for process the rest of the convolutional kernels in the AnalogNet2 filter, the Final-Goals Goal-Bag **FG** is produced:

$$\boldsymbol{FG} = \left\{ \left\langle \begin{array}{ccc} 0 & 0 & 0 \\ -3 & 1 & 0 \\ -3 & 0 & 2 \end{array} \right\rangle, \left\langle \begin{array}{ccc} -4 & -1 & -1 \\ -1 & 2 & 0 \\ 1 & 1 & 0 \end{array} \right\rangle, \left\langle \begin{array}{ccc} -1 & 2 & 0 \\ -1 & 1 & -3 \\ 0 & -3 & 0 \end{array} \right\rangle \right\} \tag{3}$$

Since, in our example, $d = 2$; the Goal representation of the identity kernel (G_{ID}) that makes up the Initial-Goals, is based on the approximation of the Final-Goals:

$$K_{ID} = \frac{1}{4}\begin{bmatrix} 0 & 0 & 0 \\ 0 & 4 & 0 \\ 0 & 0 & 0 \end{bmatrix} \implies G_{ID} = \left\langle \begin{array}{ccc} 0 & 0 & 0 \\ 0 & 4 & 0 \\ 0 & 0 & 0 \end{array} \right\rangle \tag{4}$$

Moving a value around the processor array is expressed by translating every Atom of a Goal. Addition and subtraction can be expressed by combining two

Goals into one, making sure to cancel out positive and negative Atoms with the same coordinates. Since Cain searches backwards, we apply these operations in reverse. For 2-operand addition this means we take a Goal, G, that we wish to generate code for, then produce 2 new Goals that when added together produce G. Defining Goals as multi-sets of Atoms makes this process intuitive as we can simply split the Atoms between two Goals in every possible permutation (or fewer if we are willing to assume some are non-optimal, or willing to miss potentially better code for the sake of more efficient code generation). This definition also restricts the reverse search process since when splitting a Goal we cannot split an Atom. To compute the red Atoms in G naively, PEs must sum them and read this value from the west thus translating the Atoms eastward.

3.2 Search Strategy

Cain's reverse search algorithm works iteratively taking the state of an arbitrary PE, defined as a Goal-Bag:

$$F := \{G_1, G_2, G_2, G_3...\} \tag{5}$$

This is a node in our search graph and represents the state we aim to achieve by executing the instructions that form a path from the initial-Goals to this node. In the search graph, nodes are generated dynamically as the graph is explored. Figure 2 shows a simplified view of how a graph might look as it is generated and searched. We simplify the exploration such that in each iteration of the search algorithm we produce a Goal-Bag Pair of an **Uppers** Goal-Bag and a **Lowers** Goal-Bag as well as an instruction, with the following constraints:

$$(U, L), inst = nextPair(F) \text{ where } U \subseteq F, \ U = inst(L) \tag{6}$$

This is in contrast to AUKE's method, shown later in Eq. 16. The new child node, C, is then produced by applying the instruction in reverse using the following rule, with the instruction becoming an edge in the graph:

$$C = (F \setminus U) \cup L \tag{7}$$

Following our AnalogNet2 example from Eq. 3, the first iteration of the search algorithm will start with FG and the Pair of Goal-Bags Cain produces is as follows:

$$U = \left\{ \left\langle \begin{smallmatrix} -1 & 2 & 0 \\ -1 & 1 & -3 \\ 0 & -3 & 0 \end{smallmatrix} \right\rangle \right\}, \quad L = \left\{ \left\langle \begin{smallmatrix} -1 & 2 & 0 \\ -1 & 1 & 0 \\ 0 & 0 & 0 \end{smallmatrix} \right\rangle, \left\langle \begin{smallmatrix} 0 & 0 & 0 \\ 0 & 0 & -3 \\ 0 & 0 & 0 \end{smallmatrix} \right\rangle, \left\langle \begin{smallmatrix} 0 & 0 & 0 \\ 0 & 0 & 0 \\ 0 & -3 & 0 \end{smallmatrix} \right\rangle \right\} \tag{8}$$

$$inst = U \leftarrow add(L_1, L_2, L_3) \tag{9}$$

$$C = \left\{ \left\langle \begin{smallmatrix} 0 & 0 & 0 \\ -3 & 1 & 0 \\ -3 & 0 & 2 \end{smallmatrix} \right\rangle, \left\langle \begin{smallmatrix} -4 & -1 & -1 \\ -1 & 2 & 0 \\ 1 & 1 & 0 \end{smallmatrix} \right\rangle, \left\langle \begin{smallmatrix} -1 & 2 & 0 \\ -1 & 1 & 0 \\ 0 & 0 & 0 \end{smallmatrix} \right\rangle, \left\langle \begin{smallmatrix} 0 & 0 & 0 \\ 0 & 0 & -3 \\ 0 & 0 & 0 \end{smallmatrix} \right\rangle, \left\langle \begin{smallmatrix} 0 & 0 & 0 \\ 0 & 0 & 0 \\ 0 & -3 & 0 \end{smallmatrix} \right\rangle \right\} \tag{10}$$

The multi-set semantics here mean that if the Goals in L are all already part of F then the number of Goals to solve is reduced, and so by applying more pairs (U, L) we traverse the graph of Goal-Bags, until we reach the initial-state, where the only Goal in the Goal-Bag is the identity Goal. In our example (Eq. 10) we see that the sub-expression of 3 negative Atoms is reused in C_4 and C_5 since applying a mov2x next could eliminate C_5 from C. There is also further potential to reuse this by how we split C_1. Once the initial Goal-Bag is found the path from the initial Goal-Bag back to the Final-Goals becomes the list of instructions that form our generated program.

After this point Cain continues searching for shorter paths, and can cull any nodes with longer paths. During the search the same Goal-Bags may be reproduced in different ways, we cull the current node any time a Goal-Bag is produced that has already been seen at a lower or equal cost, or if the Goal-Bag has more Goals than available registers.

The second part of the search strategy defines the search order. Each invocation of the reverse search algorithm produces one new node, C, and the input node is incremented to know how many of its children have been produced so far. Cain uses this simple definition to allow several graph traversal algorithms to be implemented. Using Depth-First-Search (DFS), Cain can simply maintain a stack of the nodes. On each cycle the top node is popped off the stack and given to the reverse search algorithm. Then the incremented parent node is put back on the stack, followed by the new child node.

While DFS performs well in AUKE, it struggles in Cain because the number of child nodes at every level is far greater, since each edge is only one instruction and there are multiple kernels to consider. This means the size of the graph we would like to search is much larger and we are unable to search even a small fraction of it. To overcome this we use a graph-traversal algorithm that, for our purposes, we call Child-Generator-Deque-Search (CGDS). The aim of this algorithm is to ensure that the search does not end up 'trapped' in one small part of the graph, but can effectively search traverse many children of many of the nodes that are found where DFS will search all of the children of nodes at

---

Algorithm 1: CGDS Graph Search

Input: s
1. $deque \leftarrow [(s, null)]$
2. **while** $deque \neq []$ **do**
3. $\quad n, g \leftarrow deque[0]$
4. $\quad deque \leftarrow deque[1..]$
5. $\quad$ **if** $g = null$ **then**
6. $\quad\quad$ do node computation on n
7. $\quad\quad g \leftarrow childGenerator(n)$
8. $\quad$ **end**
9. $\quad c \leftarrow g.yield()$
10. $\quad$ **if** $c \neq null$ **then**
11. $\quad\quad deque \leftarrow [(c, null)] + deque + [(n, g)]$
12. $\quad$ **end**
13. **end**

---

the extent of the paths it searches before searching the second children of nodes earlier in the graph. Algorithm 1 shows a pseudo-code implementation of CGDS. In each cycle the front of the queue is polled, if the node has not been seen before, Cain checks to see if it can be directly transformed from the initial-state Goal-Bag, this is the 'node computation'. The node is then passed to the reverse search algorithm to attempt to produce the next new child node and to increment parent node – this is implicit in calling '*yield()*' on *g*. The child node, if it exists, is put on the front of the queue and the incremented parent node is put on the back. We do not claim that CGDS is novel, but we have found it superior to obvious alternatives, and the strategy used in [2]; for details see [18].

3.3   Cost Function

In the reverse search algorithm we see that the pairs of **Uppers** and **Lowers** are produced one at a time. While this simplification allows us to produce more generic graph traversal implementations; what allows Cain to efficiently find solutions, are the heuristics that allow us to order the pairs that are produced for a node from the most promising to the least. This type of heuristic provides the order of siblings to search so we call it a 'local heuristic'. It doesn't compare nodes in different parts of the graph, which we would call a 'global heuristic'. We found that we were unable to find effective global heuristics because traversal algorithms that take advantage of such heuristics end up producing huge frontier sets of nodes making the memory requirements too large. The use of local heuristics drives the SCAMP-5 code generation in Cain instead, though support for best-first-search with global heuristics is available in Cain. The local heuristics used for SCAMP-5 are based on generating every child node of the parent and then ordering them based on a cost function. There are 3 main components considered for the cost: Atom distance, repeated Goals, and divisions. A simplified formula is shown in Eq. 11.

$$cost(\boldsymbol{C}) = dists(\boldsymbol{C}) + reps(\boldsymbol{C}) + divs(\boldsymbol{C}) \tag{11}$$

$$dists(\boldsymbol{C}) = \sum_{G \in C} \left(|G| + \sum_{a \in G} (|a.x| + |a.y|) \times \left\{ \begin{matrix} \frac{1}{2} \text{ if } & \nexists B \in \boldsymbol{C}.G \subset B \\ 1 & \text{otherwise.} \end{matrix} \right\} \right) \tag{12}$$

$$reps(\boldsymbol{C}) = \sum_{\{G \in C \,:\, G \text{ is unique wrt any translations}\}} \left\{ \begin{matrix} |G|^2 & \exists a, b \in G.a \neq b \\ 0 & \text{otherwise.} \end{matrix} \right\} \tag{13}$$

$$divs(\boldsymbol{C}) = \frac{2^d}{\min(multiplicity(a) \forall a \in G.\forall G \in \boldsymbol{C})} \tag{14}$$

The Atom distance part counts up how many Atoms every Goal in $\boldsymbol{C}$ has, and how far from the centre they are, with some relief if the Goal is a sub-Goal of another Goal in $\boldsymbol{C}$. The repeated Goals portion of the cost penalises $\boldsymbol{C}$ by the square of number of Atoms in each Goal, unless that Goal is equal to a translation of another Goal in $\boldsymbol{C}$. The divisions component penalises $\boldsymbol{C}$ for the number of division operations that would be required to produce the Goals from the identity-kernel Goal, G_{ID}.

4   Evaluation

All performance evaluation is conducted on an Intel Core i7-7700HQ CPU (4 cores, 8 threads) with a base frequency of 2.80GHz. The computer has 16GB of RAM, runs Ubuntu 18; as well as Java 1.8 (Oracle) and Python 3.6 to run Cain and AUKE respectively. The implementation of AUKE used, as developed by Debrunner, can be found on Github[2]. Cain source code can be found at github.com/ed741/cain, and the specific version and sources for experimental setups presented in this evaluation can be found at [19].

4.1 Performance Evaluation Against AUKE

Comparison of our work Cain against AUKE is performed by comparing resulting code generated from the respective compilers, given the same input filters. Both compilers are given 60 s to find a solution using all 6 registers. Note as Cain supports multi-threading, it spawns 4 worker threads to perform the search.

As shown in Table 1, Cain significantly outperforms AUKE. Cain supports a wider set of instructions in contrast of AUKE, enabling generation of more efficient code. Not only this, the search strategy used by Cain is better than AUKE's, as shown in 5×5 Gaussian Kernel, were using the same set of instructions (Basic), code generated by Cain is half in length when compared to output of AUKE's. Although, in further testing, AUKE is able to produce less inefficient code for this kernel given fewer registers. When given multiple kernels, Cain is able to perform simultaneous kernel optimisation. For example when combining 3×3 and 5×5 Gaussian, unlike AUKE, Cain is implemented to utilise the common sub-expressions between the kernels, thus, generating shorter code than naively concatenating the code for each of the Gaussian kernels. Neither Cain or AUKE perform a compete exhaustive search.

The AnalogNet2 filter is the kernels used in AnalogNet2 [20][12], which is a CNN for SCAMP-5, capable of MNIST digit recognition. Cain requires only 21 instructions whereas AUKE produces kernel code which has in total 49 instructions. Reduced code not only improves the execution time, but also reduces the noise build up, which is significant problem as discussed in [20]. If the aim of finding sub-expressions is to eliminate redoing work, then the number of add and subtract operands is a proxy for how effective the search for sub-expressions is, regardless of how translations are handled. Table 2 shows that AUKE's code has 40 add or subtract operands whereas Cain's code has only 27. We have compared the runtime of AnalogNet2's convolution kernels, generated by AUKE and Cain on the physical SCAMP-5. Note, as AUKE produces code which performs invalid register manipulation, the fixed code as used in [12], which executes on the device is 81 instructions long. The execution time of the code produced by AUKE and Cain for the convolution kernels were $35\mu s$ and $9\mu s$ respectively, showing almost 4 times speedup.

---

[2] github.com/najiji/auto_code_cpa/tree/75c017e5ad28c0f3f040fb9f84d7f8727d035baa.

Table 1. Kernels tested in AUKE and Cain. Values on the righthand side of the table refer to the number of SCAMP-5 macro instructions in the programs generated by AUKE and Cain for each filter. AUKE can only use the 'basic' macro instructions, so Cain is run twice; to compare its effectiveness under the same restrictions as AUKE. Since AUKE does not offer a way to compile multiple kernels at once, values for each kernel are given separately.

Name	Approximated Filter	AUKE	Cain	
		Basic	All	Basic
3×3 Gauss	$\left\{\frac{1}{16}\begin{bmatrix}1&2&1\\2&4&2\\1&2&1\end{bmatrix}\right\}$	12	**10**	12
5×5 Gauss	$\left\{\frac{1}{64}\begin{bmatrix}0&1&2&1&0\\1&4&6&4&1\\2&6&10&6&2\\1&4&6&4&1\\0&1&2&1&0\end{bmatrix}\right\}$	50	**19**	25
5×5 and 3×3 Gauss	$\left\{\frac{1}{64}\begin{bmatrix}0&1&2&1&0\\1&4&6&4&1\\2&6&10&6&2\\1&4&6&4&1\\0&1&2&1&0\end{bmatrix},\frac{1}{64}\begin{bmatrix}0&0&0&0&0\\0&4&8&4&0\\0&8&16&8&0\\0&4&8&4&0\\0&0&0&0&0\end{bmatrix}\right\}$	$(50+12)$	**26**	39
AnalogNet2	$\left\{\frac{1}{4}\begin{bmatrix}0&0&0\\-3&1&0\\-3&0&2\end{bmatrix},\frac{1}{4}\begin{bmatrix}-4&-1&1\\-1&2&0\\1&1&0\end{bmatrix},\frac{1}{4}\begin{bmatrix}-1&2&0\\-1&1&-3\\0&-3&0\end{bmatrix}\right\}$	$(13+21\\+15)$	**21**	30

Table 2. Comparison of Code for the AnalogNet2 filter generated by AUKE and Cain. The Input Register is 'A' and the output registers for the 3 kernels are 'A','B','C' respectively. For AUKE, kernel 2 is run first since testing showed it was longest so this gives AUKE more registers to use.

AUKE						Cain	

```
              AUKE                                                    Cain
Kernel 2                Kernel 3                Kernel 1          1   diva(A,D,E);
1   mov(B,A);       22  mov(C,A);           38  divq(A,A);        2   div(D,E,C,A);
2   divq(B,B);      23  divq(C,C);          39  divq(A,A);        3   movx(E,D,west);
3   divq(B,B);      24  divq(C,C);          40  movx(D,A,west);   4   movx(C,E,north);
4   movx(C,B,north);25  movx(D,C,south);    41  neg(D,D);         5   neg(F,E);
5   neg(C,C);       26  neg(D,D);           42  movx(E,D,south);  6   subx(B,F,east,A);
6   neg(D,C);       27  movx(E,C,east);     43  add(D,D,E);       7   addx(E,E,D,south);
7   movx(E,D,west); 28  sub(D,D,E);         44  add(E,A,D);       8   add2x(D,F,D,north,north);
8   neg(E,E);       29  movx(E,C,north);    45  movx(A,A,south);  9   sub2x(F,D,south,south,C);
9   add(F,B,E);     30  add(E,E,D);         46  movx(A,A,east);   10  add2x(D,C,D,east,south);
10  movx(B,D,east); 31  add(D,D,D);         47  add(A,D,A);       11  add(E,E,D);
11  add(B,B,E);     32  add(D,E,D);         48  add(A,A,A);       12  movx(D,A,north);
12  movx(D,E,south);33  movx(E,C,west);     49  add(A,E,A);       13  add2x(A,C,A,east,east);
13  movx(D,D,south);34  sub(C,C,E);                               14  movx(C,B,east);
14  sub(B,B,D);     35  add(D,D,C);                               15  add(D,F,D);
15  add(B,B,F);     36  movx(C,C,north);                          16  add2x(F,F,E,east,south);
16  add(B,C,B);     37  add(C,D,C);                               17  movx(E,B,south);
17  movx(C,C,west);                                               18  addx(A,B,A,south);
18  add(B,B,C);                                                   19  addx(A,B,A,west);
19  movx(C,F,south);                                              20  add2x(B,F,B,north,west);
20  add(B,C,B);                                                   21  add(C,D,C,E);
21  add(B,B,F);
```

4.2   Effectiveness of the Search Strategy

If Cain has an effective heuristic we will quickly see a point of diminishing returns in code length, as Cain continues to search new nodes and takes more time. We can track the number of nodes that are explored before finding any plan in Cain, and so use this as a measure of the search strategy and heuristics that is more independent of physical compute performance. With this in mind we test the effectiveness of our heuristic by constructing 100 samples of randomly generated single kernel filters as in Eq. 15. Running Cain as per the following

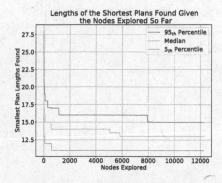
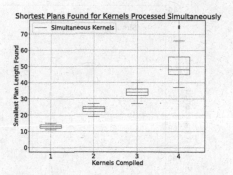

Fig. 3. Left: Graph showing the median number of instructions in the best plans found before n nodes have been explored by Cain. With 100 samples of randomly generated singular 3×3 kernel filters. Right: Graph showing the number of instructions in the shortest programs found by Cain for filters with 1, 2, 3, and 4 random 3×3 kernels. 25 samples were produced for each kernel count.

configuration – Maximum Nodes to Explore: 20000, Maximum Search Time: 60 s, Worker Threads: 1 – allows us to collect as many plans as can be found in the given time limit. We then ran Cain again, but with Cain's SCAMP-5 heuristic disabled and replaced with a random sort. This allows us to compare Cains heuristics against an unaided benchmark.

$$\frac{1}{8} \begin{bmatrix} u_1 & u_2 & u_3 \\ u_4 & u_5 & u_6 \\ u_7 & u_8 & u_9 \end{bmatrix}$$

Given $u_1..u_9$ are integers sampled uniformly from the range $[0..8]$. \hfill (15)

We found that Cain was unable to find any plan for any of the 100 sample filters without its heuristics, principally demonstrating that effective heuristics are required in Cain for any tangible progress to be made. We plot the lengths of the best plans found against the number of nodes expanded before the plan is found in Fig. 3. We can see that improvements are fewer and further between after the first 2500 nodes are explored. After this we see that we can expect at most a reduction equal to the reduction seen at 2500 for the rest of the nodes explored. This clearly demonstrates a point of diminishing returns for these filters. If the heuristic is effective we expect it to direct the search towards short plans first, and try instructions less likely to be optimal later. This model fits the data well as we see short plans are found quickly, and while improvements can be made, it is clear that they are found less often as the search continues.

4.3   Effectiveness of the Simultaneous Kernel Optimisation

One of the significant features of Cain is to efficiently generate code for filters with multiple kernels, and do this simultaneously such that shared common sub-expressions can be reused. As it is possible for Cain to perform exhaustive

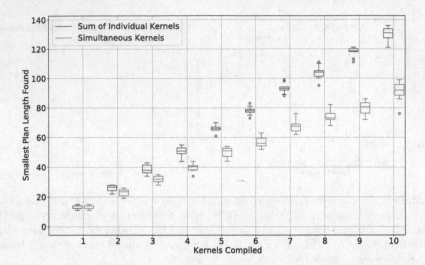

Fig. 4. Graph comparing the sum of the shortest SCAMP-5 code lengths found for kernels compiled individually, against the same kernels compiled simultaneously as one filter. For each filter a total of 18 registers were made available (more than in SCAMP-5) to reduce register availability as a limiting factor. In total 100 filters are produced, 10 for each number of kernels per filter. Each kernel is a randomly generated 3×3 kernel with coefficients uniformly selected in eighths from 0 to 1 (inclusive).

searches for plans, given sufficient time, it will find a solution that simply computes the individual kernels independently, or find a solution with lower cost – utilising the common sub-expressions.

First, we wish to test whether the length of generated code is sub-linear to the number of input kernels. To test this, we again generate kernels using the using the method in Eq. 15. For kernel counts from 1 to 4 we generated 25 filters each and test them all using the same configuration as before except that we remove the maximum nodes explored constraint, and allow 4 worker threads. We plot the results in Fig. 3 and see that the results appear worse than linear, suggesting that common sub-expressions are not effectively being taken advantage of.

We hypothesise that the limited number of registers in the SCAMP-5 architecture is the major limiting factor in producing efficient code. To test this we increase the number of available registers to 18. For filters with 1 kernel up to 10 kernels we generate 10 samples each. Every kernel in the 100 filters is produced as in Eq. 15. For each sample, Cain compiles the kernels individually, given the appropriate number of registers such that other kernels in the filter would not be overwritten. Then we compile the kernels simultaneously using Cain. All compilations are given 60s to run, with 4 worker threads.

Figure 4 shows the results of this test. We see clearly that when register limitations are not a restricting factor Cain is able to consistently improve the performance of filter implementations by compiling them simultaneously. We see that improvements grow with more kernels, and it appears that the length of code generated for simultaneously compiled kernels increases sub-linearly. This supports the idea that with more kernels, ever more common-sub expressions can be exploited.

5   Related Work: AUKE

In this section we look at how AUKE operates to provide extra context and contrast for Cain. Automatic Kernel Code Generation for Analogue SIMD (AUKE) is an algorithm for generating code given a single convolutional kernel created by T. Debrunner [11]. It can be characterised by 4 main steps: kernel approximation; the reverse split algorithm; graph relaxation; and finally register allocation. First, AUKE approximates the input kernel into the Goal representation. In this process Cain is similar to AUKE and the reasoning and mechanics have been discussed in Sect. 3.1.

Unlike in Cain, multiple instructions are represented by a single elemental transformation of Goals. These elemental transformations form edges of a graph that describe the translation, addition, subtraction and division of Goals to produce the desired convolutions filter. This abstraction allows AUKE to reduce the effective size of the search space at the cost of granularity in instruction selection and being extensible to hardware features such as 3-operand addition. Debrunner called this the 'Reverse-Split Algorithm'.

The graph of elemental transformations is dynamically generated via a recursive depth-first search that tries to split a Goal G, that needs to be produced, into 3 sub-Goals:

$$G = U \cup L \cup R \quad \text{where } U = elementalTransformation(L) \qquad (16)$$

This recursive algorithm then means that if the search can find solutions for L and R (two smaller problems) it can trivially create U and therefore the desired Goal.

In the ideal case $R = \emptyset$ and so only L needs to be produced and we save one addition. In the worst case $L = U = \emptyset$ and R is a transformation of G and so less useful work is done in that step. If two Goals are equal they are merged such that they aren't calculated twice, to exploit common sub-expressions in the Goals. This process is repeated until a single Goal, the initial-Goal, is left. This algorithm is able to entirely search the relevant problem space, given a couple of assumptions. Most notably, the assumption that every sub-Goal generated is a subset of the Final-Goal. This reduces the search space significantly to the most promising but not necessarily the best solutions, allowing AUKE to find generally effective solutions.

The algorithm is made efficient and useful by intelligently selecting the order with which Us, Ls, and Rs are generated at every recursive step. By selecting pairs of U and L that are likely to lead to efficient code, the algorithm can quickly find some path to the initial-Goal. From then on the recursive search can stop early if a lower cost solution has already be found.

The Graph Relaxation step aims to mitigate missing optimal solutions because of the assumption that sub-Goals are always subsets of the Final-Goal by using a 'retiming' algorithm used in integrated circuit design. This is not needed in Cain since Cain searches instruction by instruction, and so any optimisations found via graph relaxation are already a part of the search space.

The final step is to perform register allocation on the graph to be able to generate usable code. A maximum bound of registers is already accounted for in the search algorithm, since spilling is not an option for the SCAMP-5 architecture. For this task; variable liveness is considered for each node of the graph representation, and a graph colouring algorithm is used to find a solution.

6   Conclusion

We have presented Cain, a compiler which produces SCAMP-5 instructions from a set of convolutional kernels. Although the effectiveness of simultaneous kernel optimisation is limited on the current iteration of the SCAMP-5, we demonstrate, that with the increased number of registers, the length of the output of Cain is sub-linear to the number of kernels given. We have conducted extensive comparison against AUKE, and we demonstrate that the code generated by Cain is more efficient, and exhibits almost 4x speed up when the generated kernel is executed on the SCAMP-5 device. We believe that SCAMP-5 is a strong candidate for edge computation, and by providing easy to use, yet efficient code generation toolkit, we hope to accelerate the relevant research in this field.

Acknowledgements. We would like to thank Piotr Dudek, Stephen J. Carey, and Jianing Chen at the University of Manchester for kindly providing access to SCAMP-5, and their support in our work. This work was partially supported by the EPSRC, grant reference EP/P010040/1.

References

1. Abadi, M., et al.: Tensorflow: a system for large-scale machine learning. In: 12th USENIX Symposium on Operating Systems Design and Implementation OSDI 16, pp. 265–283 (2016)
2. Barthels, H., Psarras, C., Bientinesi, P.: Linnea: Automatic generation of efficient linear algebra programs (2019). https://arxiv.org/pdf/1912.12924.pdf
3. Bose, L., Chen, J., Carey, S.J., Dudek, P., Mayol-Cuevas, W.: Visual odometry for pixel processor arrays. In: 2017 IEEE International Conference on Computer Vision (ICCV), pp. 4614–4622 (October 2017)
4. Bose, L., Chen, J., Carey, S.J., Dudek, P., Mayol-Cuevas, W.: A camera that CNNs: towards embedded neural networks on pixel processor arrays. In: Proceedings of the IEEE International Conference on Computer Vision (ICCV), pp. 1335–1344 (2019)
5. Carey, S.J., Barr, D.R.W., Wang, B., Lopich, A., Dudek, P.: Locating high speed multiple objects using a SCAMP-5 vision-chip. In: 2012 13th International Workshop on Cellular Nanoscale Networks and their Applications, pp. 1–2 (August 2012)

6. Carey, S.J., Lopich, A., Barr, D.R.W., Wang, B., Dudek, P.: A 100,000 fps vision sensor with embedded 535GOPS/W 256 × 256 SIMD processor array. In: 2013 Symposium on VLSI Circuits, pp. C182–C183 (2013)
7. Chandra, A., Chattopadhyay, S.: Design of hardware efficient FIR filter: a review of the state-of-the-art approaches. Eng. Sci. Technol. Int. J. **19**(1), 212–226 (2016)
8. Chen, J.: scamp5 kernel api macro analog.hpp file reference (January 2020). https://scamp.gitlab.io/scamp5d_doc/scamp5_kernel_api_macro_analog_8hpp.html
9. Chen, Y.H., Krishna, T., Emer, J.S., Sze, V.: Eyeriss: an energy-efficient reconfigurable accelerator for deep convolutional neural networks. IEEE J. Solid-State Circuits **52**(1), 127–138 (2016)
10. Debrunner, T., Saeedi, S., Bose, L., Davison, A.J., Kelly, P.H.J.: Camera tracking on focal-plane sensor-processor arrays (2019)
11. Debrunner, T., Saeedi, S., Kelly, P.H.J.: AUKE: automatic kernel code generation for an analogue SIMD focal-plane sensor-processor array. ACM Trans. Archit. Code Optim. **15**(4), 59:1–59:26 (2019)
12. Guillard, B.: CNNs-on-FPSPs (May 2019). https://github.com/brouwa/CNNs-on-FPSPs/tree/c6b5c51839e9e3c453681e5b0a3e3ef541ba3cce
13. LeCun, Y., Bottou, L., Bengio, Y., Haffner, P.: Gradient-based learning applied to document recognition. Proc. IEEE **86**(11), 2278–2324 (1998)
14. Martel, J.: Unconventional Processing with Unconventional Visual Sensing. Ph.D. thesis, Institut National des Sciences Appliquées de Lyon (2019)
15. Martel, J.N.P., Müller, L.K., Carey, S.J., Dudek, P., Wetzstein, G.: Neural sensors: learning pixel exposures for HDR imaging and video compressive sensing with programmable sensors. IEEE Trans. Pattern Anal. Mach. Intell. **42**(7), 1642–1653 (2020)
16. Murai, R., Saeedi, S., Kelly, P.H.J.: BIT-VO: visual odometry at 300 FPS using Binary features from the focal plane. In: IEEE/RSJ International Conference on Intelligent Robots and Systems (IROS) (2020)
17. Saeedi, S., Bodin, B., Wagstaff, H., et al.: Navigating the landscape for real-time localization and mapping for robotics and virtual and augmented reality. Proc. IEEE **106**(11), 2020–2039 (2018)
18. Stow, E.: Automatic Code Generation for Simultaneous Convolutional Kernels on Cellular Processor Arrays. Master's thesis, Imperial College London (2020). http://edstow.co.uk/pub/2020/MEngThesis.pdf
19. Stow, E., Murai, R.: ed741/cain: 3.0-experiments.1 (August 2020). https://doi.org/10.5281/zenodo.3975615
20. Wong, M.Z., Guillard, B., Murai, R., Saeedi, S., Kelly, P.H.J.: AnalogNet: Convolutional Neural Network Inference on Analog Focal Plane Sensor Processors. arXiv preprint arXiv:2006.01765 (2020)
21. XIMEA: xiB - PCI Express Cameras with high speed and resolution. https://www.ximea.com/pci-express-camera/pci-express-camera
22. Zarándy, Á.: Focal-Plane Sensor-Processor Chips. SpringerLink : Bücher, Springer, New York (2011). https://doi.org/10.1007/978-1-4419-6475-5

Reordering Under the ECMAScript Memory Consistency Model

Akshay Gopalakrishnan$^{(\boxtimes)}$ and Clark Verbrugge

McGill University, Montréal, Québec, Canada
`akshay.akshay@mail.mcgill.ca`, `clump@cs.mcgill.ca`

Abstract. Relaxed memory accesses are used to gain substantial improvement in the performance of concurrent programs. A relaxed memory consistency model specifically describes the semantics of such memory accesses for a particular programming language. Historically, such semantics are often ill-defined or misunderstood and have been shown to conflict with common compiler optimizations essential for the performance of programs overall. In this paper, we give a formal description of the ECMAScript relaxed memory consistency model. We then analyze the impact of this model on one of the most common compiler optimizations, viz. *instruction reordering*. We give a conservative proof under which such optimization is allowed for relaxed memory accesses. Finally, we discuss the advantage of our conservative approach and the gaps needed to be filled in order to incorporate our results while doing such optimizations at the program level.

Keywords: Relaxed memory consistency · Optimization · ECMAScript

1 Introduction

Concurrent programs take advantage of *out-of-order* execution. Intuitively, this means more than one unrelated computations can be done "simultaneously" without having any fixed order in which they should happen. This results in concurrent programs having multiple different outcomes, the possible outcomes of which are described by a *memory consistency model*. The most intuitive and commonly relied upon model is that of *Sequential Consistency* (SC), which guarantees that every outcome of a program must be equivalent to a sequential interleaving of each thread's actions. For example, consider the program in Fig. 1 with two threads, which share memory denoted by x, y initialized to 0, where a, b are local variables. The right-hand-side are the possible values that a and b can read under sequential consistency.

© Springer Nature Switzerland AG 2022
B. Chapman and J. Moreira (Eds.): LCPC 2020, LNCS 13149, pp. 198–214, 2022.
https://doi.org/10.1007/978-3-030-95953-1_14

Fig. 1. Example program with its possible outcomes under sequential consistency.

However, the above program under SC cannot have the outcome $a = 2 \wedge b = 0$. From a program transformation standpoint, such an outcome should be possible: we can simply reorder either both the reads or both writes to x and y, as they are computations on disjoint memory. But from a consistency rule standpoint, since the outcome is not valid, it also brings with it the conclusion that such simple program transformations may not be safe or even invalid. Figure 2 shows how after doing either one of these reorderings, an outcome invalid under SC is possible.

Fig. 2. Left program is when the two reads in T1 are reordered, whereas the right program is when the two writes of T2 are reordered.

Weaker consistency models have been introduced to concurrent, shared-memory languages to leverage more of the out-of-order notion. For instance, under the ECMAScript consistency model semantics, if all the accesses are of type *unordered*, the above invalid outcome is allowed, which implies a reordering of such events is valid in the above case. The problem though is that semantics of such weak consistency can be easily misunderstood, and are sometimes defined in informal prose format, thus leading to misinterpretation of intended semantics, which leads to implementation issues. The lack of clear semantics also makes it difficult to assert when a particular program transformation is valid/safe (in our case, instruction reordering).

Our focus in this work is to offer a clarified, more concise rendition of the core ECMAScript memory model that allows for better abstract reasoning over allowed and disallowed behaviours (outcomes). We use our model to provide a straightforward, conservative proof of when reordering of independent instructions is permitted, addressing optimization in terms of its impact on observable program behaviours. Our approach can be extended to address additional optimization effects, such as redundancy removal. Specific contributions of our work include the following:

1. We provide a concise *declarative style* model of the core ECMAScript memory consistency semantics. This clarifies the existing draft presentation [4] in a manner useful for validating optimizations.
2. Using our model we show when basic reordering of independent instructions is allowed. Although conservative, this represents a formal proof that this fundamental optimization is permitted. Similar proof designs can be used to validate other basic optimization behaviours,such as removing redundant reads or writes.

2   Related Work

Sequential Consistency, which was first formulated by Lamport et al. [5], gives programmers a very intuitive way to reason about their programs running in a multiprocessor environment. However, in the practical sense, Sequential Consistency is too "strict," in the sense that it may impede possible performance benefits of using low-level 'optimization features, such as instruction reordering, or read/write buffers provided by the hardware. A tutorial by Adve et al. [1], summarizes the most common hardware features for relaxed memory that are now available in most hardware. What this tutorial also exposed is the difficulty in formalizing such features in a way that we can reason about our programs sanely without getting caught up in the complexity of multiple executions of our programs. Unsurprisingly, relaxed memory model specifications for different hardware/high-level programming languages are still sometimes written in informal prose format, which leads to several of problems in implementation [12].

Sarkar et al. [9] showed that the original x86-CC memory model was fairly informal, which they then formalized in their work. This also exposed inconsistencies between the specification and the implementation in hardware. This was shown in their subsequent work done by Owens et al. [8], wherein they proposed a new memory model x86-TSO as a remedy. Manson et al. [6], showed that the initial specifications of the Java memory model were quite informal and ill-defined, and offered a more precise formalization. Recent works such as that done by Bender et al. [3], also show us that the recent updates to the java Memory model are still relatively unclear, which they again formalize. Similarly, Batty et al. [2], clarified the specification of the C11 memory model.

Apart from the problems of ill-defined/informal specifications, these models also have an impact on the safety of program transformations which were considered safe to do in a sequential program. Ševčík et al. [11] showed that standard compiler optimizations were rendered invalid under the respective memory model of Java. Vafeiadis et al. [13] showed that common compiler optimizations under C11 memory model are also invalid, followed by proposing some changes to allow them.

With respect to instruction reordering in shared memory programs, Ševčík et al. [10] recently gave a proof design on how to show such optimizations are valid. However, this approach relies on the idea of reconstructing the original execution of a program given the optimized one, while also showing the well known SC-DRF guarantee holds—programs that are *data race free* (DRF) must exhibit

SC semantics. Our approach is, in fact, the other way round; we show that the optimized program does not introduce new behaviours, by explicitly using the consistency rules to show that relevant ordering relations are preserved.

ECMAScript has also had some attention in this respect. Watt et al. [14] uncovered and fixed a deficiency in the previous version of the model, repairing the model to guarantee SC-DRF. Our analysis is based on this corrected model which is incorporated in the ECMAScript draft specification. As far as our knowledge goes, no analysis has been done on this model to identify its implications on standard compiler optimizations.

3   The ECMAScript Memory Consistency Model

We give a relatively more formal and concise axiomatic description of Section 28 of the ECMAScript standard. The version we are referring to is the current working draft [4]. It is important to note that this working draft has not changed the memory model specifics since the time we started our work on this.

3.1   Agents and Agent Clusters

Agents for our context could be thought analogous to different threads/processes running concurrently. Every agent is mapped to a list of events. (defined below) Collection of agents using a common shared memory for communication form an agent cluster. There can be multiple agent clusters, however, an agent can only belong to one agent cluster.

3.2   Events

Agent execution is modelled in terms of events. An event, in our context, is either an operation that involves (shared) Read/Write memory access or Synchronize events that constrains the order of execution of multiple events. We define E as the set of events involved in an agent cluster. We refer to SM, R, W, S as sets of Shared Memory, Read, Write and Synchronize events respectively. Shared Memory events are composed of Read and Write event sets. Read-Modify-Write events belong to both R and W.

Range ($\Re$). Each of the *shared memory events* are associated with a contiguous range of memory on which it operates. $\Re$ is a function that maps a shared memory event to the range of memory indices it operates on which we represent as a starting index i and a size s. As an example, the range of event e would be like:

$$\Re(w) = (i, s)$$

We define two binary operators $\cap_\Re$ and $\cup_\Re$ to give the intersection and union respectively of the set of the byte indices, in order to describe disjoint, overlapping and equal ranges.

Types of Events Based on Order. There are 3 types (or access modes) which play a role in the sequence in which event actions are visible to different agents

1. **Sequentially Consistent** (*sc*) - Events of this type are *atomic* in nature. There is a strict global total ordering of such events which is agreed upon by all agents in an execution.
2. **Unordered** (*uo*) - Events of this type are considered non-atomic and can occur in different orders for each agent.
3. **Initialize** (*init*) - Events of this type are used to initialize the values in memory ordered before events in an agent cluster.

All events of type *init* are writes and all read modify write events are of type *sc*. We represent the type of events in the memory consistency rules in the format "*event : type*". When representing events in a figure, the type would be represented as a subscript: $event_{type}$.

Tearing (or not). Additionally, each shared-memory event is also associated with a tearing factor. Events that tear are non-aligned accesses requiring more than one memory access. Events that are tear-free are aligned and should *appear* to be serviced in one memory access. The implication of tearing is better understood with the consistency rule that will later be shown.

3.3   Relation Among Events

We now describe a set of relations between events. These relations help us describe the consistency rules.

Read-Write Event Relations. There are two basic relations that assist us in reasoning about read and write events.

Read-Bytes-From ($\overrightarrow{rbf}$). This relation maps every read event to a list of tuples each of which consist a write event and the corresponding byte index that is read. For instance, consider a read event e and corresponding write events $d1$, $d2$ all of whose ranges have byte index i and size 3. One possible $\overrightarrow{rbf}$ relation could be represented as

$$e \overrightarrow{rbf} \{(d1, i), (d2, i+1), (d2, i+2)\}$$

or having individual binary relation with each write-index pair as

$$e \overrightarrow{rbf} (d1, i), \ e \overrightarrow{rbf} (d2, i+1) \text{ and } e \overrightarrow{rbf} (d2, i+2).$$

Reads-From ($\overrightarrow{rf}$). This relation, is similar to the above relation, except that the byte index details are not involved in the composed list. So for the above example, the *rf* relation would be represented either as $e \overrightarrow{rf} (d1, d2)$ or individual binary read-write relation as $e \overrightarrow{rf} d1$ and $e \overrightarrow{rf} d2$.

Agent-Synchronizes With (ASW). A list for each agent that consist of ordered tuples of synchronize events. These tuples specify ordering constraints among agents at different points of execution. We represent such a list for an agent k as

$$ASW_k = \{\langle s_1, s_2 \rangle, \langle s_3, s_4 \rangle ... \}$$

3.4   Ordering Relations Among Events

Agent Order $(\overrightarrow{ao})$. A total order among events belonging to the same agent event list. It is analogous to intra-thread ordering. For example, if two events e and d belong to the same agent event list, then either $e \overrightarrow{ao} d$ or $d \overrightarrow{ao} e$.

Synchronize-With Order $(\overrightarrow{sw})$. Represents the synchronizations among different agents through relations between their events. It is a composition of two sets as below:

$$\forall i, j > 0, \ \langle s_i, s_j \rangle \in ASW \ \Rightarrow \ s_i \overrightarrow{sw} s_j$$
$$(e \overrightarrow{rf} d) \wedge e\text{:}sc \wedge d\text{:}sc \wedge (\Re(e) = \Re(d)) \ \Rightarrow \ (d \overrightarrow{sw} e)$$

Happens Before Order $(\overrightarrow{hb})$. A transitive order on events, composed of the following:

$$e \overrightarrow{ao} d \ \Rightarrow \ e \overrightarrow{hb} d$$
$$e \overrightarrow{sw} d \ \Rightarrow \ e \overrightarrow{hb} d$$
$$\forall e, d \in SM, \ e\text{:}init \wedge (\Re(e) \cap_{\Re} \Re(d) \neq \phi) \ \Rightarrow \ e \overrightarrow{hb} d$$

Memory Order $(\overrightarrow{mo})$. This is a total order on all events which respects happens-before

$$e \overrightarrow{hb} d \ \Rightarrow \ e \overrightarrow{mo} d$$

3.5   Some Preliminary Definitions

Before we go into the consistency rules. we define certain preliminary definitions that create a separation based on a program, the axiomatic events and the various ordering relations defined above. This will help us understand where the consistency rules actually apply.

Definition 1. *Program. A program is the source code without abstraction to a set of events and ordering relations. In our context, it is the original ECMAScript program.*

Definition 2. *Candidate. This is a collection of abstracted set of shared memory events of a program involved in one possible execution, with the added $\overrightarrow{ao}$ relations. We can think of this as each thread having a set of shared memory events to run in a given intra-thread ordering.*

Definition 3. *Candidate Execution. A Candidate with the addition of $\overrightarrow{sw}$, $\overrightarrow{hb}$ and $\overrightarrow{mo}$ relations. This can be viewed as the witness/justification of an actual execution of a Program. Note that there can be many Candidate Executions for a given Candidate.*

Definition 4. *Observable Behavior. The set of pairwise $\overrightarrow{rf}$ and $\overrightarrow{rbf}$ relations that result in one execution of the program. Think of this as our outcome of a program execution.*

3.6 Valid Execution Rules (the Axioms)

We now state the memory consistency rules. The rules are on *Candidate Executions* which will place constraints on the possible *Observable behaviors* that may result from it.

Coherent Reads. There are certain restrictions of what a read event cannot see in an execution based on $\overrightarrow{hb}$ relation with write events.

Consider a read event e and a write event d having at least overlapping ranges:

$$e \in R \wedge d \in W \wedge (\Re(e) \cap_\Re \Re(d) \neq \phi).$$

A read (e) value cannot come from a write (d) that has happened after it or if there is a write (g) that happens between them, writing to the same memory:

$$e \overrightarrow{hb} d \Rightarrow \neg e \overrightarrow{rf} d.$$

$$d \overrightarrow{hb} e \wedge d \overrightarrow{hb} g \wedge g \overrightarrow{hb} e \Rightarrow \forall x \in (\Re(d) \cap_\Re \Re(g) \cap_\Re \Re(e)), \neg e \overrightarrow{rbf} (d,x).$$

Tear-Free Reads. If two tear-free writes (d and g) and a tear-free read (e) all with equal ranges exist, then e can read only from one of them

$$d:tf \wedge g:tf \wedge e:tf \wedge (\Re(d) = \Re(g) = \Re(e)) \Rightarrow ((e \overrightarrow{rf} d) \wedge (\neg e \overrightarrow{rf} g)) \vee ((e \overrightarrow{rf} g) \wedge (\neg e \overrightarrow{rf} d)).$$

Sequentially Consistent Atomics. To specifically define how events that are sequentially consistent affects what values a read cannot see, we assume the following memory order among writes d and g and a read e to be the premise for all the rules:

$$d \overrightarrow{mo} g \overrightarrow{mo} e.$$

There are three separate cases that restrict e to read from d, which are as below:

- If all events are sequentially consistent with equal ranges.
- If both g and d are sequentially consistent with equal ranges and they happen before e.
- If both e and g are sequentially consistent with equal ranges and d happens before them.

The above cases can be summarized concisely by the rules below:

$$d: sc \;\land\; g: sc \;\land\; e: sc \;\land\; (\Re(d) = \Re(g) = \Re(e)) \;\Rightarrow\; \neg\, e \xrightarrow{rf} d.$$

$$d: sc \;\land\; g: sc \;\land\; (\Re(d) = \Re(g)) \;\land\; d \xrightarrow{hb} e \;\land\; g \xrightarrow{hb} e \;\Rightarrow\; \neg\, e \xrightarrow{rf} d.$$

$$g: sc \;\land\; e: sc \;\land\; (\Re(g) = \Re(e)) \;\land\; d \xrightarrow{hb} g \;\land\; d \xrightarrow{hb} e \;\Rightarrow\; \neg\, e \xrightarrow{rf} d.$$

3.7   Race

Race Condition (RC). We define RC as the set of all pairs of events that are in a race. Two events e and d are in a race condition when they are shared memory events ($e, d \in SM$), having overlapping ranges, not having a $\xrightarrow{hb}$ relation with each other, and which are either two writes or the two events are involved in a $\xrightarrow{rf}$ relation with each other. This can be stated concisely as,

$$\neg\, (e \xrightarrow{hb} d) \;\land\; \neg\, (d \xrightarrow{hb} e) \;\land\; (\, (e, d \in W \;\land\; (\Re(d) \cap_{\Re} \Re(e) \neq \phi)) \;\lor\; (d \xrightarrow{rf} e) \;\lor\; (e \xrightarrow{rf} d) \,).$$

Data Race (DR). We define DR as the set of all pairs of events that are in a data-race. Two events are in a data race when they are already in a race condition and when the two events are not both of type sc, or they have overlapping ranges. This is concisely stated as:

$$e, d \in RC \;\land\; ((\neg e: sc \;\lor\; \neg d: sc) \;\lor\; (\Re(e) \cap_{\Re} \Re(d) \neq \Re(e) \cup_{\Re} \Re(d)))$$

Data-Race-Free (DRF) Programs. An execution is considered data-race free if none of the above conditions for data-races occur among events. A program is data-race free if all its executions are data race free. *The memory model guarantees Sequential Consistency for all data-race free programs (SC-DRF).*

3.8   Consistent Executions (Valid Observables)

A valid observable behaviour is when:

1. No $\xrightarrow{rf}$ relation violates the above memory consistency rules.
2. $\xrightarrow{hb}$ is a strict partial order.

The memory model guarantees that every program must have at least one valid observable behaviour.

4   Instruction Reordering

Instruction reordering is a common operation in compiler optimization, essential to instruction scheduling of course, but also implicit in loop invariant removal, partial redundancy elimination, and other optimizations that may move instructions. However, we saw previously how concurrent programs, under sequential consistency, may not be allowed to reorder certain events. Understanding precisely when we can safely reorder requires information on what instructions threads may be executing concurrently, which requires impractically expensive whole program analysis.

4.1   Our Approach

Our solution to this is to construct a proof that would expose/specify the conditions under which reordering is possible given the relaxed memory semantics, while using information restricted to only the thread whose events are reordered. We construct the proof on candidate executions of a program. To keep things simple, assume that:

1. All events are tear-free
2. No synchronize events exist
3. No Read-Modify-Write events exist
4. All executions of the candidate before reordering have happens-before as a strict partial order

We first consider when consecutive events in the same agent can be reordered, followed by non-consecutive cases. The crux of the proof is to guarantee that reordering does not bring any new observable behaviors.

4.2   Preliminaries

Before we go about proving when reordering is valid, we would like to have two additional definitions which would prove useful.

Definition 5. *Consecutive pair of events (cons)*
    We define cons *as a function, which takes two events as input, and gives us a boolean indicating if they are consecutive pairs. Two events e and d are consecutive if they have an $\overrightarrow{ao}$ relation among them and are 'next to each other' in the same agent (thread), which can be defined formally as*

$$(e \overrightarrow{ao} d \land \nexists k \text{ s.t. } e \overrightarrow{ao} k \land k \overrightarrow{ao} d) \lor (d \overrightarrow{ao} e \land \nexists k \text{ s.t. } d \overrightarrow{ao} k \land k \overrightarrow{ao} e)$$

Definition 6. *Direct happens-before relation (dir)*
    We define dir *to take an ordered pair of events (e, d) such that $e \overrightarrow{hb} d$ and gives a boolean value to indicate whether this relation is direct which can be defined formally as*

$$\nexists g. \, e \overrightarrow{hb} g \land g \overrightarrow{hb} d$$

We can infer certain relations/conditions that must hold using this function based on some information on events e and d.

- *If e:uo, then $dir(e,d) \Rightarrow cons(e,d)$*
- *If d:uo, then $dir(e,d) \Rightarrow cons(e,d)$*
- *If e:sc $\land$ $e \in R$, then $dir(e,d) \Rightarrow cons(e,d)$*
- *If e:sc $\land$ $e \in W$, then $dir(e,d) \Rightarrow cons(e,d) \lor e \overrightarrow{sw} d$*
- *If d:sc $\land$ $d \in W$, then $dir(e,d) \Rightarrow cons(e,d)$*
- *If d:sc $\land$ $e \in R$, then $dir(e,d) \Rightarrow cons(e,d) \lor e \overrightarrow{sw} d$*

4.3   Lemmas to Assist Our Proof

In order to assist our proof, we define two lemmas based on the ordering relations.

Lemma 1. *Consider three events e, d, and k.*

If

$$cons(e,d) \ \wedge \ e \xrightarrow{ao} d \ \wedge \ ((d:uo) \ \vee \ (d:sc \ \wedge \ d \in W))$$

then,

$$k \xrightarrow{hb} d \ \Rightarrow \ k \xrightarrow{hb} e.$$

Proof. We have the following to be true :

$$cons(e,d) \ \wedge \ e \xrightarrow{ao} d.$$

In both cases where d is unordered or a sequentially consistent write, for any event k

$$dir(k,d) \ \Rightarrow \ cons(k,d).$$

An event that satisfies the above with d is e. Because $\xrightarrow{ao}$ is a total order, e will be the only event. This would mean that for any other $k \neq e$,

$$k \xrightarrow{hb} d \ \Rightarrow \ k \xrightarrow{hb} e.$$

Note that although there could be a direct *happens-before* relation with some event k from *another* agent, they are only relations satisfying $dir(d,k)$.

Lemma 2. *Consider three events e, d and k.*

If

$$cons(e,d) \ \wedge \ e \xrightarrow{ao} d \ \wedge \ ((e:uo) \ \vee \ (e:sc \ \wedge \ e \in R))$$

then,

$$e \xrightarrow{hb} k \ \Rightarrow \ d \xrightarrow{hb} k.$$

Proof. The proof is symmetric to that of Lemma 1.

Note that the above lemmas are only for events k which are not of type init

4.4   Valid Reordering

We view reordering as manipulating the agent-order relation among two events. In that sense, reordering two events e and d with $e \xrightarrow{ao} d$ effectively flips the relation around to $d \xrightarrow{ao} e$. What implications this change has on the other ordering relations depends what events e and d are and would require an analysis of each Candidate Execution. We begin by first defining a reorderable pair of events. We then formulate a theorem (with proof) on the set of observable behaviors of a Candidate before and after reordering a pair of consecutive events that are reorderable. We consider reordering valid if the set of observable behaviours after reordering are a subset of the original.

Definition 7. *Reorderable Pair (Reord)* *We define a boolean function* Reord *that takes two ordered pair of events e and d such that* $e \overrightarrow{ao} d$ *and gives a boolean value indicating if they are a reorderable pair:*

$$Reord(e, d) =$$
$$(((e : uo \wedge d : uo) \wedge ((e \in R \wedge d \in R) \vee (\Re(e) \cap_\Re \Re(d) = \phi)))$$
$$\vee$$
$$((e : sc \wedge d : uo) \wedge ((e \in W \wedge (\Re(e) \cap_\Re \Re(d) = \phi))))$$
$$\vee$$
$$((e : uo \wedge d : sc) \wedge ((d \in R \wedge (\Re(e) \cap_\Re \Re(d) = \phi)))))$$

Theorem 1. *Consider a candidate C of a program and its possible Candidate Executions where $\overrightarrow{hb}$ is strictly partial order. Consider two events e and d such that cons(e, d) is true in C and $e \overrightarrow{ao} d$. Consider another candidate C' resulting after reordering e and d. Then if* Reord(e,d) *is true in C, the set observable behaviors possible due to Candidate Executions of C' is a subset of that of C.*

Proof. We look at this in terms of performing an instruction reordering on a candidate execution of C. We would want the resulting candidate execution to preserve all the other $\overrightarrow{hb}$ relations (except $e \overrightarrow{hb} d$) and that any new $\overrightarrow{hb}$ relations strictly reduce possible observable behaviors. This can be summarized as addressing four main questions for any *CandidateExecution* of C':

1. Apart from $e \overrightarrow{hb} d$, do other *happens-before* relations remain intact?
2. Apart from $d \overrightarrow{hb} e$, are any new *happens-before* relations established?
3. Are any *happens-before* cycles introduced?
4. Do the new relations bring new *observable behaviors?*

1. Preserving *happens-before* Relations. If some $\overrightarrow{hb}$ relations among events are missing in Candidate Executions of C' as compared to that of C, we may introduce new observable behaviors.

The relations that could be lost can be addressed by considering two disjoint sets of events in any *Candidate Execution* of C defined as below.

$$K_e = \{k \mid k \overrightarrow{hb} e\}.$$
$$K_d = \{k \mid d \overrightarrow{hb} k\}.$$

Consider two events $p1 \in K_e$ and $p2 \in K_d$ (When e is the first event or d is the last event, assume dummy events that can act as $p1$ or $p2$.) belonging to the same agent as that of e and d such that in C:

$$dir(p1, e) \wedge dir(d, p2).$$

We consider $<p1, p2>$ as a pivot pair. This pair is *valid* if

$$\forall k \in K_e - \{p1\}, \ k \overrightarrow{hb} p1, \text{ and}$$
$$\forall k \in K_d - \{p2\}, \ p2 \overrightarrow{hb} k.$$

The intuition is to *pivot* the $\overrightarrow{hb}$ relations to $p1$ and $p2$, such that after reordering e and d, we can "flow" the relations back to retain all of them (due to transitivity of happens-before).

By Lemma 1, we have for C, the following condition on e where $p1$ is a valid pivot

$$e : uo \ \lor \ (e : sc \ \land \ e \in W).$$

Similarly, by Lemma 2, we have for C, the following condition on d where $p2$ is a valid pivot

$$d : uo \ \lor \ (d : sc \ \land \ d \in R).$$

Table 1 summarizes the cases where we have a valid pair of pivots $<p1, p2>$

Table 1. Table summarizing whether we have valid pair of pivots based on e and d.

<p1, p2>	R-R	R-W	W-R	W-W
uo-uo	Y	Y	Y	Y
uo-sc	Y	N	Y	N
sc-uo	N	N	Y	Y
sc-sc	N	N	Y	N

Note that the relations preserved are those other than $e \ \overrightarrow{hb} \ d$. Note also that relevant happens-before relations with initialize events are always preserved.

2. Additional *happens-before* Relations. Among cases that have valid pair of pivots, some may introduce new $\overrightarrow{hb}$ relations in Candidate Executions of C'. As an example, for the case when d is a sequentially consistent read, by Lemma 1, in any Candidate Execution of C,

$$k \ \overrightarrow{hb} \ d \ \not\Rightarrow \ k \ \overrightarrow{hb} \ e.$$

But in those of candidate C', by transitivity, we have

$$k \ \overrightarrow{hb} \ d \ \Rightarrow \ k \ \overrightarrow{hb} \ e.$$

This is because there are sets of relations that come through $\overrightarrow{sw}$ relations. Table 2 summarizes the cases where new relations could be introduced, assuming valid pivot pairs.

Table 2. Table summarizing when new *happens-before* relations could be introduced based on having valid pair of pivots.

New Reln	R-R	R-W	W-R	W-W
uo-uo	N	N	N	N
uo-sc	Y	N	Y	N
sc-uo	N	N	Y	Y
sc-sc	N	N	Y	N

3. Presence of Cycles? Before we go into analyzing whether new relations introduce observable behaviours, we first ensure there are no $\overrightarrow{hb}$ cycles introduced in the process. Note that if a cycle exists in Candidate Executions of C', then

1. The relations preserved do not themselves create a cycle
2. Additional new relations may introduce cycles

The first part is straightforward as we assume Candidate Executions of C have $\overrightarrow{hb}$ as a strict partial order. For the second part, we first address the case where $d \overrightarrow{hb} e$ may be part of the cycle. The other event k, may be either from the set K_e, K_d or a new relation that is formed.

1. Event k cannot belong to K_e or K_d, as by transitive property of $\overrightarrow{hb}$, a cycle would not exist.
2. For cases where $k \overrightarrow{hb} e$ is in the set of new relations, note that, $k \overrightarrow{hb} d$ already existed in the original Candidate Execution. On similar lines, for cases where $d \overrightarrow{hb} k$ is the set of new relations, $e \overrightarrow{hb} k$ exists. Thus, for both these cases also, a cycle with $d \overrightarrow{hb} e$ cannot exist.
3. For the last case where we have two new sets of relations formed, i.e. $d \overrightarrow{hb} k$ and $k \overrightarrow{hb} e$, we could have a case where k is a common event for both sets. By Lemma 1, we also have $k \overrightarrow{hb} d$ and by Lemma 2, $e \overrightarrow{hb} k$. Thus, we have a cycle.

For the case when $d \overrightarrow{hb} e$ may not be part of the cycle, consider the first scenario where the new set of relations are of the form $k \overrightarrow{hb} e$. Suppose a cycle exists with another event k', then

$$k \overrightarrow{hb} e \wedge e \overrightarrow{hb} k' \wedge k' \overrightarrow{hb} k.$$

By Lemma 1, we also have $k \overrightarrow{hb} d$ and by transitivity we also have $d \overrightarrow{hb} k'$. So, the following is also a cycle

$$k \overrightarrow{hb} d \wedge d \overrightarrow{hb} k' \wedge k' \overrightarrow{hb} k.$$

But these relations already existed in the original Candidate Execution, which implies a cycle existed in Candidate Execution of C. Thus, by contradiction, a cycle cannot exist. In similar lines we can show for the set $d \overrightarrow{hb} k$ that there cannot be any cycles.

4. Do New Relations Introduce New Observable Behaviours. In any candidate execution, reordering events e and d eliminates the relation $e \overrightarrow{hb} d$ and introduces the new relation $d \overrightarrow{hb} e$. New behaviours created by the latter directly, if any, are of course intentional (and should normally be avoided by ensuring e and d are independent), but we need to ensure that this does not also result in new behaviours indirectly.

On observing the role of the axioms on this relation, notice that if both e and d are read events then the range does not matter. For all other cases, if events e

and d have overlapping ranges, one could introduce a new observable behavior after reordering them (a simple use of Coherent Reads/Sequentially Consistent Atomics). Any other new relations that are introduced can be divided into 4 cases, in terms of our events e and d and the new relation with some event k:

a) $e : uo \land e \in R \land k \xrightarrow{hb} e$.

b) $e : uo \land e \in W \land k \xrightarrow{hb} e$.

c) $d : uo \land d \in R \land d \xrightarrow{hb} k$.

d) $d : uo \land d \in W \land d \xrightarrow{hb} k$.

In each of the above cases, note that we need to only consider cases where their ranges are overlapping/equal.

Figure 3 shows a breakdown of sub-cases for the first case (a), varying based on the nature of event k.

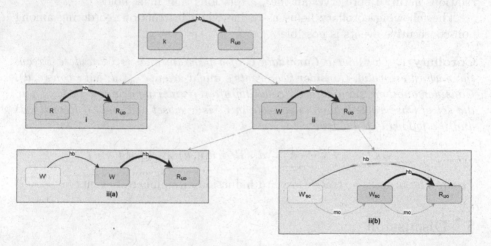

Fig. 3. The role of the axioms on introducing a new relation between an unordered read (purple box) and a preceding (by hb) event k (red box), varying based on whether k is a read, write, or sequentially consistent write. (Color figure online)

1. For (i), when k is a read, none of the rules have any implications on observable behaviors.
2. For (ii), when k is a write, the rule of coherent reads (ii(a)) or sequentially consistent atomics (ii(b)) could restrict the read (e) from reading overlapping ranges of W' with W.

The above case analysis shows us that the new relation could 'trigger' the consistency rules, only to restrict possible reads-from relations, thus restricting possible observable behaviors.

Similarly, for other cases, the new relations could also 'trigger' the consistency rules, but again, only *restricting* $\xrightarrow{rf}$ relations.

Table 3 summarizes the valid cases where, we have a pair of valid pivots, where new relations do not introduce any $\xrightarrow{hb}$ cycles and may only restrict possible observable behaviors.

Table 3. The final table summarizing the valid cases where observable behaviors will only be a subset after reordering.

Final	R-R	R-W	W-R	W-W
uo-uo	Y	Y	Y	Y
uo-sc	Y	N	Y	N
sc-uo	N	N	Y	Y
sc-sc	N	N	N	N

The table above, precisely is the definition of a reorderable pair (Definition 7).

□

Note that in the above we did not consider the $\overrightarrow{mo}$ relation, as preserving $\overrightarrow{hb}$ relations naturally preserves all the $\overrightarrow{mo}$ relations that must hold.

The following corollary helps us define when instruction reordering among non-consecutive events is possible.

Corollary 1. *Consider a Candidate C of a program and its Candidate Executions which are valid. Consider two events e and d where e $\overrightarrow{ao}$ d, but ¬cons(e, d). Consider another Candidate C' resulting after reordering e and d in C. Then, the set of Observable behaviors possible in C' is a subset of C only if Reord(e, d) and the following holds true.*

$$\forall k \ s.t. \ e \overrightarrow{ao} k \ \wedge \ k \overrightarrow{ao} d \ . \ Reord(e, k) \ \wedge \ Reord(k, d)$$

Proof. The proof is a straightforward induction on number of events k. □

5   Discussion

Theorem 1 and its corollary together give us a set of conditions that just need to be checked in addition while performing reordering of relaxed memory events. Having these set of conditions helps us avoid addressing the data-flow complexity due to different executions of the program using such accesses.

It is important to note that our approach is conservative, and one might be able to do reordering without causing new observable behaviors to occur even in cases that do not satisfy our conditions. This is possible because certain happens-before relations may not be essential and hence discarding them will not result in any invalid observable behavior. Getting such information would require an analysis that takes into account relations that we cannot obtain using just intra-thread information, which in practice might be infeasible as the number of threads and events increase. (One such well studied analysis is May-Happen-In-Parallel, whose origins come from the work done by Naumovich et al. [7]).

It is also important to note that we focus on Candidates rather than the Program. We do not in this work consider the specifics of identifying all possible candidates of a given program, and we assume that whatever candidate considered is a possible one for the original program. This translation from program to a set of candidates is something that would be needed in order to practically incorporate our set of conditions in practice while doing transformations.

6   Conclusion and Future Work

Our more declarative approach to the ECMAScript memory consistency model results in a relatively compact and concise description of the semantics. This better facilitates mathematical reasoning, which we have used to investigate the conditions on basic optimization operations such as instruction reordering.

Future work is aimed at extending our analysis to validate the conditions for redundancy elimination.

We are also interested in further exploring the constraints implied by the potential for multi-byte (non-atomic) accesses. The current standard imposes only very weak conditions on overlapping accesses, but stronger conditions are likely necessary to reflect actual programming practice.

Acknowledgements. We acknowledge the funding in part by the NSERC-COHESA project, under Strategic Networks grant number NETGP485577-15. We would like to thank Conrad Watt for his keen insights and suggestions throughout and Aarti Kashyap for many useful comments and questions that helped more clearly shape the ideas in this paper.

References

1. Adve, S.V., Gharachorloo, K.: Shared memory consistency models: a tutorial. IEEE Comput. **29**, 66–76 (1996)
2. Batty, M., Owens, S., Sarkar, S., Sewell, P., Weber, T.: Mathematizing C++ concurrency. In: POPL, Austin, TX, USA (2011)
3. Bender, J., Palsberg, J.: A formalization of Java's concurrent access modes. OOPSLA **3** (2019). Article No. 142
4. Draft: ECMAScript language specification (2020). https://tc39.es/ecma262/#sec-memory-model
5. Lamport, L.: How to make a multiprocessor computer that correctly executes multiprocess programs. IEEE Trans. Comput. **C-28**, 690–691 (1979)
6. Manson, J.: The design and verification of Java's memory model. In: OOPSLA (2002)
7. Naumovich, G., Avrunin, G.S.: A conservative data flow algorithm for detecting all pairs of statement that may happen in parallel. In: FSE, Lake Buena Vista, FL, USA (1998)
8. Owens, S., Sarkar, S., Sewell, P.: A better x86 memory model: x86-TSO. In: Berghofer, S., Nipkow, T., Urban, C., Wenzel, M. (eds.) TPHOLs 2009. LNCS, vol. 5674, pp. 391–407. Springer, Heidelberg (2009). https://doi.org/10.1007/978-3-642-03359-9_27
9. Sarkar, S., et al.: The semantics of x86-cc multiprocessor machine code. In: POPL, Savannah, GA, USA (2009)
10. Ševčík, J.: Safe optimisations for shared-memory concurrent programs. In: PLDI, San Jose, USA (2011)

214   A. Gopalakrishnan and C. Verbrugge

11. Ševčík, J., Aspinall, D.: On validity of program transformations in the Java memory model. In: ECOOP, Paphos, Cyprus (2008)
12. Sewell, P.: Memory, an elusive abstraction. In: ISMM, Toronto, Ontario, Canada (2010)
13. Vafeiadis, V., Balabonski, T., Chakraborty, S., Morisset, R., Nardelli, F.Z.: Common compiler optimisations are invalid in the C11 memory model and what we can do about it. In: POPL, Mumbai, India (2015)
14. Watt, C., et al.: Repairing and mechanising the JavaScript relaxed memory model. In: PLDI, London, UK (2020)

Verification of Vectorization of Signal Transforms

Patrick Brinich$^{(\boxtimes)}$ (ID) and Jeremy Johnson

Drexel University, Philadelphia, PA 19104, USA
{pjb338,johnsojr}@drexel.edu

Abstract. This paper proves properties of the vectorized code generated by the SPIRAL system for implementing, optimizing, and tuning fast signal transforms. In particular, it is shown that the generated code is correct and fully vectorized. The SPIRAL system uses multiple rewrite systems with varying levels of abstraction to generate, optimize, parallelize and implement code. The proofs proceed by showing that the rules preserve semantics and lead to code with guaranteed performance and correctness properties. Unlike more general approaches, much of the work is done at a higher level incorporating the underlying mathematics. This shifts much of the verification from proving equivalence of programs to proving equivalence of mathematical expressions. Furthermore, the proofs incorporate domain specific knowledge leading to stronger guarantees than could be obtained for a more general vectorizing compiler.

1   Introduction and Related Work

Traditional compiler techniques for automatic vectorization and parallelization [1,20] analyze code to determine whether certain general-purpose transformations are applicable. While there is a diverse effort directed at verifying both traditional and novel techniques in vectorization and parallelization, significant automatic vectorization or parallelization is mostly absent in large, verified optimizing compilers such as CompCert [17].

Current work in verifying correctness of vectorizing transformations as well as vectorized implementations of scalar programs focuses on showing program equivalence. Barthe et al. [3] leverage relational verification to automatically vectorize loops while simultaneously producing a proof of program equivalence. Taking a different approach, [9], Dutta validates parallelizing and vectorizing transformations using dependence graphs. A third approach by Collingbourne et al. [8] employs symbolic execution using an extension of KLEE [7] to show bounded equivalence between scalar and vector programs. Different still, Almeida et al. [2] use EasyCrypt [4] to verify both correctness and security properties of various cryptographic algorithms including their vectorized implementations.

The approach in this paper contrasts with all of the above approaches due to nature of the SPIRAL system [12]. The SPIRAL system generates and optimizes code for a variety of signal and image processing, linear algebra, and

© Springer Nature Switzerland AG 2022
B. Chapman and J. Moreira (Eds.): LCPC 2020, LNCS 13149, pp. 215–231, 2022.
https://doi.org/10.1007/978-3-030-95953-1_15

scientific computing kernels on a variety of computer architectures. The original version of SPIRAL [18] focused on linear signal transforms. SPIRAL represents algorithms in a high-level mathematical language originally called SPL (Signal Processing Language) [21] and later extended to OL (Operator Language) [13]. High-Performance code is generated and optimized through multiple levels of rewrite systems. At the highest level, the rewrite rules work on mathematical formulas and their correctness comes from mathematical identities. At lower levels, the rewrite rules convert formulas to code, preserving the mathematical semantics, and perform code level optimizations, preserving program semantics. Work on formal proofs of correctness is outlined in [11] and described in detail in [6] and implemented in Coq [19].

When performing high-level optimizations, such as vectorization and parallelization, SPIRAL starts at the highest level, exploiting domain specific information that would be lost by starting at lower levels. As a result, this information cascades to these lower levels. For instance, many code level transformations are guaranteed to be applicable. For linear signal transforms, such as the DFT and Wavelet transform, vectorization [14] and parallelization [15] are obtained naturally from the mathematical representation that encode algorithms for their computation.

The mathematical formulas used to represent fast signal transform algorithms are transformed through a series of rewrite rules to naturally expose parallel and vector operations. As a result, much of the verification effort shifts from showing program equivalence to mathematical equivalence. Moreover, it is possible to prove properties of the resulting vector and parallel code, such as full vectorization, load balance and no false sharing, at the mathematical level.

This paper presents a formal setting for the paper [14] by Franchetti et al. on a rewriting system for vectorization of signal transforms. The mathematical rules for generating vectorized code for fast signal transforms are formally verified and the rewrite system that produces a vectorized variant is proven to terminate. Moreover, a fully vectorized program is proven to exist. Finally, the generation of code from the mathematical description is proven to preserve semantics and produce a code whose operation count is decreased by the vector size of the target architecture. The proofs and examples use the discrete Fourier transform, though the proofs carry over to similar transforms and algorithm generation rules.

2   Vectorization of Signal Transforms Through Rewriting

SPIRAL uses SPL [18] to represent algorithms for computing signal transforms as sparse matrix factorizations. For example, let DFT_n be the n-point discrete Fourier transform, $[\omega]_{0 \le k,l < n}$, where ω is a primitive n-th root of unity. The following factorization of a DFT of size 4

$$\begin{bmatrix} 1 & 1 & 1 & 1 \\ 1 & \omega & -1 & -\omega \\ 1 & -1 & 1 & -1 \\ 1 & -\omega & -1 & \omega \end{bmatrix} = \begin{bmatrix} 1 & 0 & 1 & 0 \\ 0 & 1 & 0 & 1 \\ 1 & 0 & -1 & 0 \\ 0 & 1 & 0 & -1 \end{bmatrix} \begin{bmatrix} 1 & 0 & 0 & 0 \\ 0 & 1 & 0 & 0 \\ 0 & 0 & 1 & 0 \\ 0 & 0 & 0 & \omega \end{bmatrix} \begin{bmatrix} 1 & 1 & 0 & 0 \\ 1 & -1 & 0 & 0 \\ 0 & 0 & 1 & 1 \\ 0 & 0 & 1 & -1 \end{bmatrix} \begin{bmatrix} 1 & 0 & 0 & 0 \\ 0 & 0 & 1 & 0 \\ 0 & 1 & 0 & 0 \\ 0 & 0 & 0 & 1 \end{bmatrix},$$

corresponds to the Cooley-Tukey FFT algorithm. This factorization can be succinctly represented by the formula

$$(\text{DFT}_2 \otimes I_2) T_2^4 (I_2 \otimes \text{DFT}_2) L_2^4.$$

More generally

$$\text{DFT}_{rs} = (\text{DFT}_r \otimes I_s) T_s^{rs} (I_2 \otimes \text{DFT}_s) L_r^{rs}, \tag{1}$$

where T_s^{rs} is a diagonal matrix of "twiddle" factors, L_r^{rs} is a stride permutation, and $\otimes$ denotes the Kronecker product

$$A \otimes B = [a_{ij}B] \text{ when } A = [a_{ij}].$$

Equation (1) can be thought of as a rewrite rule which replaces DFT_{rs} by smaller DFTs and as such can be used to generate algorithms, represented by a matrix factorization, for computing the DFT.

Certain factorizations naturally represent algorithms that can be implemented using v-way vector operations. The key idea is that the SPL construct

$$A \otimes I_v$$

can be implemented using v-way vector operations for an arbitrary matrix A. This implementation is a straightforward transformation of the scalar code generated for A: each scalar operation is replaced by its corresponding v-way vector operation. For example, when v is 2, the scalar operation

```
a[0]:= x[0] + x[1]
```

is replaced by

```
a[0:1:2]:= vadd(x[0:1:2], x[2:1:2]),
```

where $x[b : s : n]$ denotes a size n subvector of x at stride s starting at base address b. Furthermore, constructs of the form

$$I_m \otimes A \text{ and } AB$$

can be recursively implemented using v-way vector operations by looping over the vectorized code for A and concatenating the vectorized code for A and B respectively.

Formulas that cannot be immediately used to generate vectorized code can be transformed, using mathematical identities, into a vectorized form. For example, the Cooley-Tukey breakdown for DFT_4 can be transformed into the vectorized form,

$$(\text{DFT}_2 \otimes I_2) T_2^4 (L_2^4 (\text{DFT}_2 \otimes I_2)).$$

The following code fragment implements this form for input vector x using 2-way vector operations.

```
//(DFT_2 ⊗ I_2)
t0[0:1:2] := vadd(x[0:1:2], x[2:1:2]);
t0[2:1:2] := vsub(x[0:1:2], x[2:1:2]);
//L_2^4
t1[0:1:2] := t0[0:2:2];
t1[2:1:2] := t0[1:2:2];
//T_2^4
t2[0:1:2] := t1[0:1:2];
t2[2:1:2] := vmul(t1[2:1:2], [1, ω]);
//(DFT_2 ⊗ I_2)
y[0:1:2] := vadd(t2[0:1:2], t2[2:1:2]);
y[2:1:2] := vsub(t2[0:1:2], t2[2:1:2]);
```

In [14], a set of rewriting rules based on the matrix identities in Table 1 are introduced to manipulate formulas into a vectorizable form. For example, the following factorization,

$$DFT_8 = (DFT_2 \otimes I_4)T_4^8((I_2 \otimes DFT_4)L_2^8),$$

can be vectorized using 2-way vector operations. Each of these factors can be vectorized separately. The first factor needs only a minor adjustment. The identity matrix I_4 can be rewritten as $I_2 \otimes I_2$ and the resulting product can be reassociated such that

$$DFT_2 \otimes I_4 = (DFT_2 \otimes I_2) \otimes I_2.$$

The twiddle factor matrix is a diagonal matrix, so the corresponding vectorized code can be precomputed. The third factor $((I_2 \otimes DFT_4)L_2^8)$, can be rewritten using the identity (4). Using (3), the stride permutation is pushed to the left obtaining

$$((I_2 \otimes DFT_4)L_2^8) = (L_2^8(DFT_4 \otimes I_2)).$$

Next, identity (5) decomposes the stride permutation:

$$L_2^8 = (L_2^4 \otimes I_2)(I_2 \otimes L_2^4).$$

Recombining the factors, the original formula is transformed into the equivalent fully vectorized formula

$$((DFT_2 \otimes I_2) \otimes I_2)T_4^8((L_2^4 \otimes I_2)(I_2 \otimes L_2^4)(DFT_4 \otimes I_2)).$$

A formula (see definition 1 of [14]) is fully vectorized if it is of the form $A \otimes I_v$, is a product or tensor product of fully vectorized formulas, or consists of special forms like L_v^{2v}, L_2^{2v}, and $L_v^{v^2}$ which are efficiently implemented on the target vector architecture.

Automatically transforming formulas to vectorized form using these mathematical identities can lead to difficulties as there are too many degrees of freedom, and it can not be guaranteed that the process will terminate in the desired form. The paper [14] introduced tags to guide the rewriting to the desired form.

Table 1. Matrix identities

$$I_{nm} = I_n \otimes I_m \tag{2}$$

$$L_n^{mn} L_m^{mn} = I_{mn} \tag{3}$$

$$(I_m \otimes A^{n \times n}) = L_m^{mn}(A^{n \times n} \otimes I_m)L_n^{mn} \tag{4}$$

$$L_n^{kmn} = (L_n^{kn} \otimes I_m)(I_k \otimes L_n^{mn}) \tag{5}$$

$$L_{km}^{kmn} = (I_k \otimes L_m^{mn})(L_k^{kn} \otimes I_m) \tag{6}$$

$$A^2 \otimes (BC) = (A \otimes B)(A \otimes C) \tag{7}$$

$$(A^{n \times n} \otimes B^{m \times m}) = (A^{n \times n} \otimes I_m)(I_n \otimes B^{m \times m}) \tag{8}$$

$$(A^{n \times n} \otimes B^{m \times m}) = (I_n \otimes B^{m \times m})(A^{n \times n} \otimes I_m) \tag{9}$$

Table 2. Vectorization rules for stride permutations

$$\underbrace{L_n^{nv}}_{vec(v)} \longrightarrow (I_{n/v} \otimes L_v^{v^2})(L_{n/v}^n \bar\otimes I_v) \tag{10}$$

$$\underbrace{L_v^{nv}}_{vec(v)} \longrightarrow (L_v^n \bar\otimes I_v)(I_{n/v} \otimes L_v^{v^2}) \tag{11}$$

$$\underbrace{L_m^{mn}}_{vec(v)} \longrightarrow (L_m^{mn/v} \bar\otimes I_v)(I_{mn/v^2} \otimes L_v^{v^2})((I_{n/v} \otimes L_{m/v}^m) \bar\otimes I_v) \tag{12}$$

The rewrite rules—shown in Tables 2 and 3—operate on tagged subexpressions. Each rule implicitly requires that the division of two numbers produces a whole number when necessary.

Rewriting may only occur at tags, so rule (13) allows factors to be considered separately by distributing a tag to each of the enclosed factors. Base case rules remove tags. For example, rule (15) produces a tensor product with a vectorized implementation—made explicit using $\bar\otimes$—when m is divisible by v.

Other rules, such as (19), bring an expression closer to a vectorized form by moving tags to smaller subexpressions. These rules apply the matrix identities in Table 1 in a organized manner, guaranteeing the rewrite process terminates. The previous DFT example illustrates rewriting with tags.

$$\mathrm{DFT}_8 = \underbrace{(\mathrm{DFT}_2 \otimes I_4)T_4^8((I_2 \otimes \mathrm{DFT}_4)L_2^8)}_{vec(v)}$$

$$\longrightarrow \underbrace{(\mathrm{DFT}_2 \otimes I_4)}_{vec(v)} \underbrace{T_4^8}_{vec(v)} \underbrace{((I_2 \otimes \mathrm{DFT}_4)L_2^8)}_{vec(v)} \qquad \text{using rule (13)}$$

$$\longrightarrow ((\mathrm{DFT}_2 \otimes I_2) \bar\otimes I_2) \underbrace{T_4^8}_{vec(v)} \underbrace{((I_2 \otimes \mathrm{DFT}_4)L_2^8)}_{vec(v)} \qquad \text{using rule (15)}$$

$$\longrightarrow ((\mathrm{DFT}_2 \otimes I_2) \bar\otimes I_2)T_4^8 \underbrace{((I_2 \otimes \mathrm{DFT}_4)L_2^8)}_{vec(v)} \qquad \text{using rule (14)}$$

$$\longrightarrow ((\mathrm{DFT}_2 \otimes I_2) \bar\otimes I_2)T_4^8(\underbrace{L_2^8}_{vec(v)} \underbrace{(\mathrm{DFT}_4 \otimes I_2)}_{vec(v)}) \qquad \text{using rule (19)}$$

$$\longrightarrow ((\mathrm{DFT}_2 \otimes \mathrm{I}_2) \,\bar{\otimes}\, \mathrm{I}_2) \mathrm{T}_4^8 ((\mathrm{L}_2^4 \,\bar{\otimes}\, \mathrm{I}_2)(\mathrm{I}_2 \otimes \mathrm{L}_2^4) \underbrace{(\mathrm{DFT}_4 \otimes \mathrm{I}_2)}_{\mathrm{vec}(v)}) \quad \text{using rule (11)}$$

$$\longrightarrow ((\mathrm{DFT}_2 \otimes \mathrm{I}_2) \,\bar{\otimes}\, \mathrm{I}_2) \mathrm{T}_4^8 ((\mathrm{L}_2^4 \,\bar{\otimes}\, \mathrm{I}_2)(\mathrm{I}_2 \otimes \mathrm{L}_2^4)(\mathrm{DFT}_4 \,\bar{\otimes}\, \mathrm{I}_2)) \quad \text{using rule (15)}$$

Table 3. Vectorization rules for composition, tensor products, and other constructs. The dimensions of the matrix A are $n \times n$ and D is a diagonal matrix of size kv.

$$\underbrace{AB}_{\mathrm{vec}(v)} \longrightarrow \underbrace{A}_{\mathrm{vec}(v)} \underbrace{B}_{\mathrm{vec}(v)} \tag{13}$$

$$\underbrace{D}_{\mathrm{vec}(v)} \longrightarrow D \tag{14}$$

$$\underbrace{A \otimes \mathrm{I}_m}_{\mathrm{vec}(v)} \longrightarrow (A \otimes \mathrm{I}_{m/v}) \,\bar{\otimes}\, \mathrm{I}_v \tag{15}$$

$$\underbrace{(\mathrm{I}_m \otimes A)}_{\mathrm{vec}(v)} \longrightarrow \mathrm{I}_{m/v} \otimes \underbrace{(\mathrm{I}_v \otimes A)}_{\mathrm{vec}(v)} \tag{16}$$

$$\underbrace{(\mathrm{I}_m \otimes A)}_{\mathrm{vec}(v)} \longrightarrow \underbrace{\mathrm{L}_m^{mn}}_{\mathrm{vec}(v)} \underbrace{(A \otimes \mathrm{I}_m)}_{\mathrm{vec}(v)} \underbrace{\mathrm{L}_n^{mn}}_{\mathrm{vec}(v)} \tag{17}$$

$$\underbrace{(\mathrm{I}_m \otimes A)}_{\mathrm{vec}(v)} \longrightarrow (\mathrm{I}_m \otimes \underbrace{A}_{\mathrm{vec}(v)}) \tag{18}$$

$$\underbrace{(\mathrm{I}_m \otimes A)\mathrm{L}_m^{nm}}_{\mathrm{vec}(v)} \longrightarrow \underbrace{\mathrm{L}_m^{mn}}_{\mathrm{vec}(v)} \underbrace{(A \otimes \mathrm{I}_m)}_{\mathrm{vec}(v)} \tag{19}$$

$$\underbrace{(\mathrm{I}_m \otimes A)\mathrm{L}_m^{nm}}_{\mathrm{vec}(v)} \longrightarrow (\mathrm{I}_{m/v} \otimes \underbrace{\mathrm{L}_v^{nv}}_{\mathrm{vec}(v)} (A \,\bar{\otimes}\, \mathrm{I}_v))(\mathrm{L}_{m/v}^{mn/v} \,\bar{\otimes}\, \mathrm{I}_v) \tag{20}$$

$$\underbrace{(\mathrm{I}_k \otimes (\mathrm{I}_m \otimes A)\mathrm{L}_m^{mn})\mathrm{L}_k^{kmn}}_{\mathrm{vec}(v)} \longrightarrow \underbrace{(\mathrm{L}_k^{km} \otimes \mathrm{I}_n)}_{\mathrm{vec}(v)}(\mathrm{I}_m \otimes \underbrace{(\mathrm{I}_k \otimes A)\mathrm{L}_k^{kn}}_{\mathrm{vec}(v)}) \underbrace{(\mathrm{L}_m^{mn} \otimes \mathrm{I}_k)}_{\mathrm{vec}(v)} \tag{21}$$

3   Verification of Rewrite Rules

The tagged rewriting system terminates with mathematically correct formulas. If the starting formula is vectorizable, the resulting formula has been vectorized. To facilitate the verification of these properties, the rewrite system is first presented formally. Table 4 gives a (subset) of the grammar of tagged and untagged SPL constructs. Since SPL constructs are a subset of tagged SPL constructs, this paper will refer to (necessarily) tag-free SPL constructs using the metavariable S and SPL expressions with zero or more tagged SPL expressions using the metavariable T where the distinction is not obvious.

In addition, the rewriting rules in Tables 2 and 3 describe a single rewrite of constructs entirely enclosed within a tag. An adaptation of contextual reduction semantics—originally used by Felleisen and Hieb to develop an equational theory for an imperative extension of the call-by-value lambda calculus [10]—is used to model multiple rewrites within subexpressions with minimal additions.

A *context* is an SPL construct with a *hole*, indicated by the symbol $\lrcorner$, which can be filled in by some tagged SPL construct. A context is defined inductively as

$$C ::= \lrcorner \mid C \cdot T \mid S \cdot C \mid C \otimes T \mid S \otimes C$$

where S is any (tag-free) SPL construct and T is any tagged SPL construct. For a tagged SPL expression T and some context C, the hole in C can be filled by T in the following manner,

$$C[T] = \begin{cases} T & C = \lrcorner \\ S \cdot C'[T] & C = S \cdot C' \\ C'[T] \cdot T_2 & C = C' \cdot T_2 \\ S \otimes C'[T] & C = S \otimes C' \\ C'[T] \otimes T_2 & C = C' \otimes T_2 \end{cases} \tag{22}$$

For example, Eq. (22) describes how to perform

$$((I_m \otimes \underbrace{\lrcorner}_{\text{vec}(v)}) \cdot \text{L}_m^{mn})[\underbrace{A}_{\text{vec}(v)}]$$

step-by-step. Since the context is of the form $C' \cdot T$, filling starts by descending into the subcontext on the left. The left subcontext itself is of the form $S \otimes C''$, so the subcontext appearing on the right of the tensor product is filled. This subcontext happens to be the hole, which is replaced by the redex.

$$((I_m \otimes \underbrace{\lrcorner}_{\text{vec}(v)}) \cdot \text{L}_m^{mn})[\underbrace{A}_{\text{vec}(v)}] = (I_m \otimes \underbrace{\lrcorner}_{\text{vec}(v)})[\underbrace{A}_{\text{vec}(v)}] \cdot \text{L}_m^{mn}$$

$$= (I_m \otimes \underbrace{\lrcorner[\underbrace{A}_{\text{vec}(v)}]}) \cdot \text{L}_m^{mn}$$

$$= (I_m \otimes \underbrace{A}_{\text{vec}(v)}) \cdot \underbrace{\text{L}_m^{mn}}_{\text{vec}(v)}$$

Decomposing large expressions into contexts and redexes provides a way to formalize rewriting subexpressions. The relation $\longrightarrow_C$ is defined for all contexts C by the inference rule

$$\frac{T \longrightarrow T'}{C[T] \longrightarrow_C C[T']}. \tag{23}$$

Finally, zero or more rewrites are modeled using the reflexive, transitive closure of (23), denoted by $\longrightarrow_C^*$. Note that this definition of a context is somewhat arbitrary: it merely forces rewriting to proceed from left to right. If rewriting can eliminate all tags from an expression, the rewriting subexpressions can be done in any order assuming the rule choices are fixed.

Verification of the rewrite system proceeds by showing that the rewriting produces mathematically equivalent formulas, terminates, and produces a vectorized formula whenever possible.

Matrix Equivalence of Rewrite Rules. Each SPL construct denotes a matrix, which can be computed exactly [18]. Parametrized symbols such as I_n and transforms such as the DFT represent their respective matrix forms. Composition is computed as matrix multiplication and tensor products as the Kronecker

Table 4. Abstract syntax of tagged SPL expressions

$s \in symbol ::=$ $t \in transform ::=$

$$I_n$$
$$DFT_n$$
$$F_2$$
$$WHT_{2^k}$$
$$L_s^n$$
$$T_s^n$$
$$\cdots$$
$$\cdots$$

$S \in spl ::=$ $T \in tagged\_spl ::=$

$$s$$
$$S$$
$$t$$
$$\underbrace{S}_{vec(v)}$$
$$S_1 \cdot S_2$$
$$T_1 \cdot T_2$$
$$S_1 \otimes S_2$$
$$T_1 \otimes T_2$$
$$S_1 \bar{\otimes} S_2$$

$$\cdots$$

product of their recursively computed operands. Tags do not change the mathematical meaning of the formula and are thus ignored. Two SPL constructs are said to be *matrix equivalent* when both constructs denote the same matrix, and a rule is correct *with respect to matrix equivalence* when the left hand and right hand sides of the rule are matrix equivalent. Moreover, matrix equivalence is an equivalence relation compatible with composition and the tensor product. This implies that the contextual rewrite relation and its reflexive, transitive closure relate two matrix equivalent SPL constructs if each of the rewrite rules do.

The matrix equivalence of the rules in Tables 2 and 3 follow from the application of the matrix identities shown in Table 1. Each of the identities in Table 1 follows by evaluation on a standard basis vector. The denotes the kth standard basis vector of size n is denoted by e_k^n and can be defined by the property

$$(e_k^n)_i = \begin{cases} 1 & k = i \\ 0 & k \neq i \end{cases} \text{ for all } 0 \leq i < n.$$

For example, the matrix equivalence of rule (11) follows after a single application of identity (5). The following evaluation of the identity requires the property $L_s^{rs}(e_i^r \otimes e_j^s) = (e_j^s \otimes e_i^r)$.

$$
\begin{aligned}
L_n^{kmn} e_{hmn+in+j}^{kmn} &= (L_n^{kn} \otimes I_m)(I_k \otimes L_n^{mn}) e_{hmn+in+j}^{kmn} \\
\Longleftrightarrow L_n^{kmn}(e_h^k \otimes e_i^m \otimes e_j^n) &= (L_n^{kn} \otimes I_m)(I_k \otimes L_n^{mn})(e_h^k \otimes e_i^m \otimes e_j^n) \\
\Longleftrightarrow e_j^n \otimes e_h^k \otimes e_i^m &= (L_n^{kn} \otimes I_m)(e_h^k \otimes L_n^{mn}(e_i^m \otimes e_j^n)) \\
\Longleftrightarrow e_j^n \otimes e_h^k \otimes e_i^m &= (L_n^{kn} \otimes I_m)(e_h^k \otimes e_j^n \otimes e_i^m)
\end{aligned}
$$

$$\Longleftrightarrow e_j^n \otimes e_h^k \otimes e_i^m \quad = (\mathrm{L}_n^{kn}(e_h^k \otimes e_j^n) \otimes \mathrm{I}_m e_i^m)$$

$$\Longleftrightarrow e_j^n \otimes e_h^k \otimes e_i^m \quad = e_j^n \otimes e_h^k \otimes e_i^m$$

Termination. Since a subexpression within an SPL construct may only be rewritten when enclosed within a tag, the rewrite process must terminate when either the entire construct is tag-free or no rules apply to any tagged subexpression. While rewriting is nondeterministic due to the presence of multiple rewrite rules for a single tagged construct, the contextual relation makes selecting the next subexpression to rewrite deterministic and unique.

Lemma 1 (Context Decomposition). *For all tagged SPL constructs T, if T is not a tag-free SPL construct, there exists a unique context C and an untagged SPL expression S such that*

$$T = C[\underbrace{S}_{\text{vec}(v)}].$$

This lemma can be shown by induction on T. As a consequence, rewriting must proceed from left to right until no tags are left or no rules apply to the left-most tagged subexpression. Focus can now be shifted to ensuring that rewriting an expression entirely enclosed within a tag will terminate.

Lemma 2. *For all SPL expressions S, there exists a tagged SPL expression T' such that,*

$$\underbrace{S}_{\text{vec}(v)} \to_C^* T'$$

and for all tagged SPL expressions T'',

$$T' \not\to {}_C T''.$$

This can be shown by induction on S. In most cases where a rule applies, a small number of subsequent rewrites will produce a tag-free expression. For example, if rule (19) or (20) is used to rewrite $(\mathrm{I}_m \otimes A)\mathrm{L}_m^{nm}$, the process will produce a tag-free expression when v divides both m and n in at most three rewrites and will stop after zero or more rewrites otherwise.

$$\underbrace{(\mathrm{I}_m \otimes A)\mathrm{L}_m^{nm}}_{\text{vec}(v)} \longrightarrow_C \underbrace{\mathrm{L}_m^{mn}}_{\text{vec}(v)} \underbrace{(A \otimes \mathrm{I}_m)}_{\text{vec}(v)}$$

$$\longrightarrow_C (\mathrm{L}_m^{mn/v} \bar{\otimes} \mathrm{I}_v)(\mathrm{I}_{mn/v^2} \otimes \mathrm{L}_v^{v^2})((\mathrm{I}_{n/v} \otimes \mathrm{L}_{m/v}^m) \bar{\otimes} \mathrm{I}_v) \underbrace{(A \otimes \mathrm{I}_m)}_{\text{vec}(v)}$$

$$\longrightarrow_C (\mathrm{L}_m^{mn/v} \bar{\otimes} \mathrm{I}_v)(\mathrm{I}_{mn/v^2} \otimes \mathrm{L}_v^{v^2})((\mathrm{I}_{n/v} \otimes \mathrm{L}_{m/v}^m) \bar{\otimes} \mathrm{I}_v)$$

$$((A \otimes \mathrm{I}_{m/v}) \bar{\otimes} \mathrm{I}_v)$$

$$\underbrace{(\mathrm{I}_m \otimes A)\mathrm{L}_m^{nm}}_{\text{vec}(v)} \longrightarrow_C (\mathrm{I}_{m/v} \otimes \underbrace{\mathrm{L}_v^{nv}}_{\text{vec}(v)} (A \bar{\otimes} \mathrm{I}_v))(\mathrm{L}_{m/v}^{mn/v} \bar{\otimes} \mathrm{I}_v)$$

$$\longrightarrow_C (\mathrm{I}_{m/v} \otimes (\mathrm{L}_v^n \bar{\otimes} \mathrm{I}_v)(\mathrm{I}_{n/v} \otimes \mathrm{L}_v^{v^2})(A \bar{\otimes} \mathrm{I}_v))(\mathrm{L}_{m/v}^{mn/v} \bar{\otimes} \mathrm{I}_v)$$

Alternatively, when rule (13) is used, an inductive case may be reached

$$\underbrace{(I_m \otimes A)L_m^{nm}}_{vec(v)} \longrightarrow_C \underbrace{(I_m \otimes A)}_{vec(v)} \underbrace{L_m^{nm}}_{vec(v)} \longrightarrow_C (I_m \otimes \underbrace{A}_{vec(v)}) \underbrace{L_m^{nm}}_{vec(v)}$$

where rewriting stops in at most one additional rewrite after A is completely rewritten.

Once each individual rule is shown to produce a terminating chain of rewrites, proving overall termination is straightforward.

Theorem 1 (Termination). *For all tagged SPL constructs T, there exists some final tagged SPL construct T' such that*

$$T \longrightarrow_C^* T'$$

and for all tagged SPL expressions T'',

$$T' \not\longrightarrow_C T''.$$

This can be shown by induction on T. If T is tag-free, it cannot be rewritten, and if T is a construct entirely enclosed in a tag, it must terminate by the previous lemma. If T is a composition or a product, rewriting T terminates when the first or both operands are completely rewritten.

Fully Vectorized Forms. Not all SPL constructs can be implemented using v-way vector operations. For example, $(A \otimes I_m)$ cannot be implemented entirely using v-way vector operations when m is not divisible by v. The final step of verifying the rewrite rules is to determine when rewriting produces a tag free SPL construct, ensuring that said SPL construct has a vectorized implementation.

Table 5 defines an inductive predicate describing when an SPL construct can be implemented using v-way vector operations. A tagged SPL expression T is *fully vectorizable* if for all tag-free S such that

$$T \longrightarrow_C^* S,$$

the predicate $VF(S)$ holds and there exists at least one such S.

Table 5. The inductively defined predicate $VF(S)$ holds when S can be implemented using v-way vector operations.

$$\frac{}{VF(L_2^{2v})} \text{ Perm1} \qquad \frac{}{VF(L_v^{2v})} \text{ Perm2} \qquad \frac{}{VF(L_v^{v^2})} \text{ Perm3} \qquad \frac{}{VF(S \otimes I_v)} \text{ AtensorI}$$

$$\frac{\text{diagonal } D^{n \times n} \quad v|n}{VF(D^{n \times n})} \text{ Diag} \qquad \frac{VF(A)}{VF(I_m \otimes S)} \text{ ItensorA} \qquad \frac{VF(S_1) \quad VF(S_2)}{VF(S_1 S_2)} \text{ Compose}$$

The left hand side of each rewrite rule is fully vectorizable under certain assumptions. This can be shown by completely rewriting as far as possible under assumptions that would allow rewriting to produce a tag-free construct, keeping track of multiple cases when multiple rules may apply. For each of these cases, constructing a proof tree shows that the resulting constructs are in a vectorized form. For example, if v divides both m and n, the stride permutation, L_m^{mn} is fully vectorizable in at most one rewrite:

$$\underbrace{L_m^{mn}}_{vec(v)} \longrightarrow_C^* L_v^{v^2} \qquad\qquad m = n = v$$

$$\underbrace{L_m^{mn}}_{vec(v)} \longrightarrow_C^* (I_{m/v} \otimes L_v^{v^2})(L_{m/v}^m \bar{\otimes} I_v) \qquad\qquad v|m, n = v, d > 0$$

$$\underbrace{L_m^{mn}}_{vec(v)} \longrightarrow_C^* (L_v^n \bar{\otimes} I_v)(I_{n/v} \otimes L_v^{v^2}) \qquad\qquad m = v, v|n$$

$$\underbrace{L_m^{mn}}_{vec(v)} \longrightarrow_C^* (L_m^{mn/v} \bar{\otimes} I_v)(I_{mn/v^2} \otimes L_v^{v^2})((I_{n/v} \otimes L_{m/v}^m) \bar{\otimes} I_v) \qquad v|m, v|n$$

Each of the resulting rewrites produces a vectorized form. As an example, the proof that the final case has a completely vectorized result can be seen in the following proof tree.

$$\cfrac{\cfrac{}{VF(L_m^{mn/v} \bar{\otimes} I_v)}\ \text{AtensorI} \quad \cfrac{\cfrac{\cfrac{}{VF(L_v^{v^2})}\ \text{Perm3}}{VF(I_{mn/v^2} \otimes L_v^{v^2})}\ \text{ItensorA}}{VF((L_m^{mn/v} \bar{\otimes} I_v)(I_{mn/v^2} \otimes L_v^{v^2}))}\ \text{Compose} \quad \cfrac{}{VF((I_{n/v} \otimes L_{m/v}^m) \bar{\otimes} I_v)}\ \text{AtensorI}}{VF((L_m^{mn/v} \bar{\otimes} I_v)(I_{mn/v^2} \otimes L_v^{v^2})((I_{n/v} \otimes L_{m/v}^m) \bar{\otimes} I_v))}\ \text{Compose}$$

For the remaining rules, Table 6 summarizes when each construct is fully vectorizable.

Table 6. Table of fully vectorizable factors with their constraints.

Tagged Factor	Size Constraints	Fully Vectorizable Subexpressions
$D^{n \times n}$	v divides n	
AB		A, B
L_m^{mn}	v divides m and n	
$(I_m \otimes A^{n \times n})$	v divides m and n	
$(I_m \otimes A^{n \times n})$		A
$(I_m \otimes A^{n \times n})L_m^{mn}$	v divides m and n	
$(A^{n \times n} \otimes I_m)$	v divides m and n	

As a result, checking that any tagged SPL expression can be fully vectorized reduces to checking when each of its factors can be fully vectorized. This method provides an easy proof that a vectorized form of the Cooley-Tukey factorization exists.

Theorem 2. *For all natural numbers n and m, if v divides m and n, the Cooley-Tukey DFT factorization, $(\mathrm{DFT}_m \otimes \mathrm{I}_n)\mathrm{T}_m^{nm}(\mathrm{I}_m \otimes \mathrm{DFT}_n)\mathrm{L}_m^{mn}$ is fully vectorizable. It is assumed that smaller transforms, DFT_m and DFT_n, stand in for fully factorized constructs.*

Proof. Each of the factors may be considered separately if the union of their constraints is satisfied. The first factor is $(\mathrm{DFT}_m \otimes \mathrm{I}_n)$, which is fully vectorizable if v divides m. The second factor, T_m^{nm}, is fully vectorizable when v divides either m or n.

The third and forth factors, $(\mathrm{I}_m \otimes \mathrm{DFT}_n)\mathrm{L}_m^{mn}$, may be considered separately or together. When considered together, they are fully vectorizable when v divides both m and n. Considered separately, $(\mathrm{I}_m \otimes \mathrm{DFT}_n)$ is fully vectorizable if v divides both m and n or if the resulting DFT_n breakdown is fully vectorizable. The forth factor, L_m^{mn}, is fully vectorizable if v divides both m and n.

The least constraining assumptions necessary to vectorize the Cooley-Tukey factorization requires that v divides m both n. If DFT_n is fully vectorizable, then additional vectorized forms may be produced by rewriting; however, this is not required to produce at least one fully vectorized form.

4   Vectorizing Compiler

Verification of the vectorizing compiler builds upon the formally verified scalar compiler presented in [6], which compiles to a simple imperative language extended with arrays of elements drawn from an arbitrary commutative ring called IMP+V. Extending the compiler to produce v-way vectorized implementations for completely vectorized formulas is straightforward. Vectorized code for $(A \bar{\otimes} \mathrm{I}_v)$ can be produced by transforming the scalar code for A to operate on v-sized blocks of its input vector. Certain SPL constructs are implemented by computing elements of the output vector as a linear combination of the input vector. Vectorizing replaces scalar operations in the linear combination with the corresponding v-way vector operations. Constructs such as $(\mathrm{I}_m \otimes B)$ produces looping code using code generated for B. Generating vectorized code for looping constructs, e.g. $((\mathrm{I}_m \otimes B) \bar{\otimes} \mathrm{I}_v)$ can be done recursively by descending into the loop, taking subvectors in v-sized blocks, and recursively replacing the scalar implementation of B with the vectorized code for $(B \bar{\otimes} \mathrm{I}_v)$. Tables 7 and 8 show the transformation from scalar code to vectorized code. Additionally, for SPL constructs representing diagonal matrices, vectorized code can be generated by replacing v scaling operations by a single vector multiplication as seen in Table 9.

Efficient Implementation. Vectorized implementations of fully vectorized formulas produces efficient code. If S is a tag free SPL formula in vectorized form, the number of vector operation in the vectorized implementation of S should be a constant factor less than the number of scalar operations in the scalar implementation. This is indeed the case.

Table 7. Transformation of scalar code to vectorized code for non-looping constructs.

Scalar Code for A	Vectorized Code for $A \bar\otimes I_v$

`y[i] := c*x[j] + x[k]`	`y[iv:1:v] := vadd(`
	`            vscale(c,x[jv:1:v]),`
	`            x[kv:v])`

`//n-length subvector at i` `t := x[i:1:n]`	`//n-block subvector at i` `t := x[iv:1:nv]`

`//n-length subvector at i`
`//by stride s`
`t := x[i:s:n]`
	`//n-block subvector`
	`//at block i by stride s`
	`t := x[i:s:v:n]`

Theorem 3. *Let S tag-free SPL construct such that $VF(S)$ holds, and let k be the number of vector operations in the vectorized implementation of S. The number of scalar operations in the scalar implementation of S is vk.*

This can be shown by induction on the structure of $VF(S)$. The structure of the proof is as follows. The base-case stride permutations are assumed to be efficient: the input vector is merely rearranged. For diagonal SPL constructs of size $n = kv$, n scalar multiplications are reduced to k vector multiplications. In the case of composed SPL constructs AB such that $VF(A)$ and $VF(B)$, assume for the sake of induction there are k_A vector operations and vk_A scalar operations respectively in the vector and scalar implementations for A. Assume similarly a k_B vector operations and vk_B scalar operations for B's implementations. Composition runs A's code on the output of B, so the total vector operations are $k_A + k_B$ and the total scalar operations are $v(k_A + k_B)$.

In the case of $(I_m \otimes A)$, where $VF(A)$ assume for the sake of induction that there are k_A vector operations and vk_A scalar operations respectively in the vector and scalar implementations for A. The looping code generated for $(I_m \otimes A)$ runs A's code for m iterations. If scalar code is generated for A, this results in mvk_A scalar operations. If vectorized code is generated for A, there are mk_A vector operations.

In the case of $A^{n \times n} \bar\otimes I_v$, the proof proceeds further by induction on A. If A is not a looping construct, the n linear combinations in A are replaced by n/v linear combinations with the same number vector operations. If A is a looping construct, e.g. $(I_m \otimes B^{k \times k})$ with $n = km$, assume for the sake of induction that the number of scalar operations for B's scalar implementation is vb and the number of vector operations in B's vector implementation is b. All looping constructs run m iterations of B's implementation, resulting in mvb scalar operations and mb vector operations.

Table 8. Transformation of scalar code to vectorized code for looping constructs, where "scalar(A, t)" represent the scalar code generated for A run on input vector t, and "vector(A, t)" represents the vectorized code generated for $A \bar{\otimes} I_v$ run on input vector t.

Scalar Code	Vectorized Code
``//(I_m ⊗ A)
FOR (i:= 0; i < m; i++) DO
t0 := x[in:1:n];
t1 := scalar(A, t0);
y[in:1:n] := t1;
END```	```//(I_m ⊗ A) ⊗̄ I_v
FOR (i:= 0; i < m; i++) DO
t0 := x[inv:1:nv];
t1 := vector(A, t0);
y[inv:1:nv] := t1;
END```
``//(I_m ⊗ A)L_m^{mn}
FOR (i:= 0; i < m; i++) DO
t0 := x[i:m:n];
t1 := scalar(A, t0);
y[in:1:n] := t1;
END```	```//((I_m ⊗ A)L_m^{mn}) ⊗̄ I_v
FOR (i:= 0; i < m; i++) DO
t0 := x[i:m:v:n];
t1 := vector(A, t0);
y[inv:nv] := t1;
END```
``//(A ⊗ I_m)
FOR (i:= 0; i < m; i++) DO
t0 := x[i:m:n];
t1 := scalar(A, t0);
y[i:m:n] := t1;
END```	```// (A ⊗ I_m) ⊗̄ I_v
FOR (i:= 0; i < m; i++) DO
t0 := x[i:m:v:n];
t1 := vector(A, t0);
y[i:m:v:n] := t1;
END```

Correctness of Compilation. As a final task, it is important to verify that the code produced for an SPL formula S—vector or scalar implementation—is correct. That is, for a fixed input vector x, the output vector y obtained by running S's compiled code on x, should be exactly Sx. The full details of verifying the SPL compiler are beyond the scope of this paper, so the process is presented in brief.

First, the syntax of IMP+V is defined formally, and its semantics are defined using big-step operational semantics. In addition, a Hoare Logic [16] for IMP+V is created, and each of its rules are proven sound with respect to the operational semantics.

Formulas are compiled to scalar code by traversing the construct's AST from the top down to produce code fragments from parametrized templates. Subexpressions in the construct are recursively compiled using code fragment templates, and the resulting code fragments are inserted from the bottom up. The correctness of each fragment template is verified using Hoare logic. Templates that require recursively compiled subexpressions are verified under the assumption that the recursively compiled code is correct, and an inductive proof is used to show that the compilation process produces correct code overall.

Finally, the vectorization of code fragments is shown correct. That is, if a code fragment for A correctly computes Ax on input x, then the vectorized code generated for $(A \bar{\otimes} I_v)$ is verified to compute $(A \bar{\otimes} I_v)x$ on input x. Hoare

Table 9. Comparison of scalar and vector code generated for an SPL construct representing a diagonal matrix.

Scalar code	Vector code

```y[0] := c_0*x[0];```
 ...
 ```y[i] := c_i*x[i];```
 ...
 ```y[i+v-1] := c_{i+v-1}*x[i+v-1];```
 ...
 ```y[n] := c_n*x[n]```
	```y[0:v] := vmul(```
	 ```[c_0, ... , c_{v-1}], x[0:1:v]);```
	 ...
	 ```y[iv:v] := vmul(```
	 ```[c_i, ... , c_{i+v-1}], x[iv:1:v]);```
	 ...
	 ```y[(n-1)v:v] := vmul(```
	 ```[c_{n-v}, ... , c_{n-1}],```
	 ```x[(n-1)v:1:v])```

Logic is also used here to show that vectorized fragment templates are correct. The Hoare proof of the scalar template guides construction of Hoare proofs for the vectorized templates. Preconditions, postconditions, invariants, and other assertions are updated to match the vectorizing transformations.

5 Conclusion and Future Work

The rewriting system for vectorization presented in [14] by Franchetti et al. leverages higher-level abstractions using rules based matrix identities to produce vectorized implementations of signal transform algorithms. These matrix identities and rules have been formally verified. Furthermore, a formal presentation of the rewriting system using a contextual small-step relation was used to show that the process of rewriting terminates and produces vectorized algorithms. Vectorized code generation for these vectorized algorithms has been shown to preserve the matrix semantics of these algorithms while reducing the operation count by a factor of the vector size compared to scalar code.

Work on implementing these formal proofs of correctness in Coq is ongoing, extending a previous development for formalizing algorithm and code generation for scalar implementations [6]. The techniques used in the example proof for the discrete Fourier transform can be applied similarly to other transforms. Moreover, these types of proofs may be ripe for automation via proof search in Coq. Additionally, formal verification of the rewriting system optimizing for shared [15] and distributed memory systems [5] using similar techniques is planned.

References

1. Allen, R., Kennedy, K.: Optimizing Compilers for Modern Architectures: A Dependence-based Approach. Morgan Kaufmann Publishers, San Francisco (2002)
2. Almeida, J.B., et al.: The last mile: high-assurance and high-speed cryptographic implementations. In: 2020 IEEE Symposium on Security and Privacy (SP), pp. 965–982 (2020)

3. Barthe, G., Crespo, J.M., Gulwani, S., Kunz, C., Marron, M.: From relational verification to simd loop synthesis. In: Proceedings of the 18th ACM SIGPLAN Symposium on Principles and Practice of Parallel Programming, pp. 123–134. PPoPP 2013, Association for Computing Machinery, New York, NY, USA (2013). https://doi.org/10.1145/2442516.2442529
4. Barthe, G., Grégoire, B., Heraud, S., Béguelin, S.Z.: Computer-aided security proofs for the working cryptographer. In: Rogaway, P. (ed.) CRYPTO 2011. LNCS, vol. 6841, pp. 71–90. Springer, Heidelberg (2011). https://doi.org/10.1007/978-3-642-22792-9_5
5. Bonelli, A., Franchetti, F., Lorenz, J., Püschel, M., Ueberhuber, C.W.: Automatic performance optimization of the discrete fourier transform on distributed memory computers. In: Guo, M., Yang, L.T., Di Martino, B., Zima, H.P., Dongarra, J., Tang, F. (eds.) ISPA 2006. LNCS, vol. 4330, pp. 818–832. Springer, Heidelberg (2006). https://doi.org/10.1007/11946441_74
6. Brinich, P.: Formal Verification of SPIRAL Generated Code. Master's thesis, Drexel University (2020)
7. Cadar, C., Dunbar, D., Engler, D.: Klee: unassisted and automatic generation of high-coverage tests for complex systems programs. In: Proceedings of the 8th USENIX Conference on Operating Systems Design and Implementation, pp. 209–224. OSDI 2008, USENIX Association, USA (2008)
8. Collingbourne, P., Cadar, C., Kelly, P.H.: Symbolic crosschecking of floating-point and simd code. In: Proceedings of the Sixth Conference on Computer Systems, pp. 315–328. EuroSys 2011, Association for Computing Machinery, New York, NY, USA (2011). https://doi.org/10.1145/1966445.1966475
9. Dutta, S.: Validation of parallelizing transformations of sequential programs. Concurr. Comput. Pract. Exp. **29**(8), e3958 (2017). https://doi.org/10.1002/cpe.3958, https://onlinelibrary.wiley.com/doi/abs/10.1002/cpe.3958, e3958 cpe.3958
10. Felleisen, M., Hieb, R.: The revised report on the syntactic theories of sequential control and state. Theor. Comput. Sci. **103**(2), 235–271 (1992). https://doi.org/10.1016/0304-3975(92)90014-7
11. Franchetti, F., et al.: High-assurance SPIRAL: end-to-end guarantees for robot and car control. IEEE Control Syst. Mag. **37**(2), 82–103 (2017)
12. Franchetti, F., et al.: SPIRAL: extreme performance portability. Proc. IEEE **106**(11), 1935–1968 (2018)
13. Franchetti, F., de Mesmay, F., McFarlin, D., Püschel, M.: Operator language: a program generation framework for fast kernels. In: Taha, W.M. (ed.) DSL 2009. LNCS, vol. 5658, pp. 385–409. Springer, Heidelberg (2009). https://doi.org/10.1007/978-3-642-03034-5_18
14. Franchetti, F., Voronenko, Y., Püschel, M.: A rewriting system for the vectorization of signal transforms. In: Daydé, M., Palma, J.M.L.M., Coutinho, Á.L.G.A., Pacitti, E., Lopes, J.C. (eds.) VECPAR 2006. LNCS, vol. 4395, pp. 363–377. Springer, Heidelberg (2007). https://doi.org/10.1007/978-3-540-71351-7_28
15. Franchetti, F., Voronenko, Y., Püschel, M.: FFT program generation for shared memory: SMP and multicore (January 2006). https://doi.org/10.1145/1188455.1188575
16. Hoare, C.A.R.: An axiomatic basis for computer programming. Commun. ACM **12**(10), 576–580 (1969). https://doi.org/10.1145/363235.363259
17. Leroy, X.: Formal verification of a realistic compiler. Commun. ACM **52**(7), 107–115 (2009). https://doi.org/10.1145/1538788.1538814
18. Püschel, M., et al.: SPIRAL: code generation for dsp transforms. Proc. IEEE **93**(2), 232–275 (2005)

19. The Coq Development Team: The Coq Reference Manual, version 8.9.1 (2019). available electronically at https://coq.inria.fr/distrib/V8.9.1/refman/
20. Wolfe, M., Wolfe, M.: High Performance Compilers for Parallel Computing. Addison-Wesley, Boston (1996)
21. Xiong, J., Johnson, J., Johnson, R., Padua, D.: SPL: a language and compiler for DSP algorithms. In: Proceedings of the ACM SIGPLAN 2001 Conference on Programming Language Design and Implementation (PLDI 2001), pp. 298–308. Snowbird, Utah (June 2001). https://doi.org/10.1145/378795.378860

Author Index

Printed in the United States
by Baker & Taylor Publisher Services